Feather Bed & Shive of Cheese

*Names in the landscape of
Finsthwaite, Lakeside, Stott Park and Ealinghearth*

Sophia Martin, Pat Jones and Liz Kingston

Published in 2019 by Sophia Martin, Pat Jones, Liz Kingston

© Copyright Sophia Martin, Pat Jones, Liz Kingston

ISBN: 978-1-9160217-1-6

Book & Cover Design by Russell Holden

www.pixeltweakspublications.com

A Catalogue record for this book is available from the British Library.

Printed by Ingram

All rights reserved without limiting the rights under copyright reserved above, no parts of this publication may be reproduced, stored in or introduced into a retrieval system, or transmitted in any form, or by any means (electronic, mechanical, photocopying, recording or otherwise) without the prior written permission of both the copyright owner and the publisher of this book.

The Open Gate

Step into the field and wonder
Who owns this land and does it have a name?
Was it always his or did his father gain it
In exchange for some far flung acres,
As he gathered all his fields around the farm,
Just as he gathered all his sheep
From the summer pastures on the fell?
Did the woods beyond ring with the sound
Of bill-hooks, as men coppiced the hazel
Or the voices of the charcoal burners
Camped out in their wooden wigwams?
Did the village folk follow this footpath
To the old grey church down in the valley?
Step into the field and listen
And you may hear the echoes of the past.

Pat Jones

August 2018

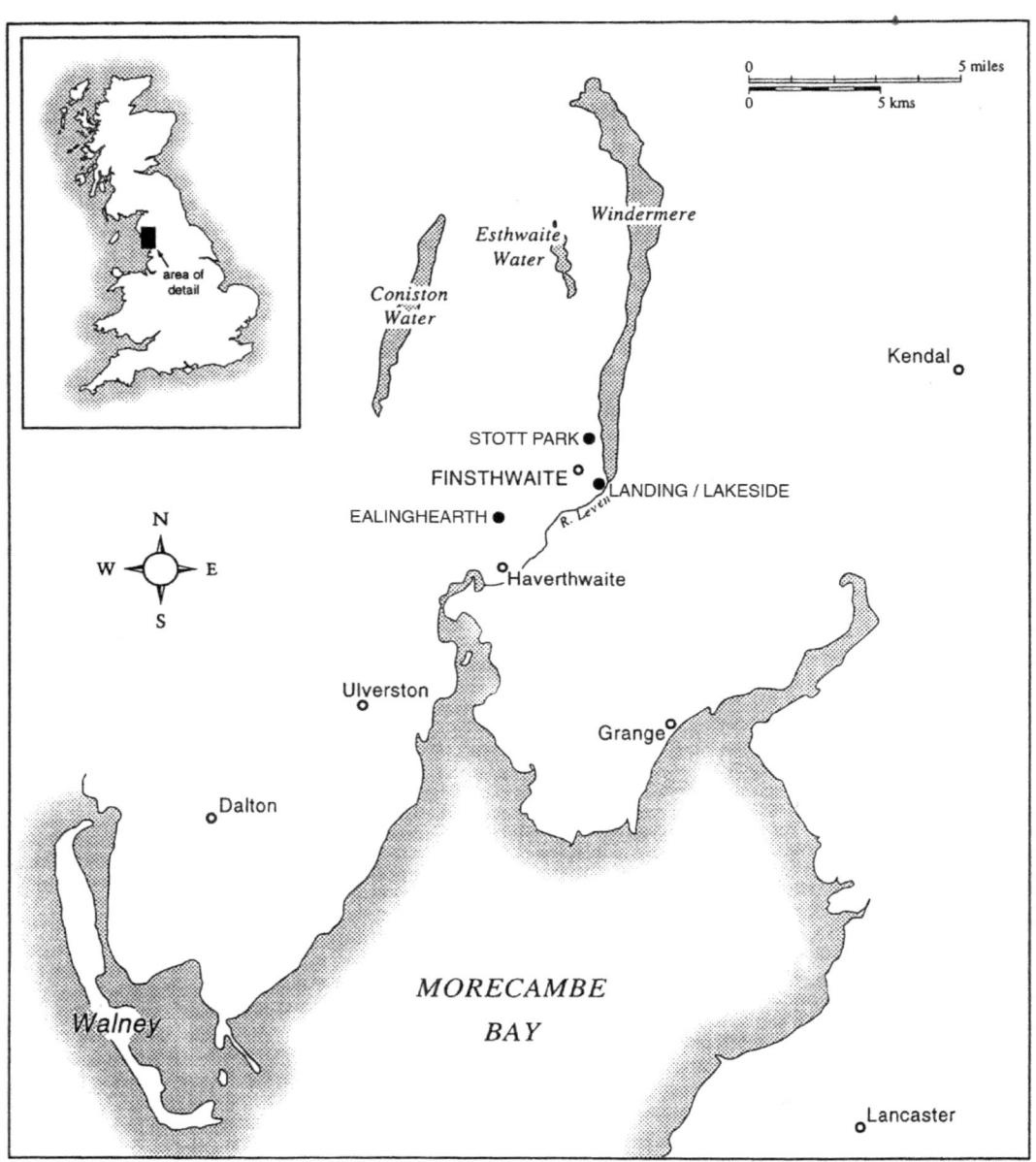

Adapted with permission from Janet Martin

Contents

Introduction 1
Finding and Interpreting Names 5
Village Histories 19
      Finsthwaite 21
      Newby Bridge and the Knott 30
      Landing and Lakeside 33
      Stott Park 38
      Ealinghearth 44
The Maps 49

FINSTHWAITE
Plum Green 51
Chapman House and Jolliver Tree 64
Finsthwaite House 77
Lower Finsthwaite and Town End 87
The Haggs and Waterside. 99
Finsthwaite Heights 106

NEWBY BRIDGE & THE KNOTT
Newby Bridge and the Knott 114

LAKESIDE
Landing and Lakeside 118

STOTT PARK
Low Stott Park 128
High Stott Park 132

EALINGHEARTH
Linsty Green and Hill Top 146
The Ellersides and Yewbarrow 150
The Parrocks and Fearing Brow 154
Ealinghearth and Border Moss 160
St Helens and Hall Brow Wood 170

The journey continues.... 174

Introduction

This book is about names – over 500 of them – the names given to fields, woods and some minor landscape features like bridges and hills, in an area of the Rusland Valley in South Cumbria. The identification of these names has been a journey of discovery among archive documents and maps, and through conversations with people who live, work and continue to name the landscape, in the four villages we surveyed.

Naming something is not a neutral act. It is based on observations, sometimes joking ones, about the character of the land, and the generations-old work of farming in this place. It is also very often a memorial to people: neighbours, family, friends, tenants, owners, and their occupations on the land. Names in the landscape are documented back to 1552 but it is also a current and continuing process among the people who work the fell, fields and woods today, and they have contributed much to our work. This book presents the results of a two-year search among maps, archives and memories.

The Mapped Histories Project

Our research has been carried out as part of the Mapped Histories project, itself one element of *Rusland Horizons*. This Heritage Lottery Fund scheme has worked on many fronts: ecology and wildlife projects, woodland management skills training, and history and archaeology projects involving local people. Mapped Histories, which began in the autumn of 2016, recruited and trained volunteers to search archive sources for historic field and woodland names, to interpret the meanings behind those names, and to present them on a digital map. The volunteers' work was coordinated by Clare Dyson and overseen by Angus Winchester of Lancaster University, who provided archive training and advice on interpreting names. His *Lake District Field-Names,* published during the time of the project, provided the pattern for our work. The map was launched on the *Rusland Horizons'* website in November 2017.

One objective of Mapped Histories, and other initiatives of *Rusland Horizons*, was to understand the historical interaction between local people and their landscape, and to capture names before they were forgotten. By getting involved in the project, we have had the satisfaction of a very successful search for names, but have also deepened our appreciation of the way people lived and worked in the area, and the continuity of parts of that way of life in our present-day community. This book presents the findings of a team of three volunteers, who surveyed the village of Finsthwaite, where two of the authors live, together with the outlying hamlets of High and Low Stott Park, Lakeside, and Ealinghearth.

Janet Martin, a Finsthwaite archivist and historian, offered access to her research, carried out over several decades. Her work, both published and in note form, was made available to us – and indeed was the primary driver of Sophia's involvement in Mapped Histories. Janet had recorded Finsthwaite field names during conversations with landowners in the 1970s and had annotated the large sheets of the 25" Ordnance Survey map with her findings. Sophia originally attended a Mapped Histories meeting to show the maps to anyone interested – but instead, of course, found herself signed up as a volunteer.

We have repeated much of Janet's work, following in her footsteps to consult archives and re-interview neighbours. We have used her analysis of the archives of Finsthwaite House, especially the collection in the Lancashire Record Office, to establish the oldest of the names we collected. Her painstaking reading of parish records, census returns and wills provided us with a wealth of genealogical and historical detail, which assisted us greatly when we began interpreting field names. Her notes identified people whose own names survive in association with the land they farmed, worked and traded. The stories she uncovered are the source of the additional information we have written up here, and helped make our experience of Mapped Histories so rewarding. We have been most grateful for her generosity in letting us use her notes. Ever competitive, she cheerfully issued a challenge at the outset that if we found anything she hadn't already made a note of then we would win £5. After over two years' searching, her money is safe.

Change and continuity in the landscape

The landscape in our survey area is still largely agricultural, and so the project naturally extended into including modern names captured through conversations with farmers and landowners. In Finsthwaite both farming families have been generous with their time, as well as their archives, and have explained the rationale behind field names now. John Chaplin and his daughter Charlotte Dean, and Iain Kellett and his nephew Stephen Watson have made significant contributions to our survey, and we are thankful for their interest and insights. At Finsthwaite in particular, the sixteenth and seventeenth century farming landscape is still highly visible, with both farms continuing to use, and hence to conserve, a much more ancient tradition. Although arable farming has been a thing of the past since the Second World War, Finsthwaite farmers continue to keep sheep in the same way as their forebears, following the same seasonal routines of lambing, shearing and gathering. There has been some clearance of trees from fields, but the basic pattern is much as it was when 'intakes' and 'parrocks' were first created. Ealinghearth is also still farmed, so here, as at Finsthwaite, there is a strong element of continuity to the landscape we see. Although the woods are not now worked with the same intensity, woodland is still a dominant feature of the area. The old woodland industries, like swill making and charcoal burning, have left their legacy in pitsteads and old coppice woodland. At Stott Park, where there were once three farms, there is now none but the layout of fields is still extant. It was here, in 1835, that a bobbin mill was established as a factory for the production of bobbins for the cotton industry of Lancashire and Yorkshire. It is at Lakeside that the greatest change has occurred, with the development of almost the entire community since the arrival of the railway in the 1860s.

The layout of the book

The first section of the book, Finding and Interpreting Names, gives an account of our search for names, describes the archives and maps we worked from, and outlines the way conversations with our farming neighbours played their part in the research. Then there are short histories of each settlement we covered. The histories focus on the people who lived there, together with stories which we hope show the human as well as the landscape context of our work. There are 15 map sections, sometimes with additional notes about historic farms or particular areas, like the Haggs and Finsthwaite Heights. The maps are OS 1890, marked up with plot numbers used by the Ordnance Survey. The names we have found are given in the text alongside, with the plot number as an identifier. Archival references and dates for the names we found, and an interpretation of each name, are also given.

Acknowledgements

Maps were supplied by Barrow Record Office who kindly scanned the 1890 OS map. The images were enlarged and annotated by Russell Holden, who also did the work of designing the book for us. Photographs are by Sophia Martin, Charlotte Dean, Stephen Watson and Pat Jones or from the Kellett and Bayman family albums.

None of this book, or the work of Mapped Histories, would have been possible without access to the archive collections held at County Record Offices, in our case at Cumbria (both Barrow and Kendal) and Lancashire (Preston). Local archive services hold an extraordinary treasury of material, made available to the public, which we are very grateful to have had the chance to explore and understand. Our particular thanks go to Susan Benson and her colleagues at Barrow, for their support and interest.

Angus Winchester gave us not only great encouragement, but also shared his knowledge and offered firm, but kindly guidance which has been invaluable.

He shared the same attitude too as Janet Martin, which is that the historian and researcher should get out from time to time, and walk in fields and woods, because some things really only make sense when you are on the ground.

We acknowledge the support given to us by a grant to assist with the publication of this volume from the Kirby Archives Trust. We have also had generous support from a London backer: Patrick Martin.

Various neighbours have given us additional information, in particular Vanessa Champion who offered advice about trees and woodland management and drew the picture on page 19. John Taylor kindly read and commented on the text.

We worked together during the project, something which made the ups and downs of compiling spreadsheets, researching hundreds of names, visiting archive offices and walking through fields enormous fun. Our division of labour in writing has been that Sophia drafted the text, but it has been amended and worked on by us all. Liz, a former teacher, has marked Sophia's written work enthusiastically. She strengthened our team by good will and amazing energy. Pat Jones has shown remarkable tenacity and terrier-like qualities in hunting down names, references and Old Norse words; she also kept the most orderly notes. Sophia is just glad to have followed in the maternal footsteps. In the course of our researches, she found transcriptions of two documents in her own teenage handwriting; evidence of a trip with Janet to Kendal Record Office. An early lesson in the fascinating value of archives has, finally, been learned.

Sophia Martin, Pat Jones, Liz Kingston
February 2019

Finding and Interpreting Names

The Ordnance Survey and other maps

Mapped Histories volunteers were each allocated Ordnance Survey maps: in our case OS VIII-10, 11 (west of the lake), 14 and 15 (the north-west corner only) from 1890. The 1890 25" map gives a plot number to all the woods, fields and roads surveyed. We had about 300 plots to try and name. The first step was to enter each plot, with its grid reference, on a spread sheet. We next looked at the earliest 1850 OS map, which recorded a helpful number of woodland names and some lanes and streams. Field names are not recorded by the Ordnance Survey.

We began to search archives stored by Cumbria Archive Service. Our goal was to find maps, and we uncovered several. Most were the work of local surveyors, with keys and acreages given with precision and the maps drawn with artistry. An 1843 map, prepared for an intended sale of the Landing estate, is stored at Kendal in both draft and printed form. This yielded over 70 names. The estate included farms at Finsthwaite and at Stott Park as well as the holdings at Landing. Later maps, from the late 1860s and early 1880s, showed building plots offered for sale at Lakeside, and gave us further names. Some, like Buck Yeats, can still be found as house names. An early find, at Barrow Record Office, was an 1890 map of High Stott Park estate. We found three maps of farmland at Ealinghearth which were productive, the earliest dating to sometime before 1821.

With care, even a document without a map could yield up names, if the description of where the land lies is detailed and includes some known site as a point of reference. This helped us to identify 'Water or Blumer Meadow' at Stott Park, which was described in relation to a field we knew called Cowper Ridding. Some lists of field names post-date the 1890 Ordnance Survey map and make use of the OS plot numbers we were using ourselves. One list of fields at Chapman House farm in Finsthwaite included OS plot numbers; some sets of late nineteenth and early twentieth century sales particulars also did.

The documents we studied at the Cumbria Archive Service office at Barrow were mainly from the extensive Hart Jackson collection, while at Kendal we used papers deposited by solicitors Arnold Greenwood. Collections of family papers for the Braithwaites of Stock Park, the Harrisons of Stott Park and later the Landing estate, and the Taylors and Lewthwaites of High Stott Park are preserved. These collections detail land sales and acquisitions, and other aspects of farm and land management over several generations. Archives also sometimes concerned disputes between owners, during the resolution of which a map may be sketched or names simply mentioned in passing. In this way we found an early date, 1751, for the name Star Mire, a wood on Stott Park Heights.

The Pedder Archive and Finsthwaite House estate plan

Our principal archive source was the Pedder archive, a remarkable collection of over 400 documents preserved by the Taylor family who lived in Finsthwaite from the 1530s when the village is first documented. Both its range and survival as a collection are notable. In 1724 Clement Taylor began building Finsthwaite House, and gradually amassed the estate which is still farmed at the southern end of the village. The archive collection includes his account book, a transcript of which was published by Janet Martin in 1997. Box 26 of the Pedder archive begins in 1552, and includes documents detailing sales, disputes and land management transactions over more than 300 years. It demonstrated that some names, of both fields and woodland, have endured for over 450 years. We cross-referenced the names we found in the archive with the Finsthwaite House estate plan, drawn up in 1851, two years after the Pedder family inherited the estate from the last of the Taylors. The Pedder archive is now housed at Lancashire Record Office in Preston. We relied on the detailed study of it made over several years by Janet Martin, although we also used summaries of the documents in the on-line catalogue of the National Archives.

The oldest names in the Pedder archive, Haggscar (an area of woodland on a steep slope running down to the River Leven) and land at the Knott (now Great Knott wood) both date to 1552. Fearing Brow is first mentioned in 1564. Tenancy agreements, disputes and farm lists yielded up a wealth of names of fields and woods through the centuries. The most detailed picture comes in Clement Taylor's mid-eighteenth century account book. Alongside his purchases of food, clothes and materials to build his new house, he names the fields and woods where ploughing, harvesting, hay making, lath making, charcoal burning and bark peeling were going on. Clement Taylor's successors Edward Taylor, and later Roger Taylor, also kept account books and these confirm the active management of the land, especially the woodland, through the later eighteenth and early nineteenth centuries. Roger Taylor's account book lists coppicing and felling dates for the woods on his estate at Stott Park from 1794, and later for the Finsthwaite House estate, which he inherited in 1821.

The Finsthwaite House estate plan was made for the Pedders, after they inherited the estate on the death of Roger Taylor. The map itself is annotated with some name changes, with occasional new purchases, and notes about neighbouring owners. Both ink and pencil annotations are marked on the 1851 map. In ink a couple of spelling mistakes have been firmly corrected: Light Hall, as printed, has been corrected to Light Horse (Light Horse Scar). Rather more entertainingly, Wild Brigg End has been altered to Willy Brigg End. The name Backside has been added, again in ink and apparently by the same hand, to an enclosure at the side of Finsthwaite House. This is now a concrete yard with sheep sheds on it, but is mentioned in Clement Taylor's account book in 1713 as a field where trees are to be felled. Pencil changes suggest that the estate plan was, to a limited extent, a working document. These pencil comments have been added at different times and are sometimes dated. The name Longmire has been altered to Hog House Field and an outline of the, now derelict, hog house added. 'The Cow Pastures' has been written in on Great Hagg. Both these new additions are in current use. Charmingly, the word 'donkey', presumably a resident of the field, has been added to High Paddock above Green Cottage; Charlotte Dean says that they use the name Donkey Paddock for that enclosure, although it is now wooded. In the main, however, the map remains as originally designed and is the only estate plan that we have for our survey area.

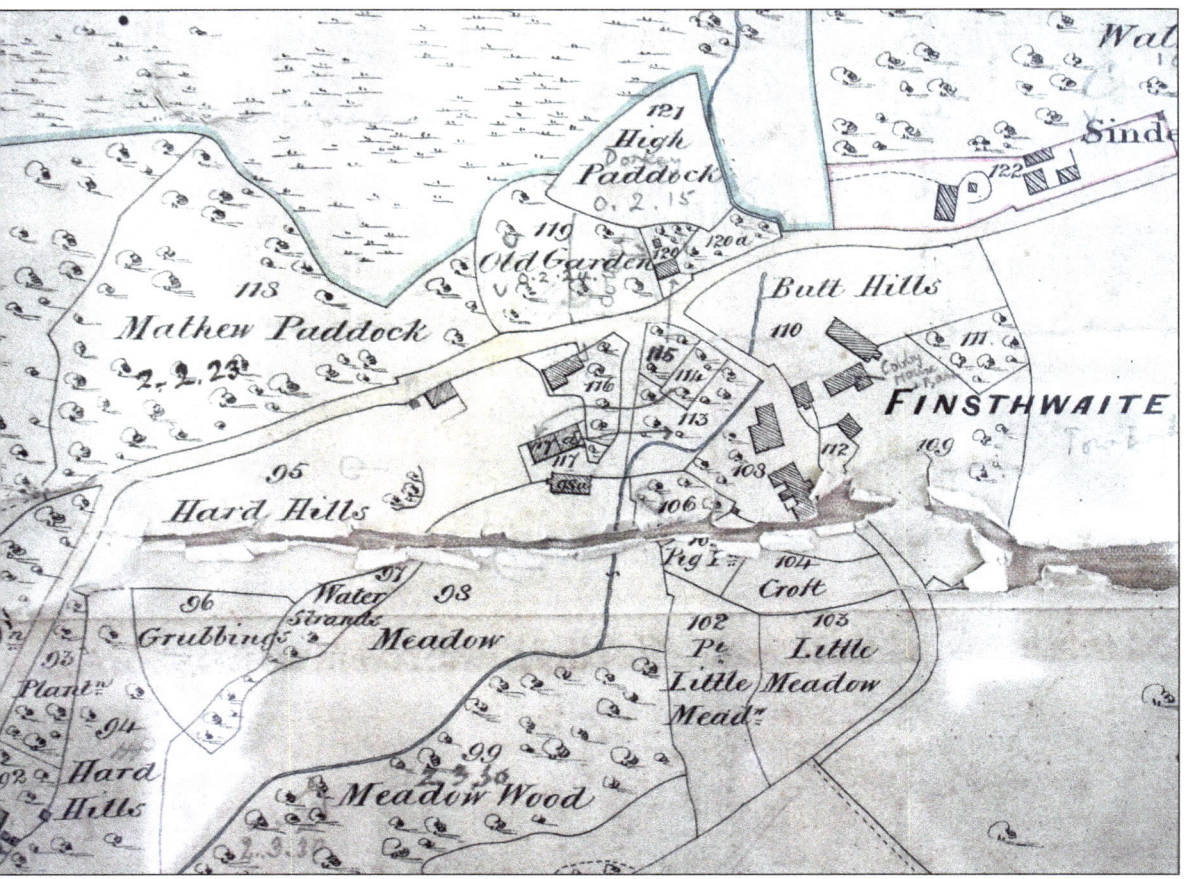

Lower Finsthwaite on the Finsthwaite House estate plan 1851

An enclosure map also exists, again in the Pedder archive. This dates to 1771, when 300 acres of land on Finsthwaite Heights was marked for enclosure by 15 local landowners and managers of land; three of the signatories are executors of an estate rather than owners in their own right. This map gave us names, like Tup Haw, Holling Hill and Windy Hawes, of features within the proposed wall. It also gave us one or two names on the enclosure boundary like Parrock of the Height, giving us one of our earliest dates for this wooded plot. In the list of holdings of Laurence Harrison in 1769 it is Parrock oth Height, which is similar to the version on a map of the Landing estate in 1843: Parrock 'eth Height. On Ordnance Survey maps it has become Parrocket Height; the OS surveyors must have written down what they heard said as the name (say it out loud with a 't for 'of the' and it will all make sense).

Wills and marriage settlements

At the northern end of Finsthwaite, in the area known as Plum Green, there is no parallel to the Pedder archive. As indicated above, two farms there were once part of the Landing estate, and so were covered by the 1843 sale map, which gave us many names with a mid-nineteenth century date. Here, Janet Martin's careful piecing together of wills and archives like marriage settlements, which list farm holdings, has pushed back the dates of some field names to the seventeenth and eighteenth centuries. Wills, which Janet studied in the Richmond Deanery archive at Lancashire Record Office, yielded many human details but relatively few field names. The earliest will is that of Edward Ashburner of Stott Park in 1576 and the last is from the early twentieth century. We found names for fields at Ealinghearth in the will of Thomas Taylor in 1803, but most wills gave only passing references. In two cases, land is named because it had been newly acquired, and in a couple of instances a single field was earmarked for use as a legacy to a specific person. In this way, we got early references to Buck Yeats Close, 1626, and Cowper Ridding, 1612. These names still persist, both as names for land and for houses that have been built since.

The main value of wills and inventories is for the human details and the glimpses into possessions and farming practices of the past. The 1615 will of Robert Barrow of Finsthwaite mentions 'cow grass in Ellersyde', referring to his right to graze cattle in that wood. The inventory mentions items we would expect among the goods of a farmer: 'gysse and hens', corn and hay. More surprisingly he also had books (valued at 30s) and 'a bowe, arrows, swords, saddles and gyrdels' (valued at 6s 8d).

Wills often include references to bees and beehives which would have provided honey as a precious sweetener for food. Jennet Taylor inherited 10s worth of bees from her husband John in 1600, as well as one-third of 'the old tenement, according to custom'. William Danson left bees too: the hives at Plum Green to his nephew and his wife, hives at Clement Taylor's house to Clement's wife Isabel (Clement himself got a 'pair of new boots' – William Danson was a shoe-maker), and a Margaret Braithwaite got possession of the 'bees at Town End'. Bee hives may have been spread around the village where there were blossom trees like crab apples in orchards or on the fellside, where they are common.

Oral traditions and local stories

We have talked to neighbours, many of whom can give a background to a name, but sometimes the origins are forgotten, even if the name itself is remembered and used. 'Washhouse Hill' in Finsthwaite is used, but not widely understood; we were able to explain it by reference to Janet Martin's notes of the 1891 census which identify the Croasdell sisters who were laundresses, living in a cottage at the bottom of the hill. Anne Watson told us that, as a child, she used to stand underneath the railway bridge at Linsty Green and shout 'cuckoo!' to make an echo. Although many people call the bridge 'Cuckoo Bridge', the game seems to have died out and the origin of the name largely forgotten.

The most striking example of the longevity of memory is Great Ealinghearth at Ealinghearth. When Sophia asked Miles Saunders whether the fields he kept his sheep in had a name he thought for some time and said 'No, it's just Ealinghearth really.' We wrote it down as a blank, but later discovered in Janet Martin's notes a will of 1803 which named those fields Great and Little Ealinghearth. When we finally appreciated the value of what we had been told about Ealinghearth we were able to identify a pattern where the field closest to a farmhouse has a simple name: The Field, opposite Rose Cottage at Plum Green (the earliest name for what was later called the Meadow behind the Barn), Meadow at Finsyke and the Field Behind the House at Stott Park. Only as you work away from the immediate vicinity of the farmhouse do names become a little more complex.

Changes over time

We have noted many more changes of field names than of woodland names. Field names have changed most rapidly in the twentieth century. The newest names are those used by the current generation of farmers. We have this information in greatest detail for Finsthwaite, where we have had the most contact with the two farming families. They use entirely the same approach to naming as was done in the past: associations with farming practice and with people.

Chapman House farm has changed the names of its holdings since we first have them recorded. The oldest names, Barn Parrock, Barn Parrock Meadow and Well Close for example, have become Bull Field, Lowside and High Side respectively; although the fields themselves remain the same. Well Close and Barn Parrock are names which date back to 1600. Chapman House has been owned by the Kellett family since 1920, when they bought the farm when it came on the market during their tenancy. The changes in field names were beginning in the late nineteenth century, probably at the start of their tenancy. The Kelletts also provided one of the newest names in our survey, the Prison Field, in reference to the fencing of a field previously called the Little Field, and at an even earlier stage in its history Corn Parrock. The fencing is meant to make it sheep-proof but the animals seem to have worked out an escape route.

In only one place have we found a significant change of field outline, in an otherwise remarkably conserved and preserved agricultural environment. At Jolliver Tree there are two lists of holdings, dating to the mid-eighteenth century, which give names like Barn Parrock and High Brow, which we can allocate with reasonable confidence to existing plots by the house. However, south of the house the field outline has changed completely. Between the OS surveys of the 1840s and 1880s a substantial reorganisation is recorded. Three square fields, with walls running east-west replaced a collection of smaller fields and one, which was called Nether Field, which ran parallel to the lane. There may have been earlier 'improvement' too, as even working to the 1850 boundaries we are hard pressed to find exact sites for some of the fields named the century before. So Christopher and George's Field and Little Meadow may be lost to us. These fields are now known as Mrs Doble's Fields, after their previous owner. She died in 2013 but her name remains linked to the land.

At Finsthwaite House, the tendency now is to group fields together rather than to preserve their older, more individual names. Town End Paddock and two fields once known as Tarn Close and Tarn Close Meadow are now called the Town End Fields. Reading and Slack are the Tower fields, because they sit under the hillside on which Finsthwaite Tower stands. A group of fields, including Meadow, Hard Hills and Grubbings, between Finsyke and Town End is now bundled together to become the Charley Crag Fields, again because they are near the house of that name. Although field walls largely still stand they have gaps and open gateways to allow sheep to graze across the whole area. The same is true of the Cow Pastures, a collective name for what were once the Haggs and Becking Garths. In the twenty-first century, Dave Wilson named a field more formally known as Swinebroach, the Bus Shelter Field because a little concrete building there looks rather like a bus shelter. The absence of public transport in Finsthwaite makes this name ironic.

Woods and orchards

One common naming-formula, that of linking a wood and a field with the same name, occurs multiple times across our survey area: Sourbutts and Sourbutts Wood, Meadow and Meadow Wood, Swinebroach Wood and Swinebroach are all examples. Brookbank (also spelled Break Bank) is both the name of a wood and a field next to it.

The field called Meadow, near Finsyke, has now been subsumed into the group called the Charley Crag Fields, but the name Meadow Wood is still used for the adjacent wood. Usually it is the field name that dominates: Sourbutts (the open field with a marsh or 'sour' ground at one end of it) would come first as the marsh is a feature of the field, then the wood is named because it is adjacent. The same is true of Meadow and Meadow Wood, and High Field and High Field Wood. However at Haggscar, because the scar is a feature of the wood, it is the wood's name that has been attached to the field opposite. Swinebroach is both the name of a wood and a field nearby. The word 'broach' means a wide area, and so it is likely that both woods and pasture were used as places to keep pigs. In one case we have relied on the frequency of this naming phenomenon to allocate a name to a field at Jolliver which was otherwise uncertain: High Brow.

The pairing of names is in part a legacy of the past, when individual trees and even quite substantial woodlands would have existed within fields. Archives often describe land as 'arable and woody' or 'woods, waste and meadow', 'woody and pasture'. Trees are a valuable resource in the area, and were not cleared from fields in a concerted way until the nineteenth and twentieth centuries. A local, and ancient, habit also exists called 'wood-pasture' where animals are grazed in woodlands. It is somewhat controversial in forestry circles, being seen as detrimental to woodland health. Newly-sprung coppice woods are obviously vulnerable to grazing damage. Roger Taylor's account book (1794-1850) detailed the dates of when woods had been cut or coppiced, which suggests that several seasons would have to elapse before livestock could be allowed to graze in each wood. He would have been keeping a record in order to plan when coppice poles would be ready to harvest, but it seems likely that grazing was also under consideration. Wood pasture would have been familiar to medieval and later farmers as 'haggs', where the valuable wood takes its place alongside subsistence farming. Hagg is derived from an Old Norse word for a clearing, and becomes attached both to areas of working woodland like coppices, and animal pasture. A large area south-west of Finsthwaite incorporates 'hagg' into the name of its fields and woods, and we have covered this as one of our map sections.

On a smaller scale, we also found many examples of 'busk' and 'bush' names, meaning small areas of woodland or bushes often found at the edge of a field such as Barn Parrock Busk, Little Field Busk, Lag Paddock Bush and Knot Busk. In some cases these have been grubbed up, but in many instances little areas of trees still stand. The words busk and bush are derived from *buskr*, another Old Norse word.

Other wooded areas which used to be common, but have now all but disappeared, are orchards, which are designated on the 1850 OS map with a different symbol from other woods: the trees appear in straight rows. Each farm at Finsthwaite had orchards and there were others at Stott Park, Landing and Ealinghearth, usually close to the farmhouse. At Low Stott Park in 1769 there were three orchards, including most of the triangular-shaped area on which the bobbin mill now stands. Late nineteenth century correspondence in the Arnold Greenwood archive mentions that Thomas Newby Wilson's grandfather was a great planter of trees, including cherry and crab apple at his Stott Park farm. These orchards, which would have served as grass pasture as well as for fruit and blossom for bees, have almost all gone. Only two still have fruit trees, both at Chapman House. The presence of orchards at Jolliver may finally explain this unusual house name, as there is a variety of apple known as the Gillyflower. It has clove-scented juice, and may have been preferred to the usual crab apple as an orchard tree. The house name is spelt variously: Joliver, Giliflowertree, Jilifloore Tree, Julyflowertree and July Flower Tree through the late seventeenth and eighteenth centuries. Pat Jones's family have planted two Cornish Gillyflower trees, to commemorate our project. Her identification of the apple tree variety was another small triumph of the persistent research at which she excelled.

Obscure names

We have drawn on the general principles for naming historic fields outlined by Angus Winchester in his booklet *Lake District Field-Names*. Land use is a key determinant, and we have examples of fields previously used for arable (Peaselands, Corn Parrock) and fodder or animal-bedding crops (Hollin, or holly, How, Brackendales). Landscape features and topography are also relevant (Hard Hills, Low Intake) as is size. Several Great Fields exist, often accompanied by a smaller Little Field, although as Great Field and Little Field at Plum Green do not differ greatly in size we have assumed that humour is at play. The name 'Far' is added to some names, denoting a piece of land at furthest distance from the farm. Far Hagg is the area of (previously) wooded pasture furthest west from Lower Finsthwaite. Far Acre is presumably another mild joke, as it is marked on an early nineteenth century map as a small strip of land immediately opposite the gate of Hill Top farm at Ealinghearth.

Some names are more mysterious, or at least not entirely clear. Feather Bed we thought originally might be humorous as there is a lump of bedrock in the field topped by a heap of stones. This may be simply field clearance, a never-ending job in Finsthwaite, but Pat's researches suggest the waller's practice of 'feathering' rock may be indicated here. The name Feather Bed is not as old as some; it is used on the Finsthwaite House estate plan in 1851, but does not appear in the Pedder archive until the 1860s. This may mean that it has more to do with some contemporary activity at the site, in this case the splitting of rock, and even breaking up the outcrop itself, for building or walling at Townend, rather than being the joking reference we originally thought.

Piet Holes may have had magpies nesting or gathering there; piet is the local name for the magpie. On the other hand, Pigeon Croft has nothing to do with pigeons. It has been called a croft throughout its documented life, which Angus Winchester suggests means it is either a field next to a farmstead, or land of particularly good quality. Against this being a croft next to a house are three points: there is no tradition of building in that part of Finsthwaite, away from the line of the lane, and no evidence on the ground of a dwelling. Most tellingly there is no fresh water to supply a house, and indeed Pigeon Croft stands close to the Ellermire, which is deep and stagnant. It is more likely that this is a croft in the sense of a good piece of farmland and Pigeon Croft is notably smoother and less rocky than the nearby haggs. The Pigeon part of the name is more convoluted. The earliest version of the name is Pynshowe (1582), then Phinchawe (1609) and Pinchway (1749) – always with the Croft part of the name included. Clement Taylor's account book gives various versions: Pincher Croft in 1725 and 1742 and Pincha Croft in 1723. 'Pigeon Croft' first appears in 1719 and is the name on the 1851 Finsthwaite House estate plan. It is also the name in current use – at the end of a long trail of what Angus Winchester calls 'Chinese whispers'. We think the name is another example of a field and wood name being paired together and that it derives from 'Finn's Shaw' – a small wood (shaw is derived from Old English *sceaga*) belonging to *Finnr* (of Finsthwaite). The Pedder archive contains a reference in 1564 to 'an area known as the shawe' which seems to be in that vicinity.

Another Chinese whisper example, albeit with a shorter sequence to the whisper, is Turn Moss Field at Lakeside, which is a twentieth century version of what was previously Twin Moss Field, in 1843 and 1868, and before that, as early as 1694, the field next to Tween Most Knott.

Lag Paddock appeared obscure at first. Lag is a dialect word for a stave, or section of a barrel. The field is not stave-shaped, and so we were left wondering if it was a place where staves might have been made, or some other split wood product worked. There is, typically, a wood alongside the field: Lag Paddock Bush. Clement Taylor's account book may have provided an answer. This area was known to him as Top of the Paddock. In September 1726, his account book records the purchase of 1,000 sapps, or sapp laths, some of which had been made at Top of the Paddock. It seems a fair guess that the name Lag Paddock memorialises this activity, albeit making use of the dialect word 'lag' rather than the version Clement Taylor wrote down. Sapps use the outer wood, which can be split more easily, and produced laths for strengthening walls that are going to be plastered (the lath part of 'lath and plaster'). Clement Taylor began building his new house, the present Finsthwaite House, in 1724. If, in September 1726, he had reached the stage of constructing the interior walls then it is not difficult to imagine him marking such a milestone by re-naming the place that produced the laths.

Finding and Interpreting Names

Lag Paddock on the Finsthwaite House estate plan 1851

The name Lag Paddock does appear in the account book, but not until 1756, in a section completed by his son, by which time the name could have become established.

The idea that a name, once given, might linger well beyond the time of the activity or person involved is more reasonable than it might at first sound. Indeed there is other evidence for it. Swinebroach must once have been an area where pigs were kept, but the name has long outlived the practice. The name Wintering Park is thought to mean a safe place to keep livestock over the winter. However, this wood has been coppiced in the past, and is mentioned as a working woodland throughout the eighteenth century. Since it is first documented in 1633, it must have had multiple uses, but it is the seasonal haven name that has stuck. Lag Paddock, Swinebroach and Wintering Park are all part of the Finsthwaite House estate, and it is perhaps more likely that a name used in the same family might endure.

Remembering the seller's name

Selling a field often led to a name, the vendor's, being fixed to a certain plot, and the name can be used long after the person is otherwise forgotten. Hatter Parrock, near Black Beck Mires, and Hatter Hag, by Little Nook at Waterside, are so called because they were sold in the 1760s by William Braithwaite, a hat maker, to his neighbours the Taylors. This human detail was revealed in the Pedder archive documents which record the transactions. Sale documents obviously identify buyers and sellers, but also often record their occupations (something which may have been particularly helpful at a period when so many of the residents of Finsthwaite were called Taylor and could only be differentiated by their trades or holdings). The Hatter name survived to be included on the Ordnance Survey maps in 1850 and 1890. An even older example may be 'Water or Bloomer Meadow' at High Stott Park. Recent archaeology (the *Windermere Reflections* project) confirms a bloomsmithy at the site, but the double name is recorded in Braithwaite family papers. They seem to have purchased the field from the Blumers, a family living at Stott Park in the 1530s.

Another early example of this practice is Walker Brow, near Sinderhill, a wooded hillside (a 'brow') plot sold by John Walker in the 1630s. John Walker married into the family of Nicholas Taylor and sold, according to various documents in the Pedder archive, much of the land he got by marrying Nicholas's daughter Isabel in a series of transactions in the early to mid 1630s. It is unclear whether he needed money, or was confident of his ability to support his family through his profession (he was a tailor) and felt he did not need to own land. Liz Kingston, a history teacher, pointed out that, following Charles I's dramatic dissolution of parliament and revival of various land and property taxes in the late 1620s, Mr Walker may have found he had liabilities that he was unable to meet without selling his holdings. Whatever the motive, the neighbour who bought a particular parcel of woodland from him remembered it as Walker Brow thereafter. It is so named on both the Finsthwaite House estate plan in 1851 and the OS map of 1890. The 1850 OS map calls it 'Fir Wood' and shows it planted with conifers – trees that remain to this day in a small remnant of plantation high up the hillside.

Jenny Hagg, a field now called Haggscar, was called so because it was sold by Clement Taylor on behalf of Jennet Taylor, who lived in Finsthwaite, to raise funds to support her in her widowhood. Clement Taylor managed finances and acted as banker for a number of neighbours, and had been chosen by Jennet (Jane) Taylor's husband as a suitable executor. His account book shows various transactions on her behalf, and payments to her; he calls her 'Old Jennet'. She lived at Charley Crag farm, and will appear again in this book, in the section on Finsthwaite Heights. She died, aged over 90, in 1728; she had been a widow for 10 years. Her name was still associated with Jenny Hagg when the Finsthwaite House estate plan was drawn up in 1851.

The practice of naming after vendors is still being followed. After the Kelletts bought fields from the Scales family, who farmed at Plum Green, the fields which had previously been called the Brow Dales (Low and High) and High Field are now referred to as Scales's Bottom Field, Scales's Middle Field and Scales's Top Field. The association with a person also means that Charlotte Dean calls some of the fields by Town End 'Dulcie's Fields' because of Dulcie Curwen and her husband Tom who lived in a nearby cottage.

Open or shared fields

We know some fields were once open or shared by a number of farmers because of their names. Angus Winchester notes that sequences of names like 'low, middle and high' denote land has been held in common or on some shared basis. This occurs twice at Finsthwaite, in the Brow Dales (which are Low and High Brow Dales) and again at the southern end of the village in a sequence of wood pastures: a group comprising Low, Middle, Far and Great Hagg. The haggs lie west of a large open field once used as arable, The Dales, a name which also suggests shared usage; so the practice was observed across both arable and pastureland. In Old English a *dael* is a share, and land called 'dales' usually denotes a place where several villagers would have had access or rights to a plot. At Bracken Dales near Ealinghearth, different people would have had rights to cut bracken for animal bedding. Yewbarrow Dale at Ealinghearth is a wood which was parcelled out between multiple owners under the terms of the 1771 enclosure award.

Dales are not the same as common land, where anyone local had some rights (to cut peat, or gather firewood), as on the top of the Heights, but rather a system of shared rights. Although a single wall might enclose the entire area of an open field, it is likely that posts or boundary stones marked out individual holdings. Some early transactions in the Pedder archive mention the trading of a 'dale or close of land' meaning that a strip within a larger field is being sold or swapped. Some tenancy agreements mention a half-share in a certain field being part of the holding of a farm. Sourbutts is another example of an open field: the 'butts' part of the name suggests that different strips 'butted up against each other' to make a whole. The acreage of fields like Sourbutts,

Making haylage in Low Brow Dale/Scales's bottom field

the Dales, and the Low and High Brow Dales are all around the 7-acre mark, and they are large fields for the area.

Dialect and Old Norse words

Dialect and words of Old Norse origin abound in the names we found – *bekkr* (a beck, as in Beck Field and Beck Meadow), *haugr* (a hill, as in Smithy Haw Wood), *knottr* (a free-standing hill, The Knott), *fjall* (land on the Heights as in Far Fell), *saur* (muddy, as in Sourbutts), *slakki* (a hollow or low-lying field as in Slack and Greenslack), *sker* (a steep cliff or scar as in Haggscar) all feature in our survey area. Old Norse words are usually used when a field or wood is named after a landscape feature or characteristic. Old English also features: like *dael*, meaning a share, as in Bracken Dales and The Dales, and the word *feld* (field) itself – but Old Norse words are more commonly the root of names.

We referred frequently to Wright's *Dialect Dictionary* to identify meanings for many words, including Fearing Brow. The 'brow' refers to the hillside slope that this wood is on, but 'fearing' is North Country dialect for a ghost or evil spirit, often associated with hollow ways and hillsides. A lane runs down the hill, with woodland on either side of the road and over-arching trees, and it is an easy place to imagine a haunting atmosphere. The Elinghearth Dobby is also said to haunt this slope, although her presence is nineteenth century. Cowper, who tells her story in his 1897 *History of Hawkshead,* also notes that ghost stories were told about this hill from much longer ago. Fearing Brow first appears in the Pedder archive in 1564, which confirms his belief.

What is now the church car park at Finsthwaite used to be the Shilla, named after the bed of small stones that used to cover it before the twenty-first century tarmac. Early in Sophia and Janet's time in Finsthwaite, a neighbour remarked that 'they were coming to shilly the yard' meaning to lay the rough pebbles that formed the surface of Plum Green yard outside her cottage. When asked the meaning of the word she explained that the area at the front of the church, covered in similar small stones, was known to her and other older residents as the Shilla. It is a name that is still used, usually as 'the Church Shilla', surviving as a dialect-based name despite the blanket of tarmac.

The field at the foot of the High Dam path now known as Beck Meadow appears as two plots, Gill Beck Field and Gill Beck Meadow, in a map of 1868. It was known as The Gillbeck in the eighteenth century, when it appears in a list of the holdings of Laurence Harrison in 1769. The gill element of the name is derived from an Old Norse word *gil* which means a small ravine, and comes to be associated with a stream in the bed of such a ravine. The stream which runs along the edge of this field comes down the hill from High Dam in a rocky ghyll.

Parks and parrocks

Three areas of parkland, shaded grey on the 1850 OS map, are shown: at Landing, Stott Park and Finsthwaite House. That at High Stott Park is in front of a now demolished house but the Low Parks is at least a seventeenth century name for the land in question. The first farms here were founded by Furness Abbey for raising stots, young cattle or possibly horses, and the grazing land was not apparently divided into small plots but left as open pasture on the gently sloping ground going down to the lake. It is a huge area, some 31 acres in all. At Landing there is a landscaped area of parkland by the mansion that was built there in 1830, and in this case it is remembered in the modern name The Parks for the large field which is let to the Kelletts of Chapman House as grazing. The parkland in front of Finsthwaite House is now called The Big Meadow, rather prosaically, but is picturesque and, at 20 acres, the largest field in Finsthwaite. It has been landscaped, and has absorbed at least one other field, Walker Parrock, into its acreage.

The name Wintering Park however, seems to be an example of parrock, a common name for a small enclosure of either woodland or field, being contracted to park. Angus Winchester's *Lake District Field Names* suggests that the small field next to a farmstead would commonly be called a croft but we found only one example of this in our survey area, at Tom Crag. We have found these small enclosures are usually called Parrock or The Parrock.

Village Histories

The following are short histories of each of the main settlements in our survey area. That for Finsthwaite is the longest, but we also have found background detail and stories about the people who lived at Landing, and what later became the village of Lakeside, High and Low Stott Park and Ealinghearth.

Our source material for this section was derived from Janet Martin's notes of her detailed study of the Pedder archive, other family archives (principally the Harrison and Braithwaite papers), parish records, census returns for each village, wills from the Richmond Deanery and the house histories and family trees she wrote. Sophia also drew on a history of Landing How, prepared for its modern owners by Carole Knight; it was Carole who tracked down the report of John Harrison's state of mind in the *Westmorland Gazette* of 1846.

Plum Green, Finsthwaite with Summersides fell grazing in the background.

Finsthwaite

Origins

Finsthwaite is a small village of about 50 houses, spread out over a mile and a quarter along a valley in the south-east of the Rusland Valley. It now has two working farms, Finsthwaite House and Chapman House and until the 1970s it had a third, a tenant farm at Tom Crag. In the 1851 census, seven people listed themselves as farmers. In 1537, when the village first appears in archival records, 15 households were paying greenhew rents and are listed as living in two groups of houses, Lower and Outer Finsthwaite. Both these are visible on the ground today, although Plum Green, the old Outer Finsthwaite, has developed slightly more substantially, has more modern houses, and is the site of the church and village hall.

The name Finsthwaite means Finn's clearing. The village, like so much of the Rusland Valley, is set in prolific woodland. Fields have been cleared along the line of the lane which runs through the valley, and the woodland, which provided a major focus of work for many villagers in the past, still covers the fellside of Finsthwaite Heights and The Knott. Finn as a personal name has Old Norse origins but no archival record of *Finnr* exists; a fact which both frustrates and inspires.

The whole origin of the village is uncertain. For all the vividness of the archives from the sixteenth century, and the first mention in the mid-fourteenth, when and how *Finnr* first came to the village, and whether it has been continuously occupied since that time, is not clear. The loss of so much of the Furness Abbey archive, which would have given us historical evidence, is galling. The two groupings of Lower and Outer Finsthwaite may follow an Irish Norse settlement pattern, with three or four farmsteads clustered around a green with a stream running through it, with arable fields nearby and with ways up onto the fellside for common grazing. Fell grazing may be a reason for the village being founded, as a *saeter* or summer grazing ground, which was later developed by *Finnr* and others to form a permanent settlement, which in course of time spread northwards as the extended family grew. Modern public footpaths follow the routes from these little centres out to the old open fields and, in the case of the paths to High Dam, onto the fell in a way which suggests that these mirror age-old routes followed by the inhabitants of Finsthwaite.

We have a handful of examples of Fin as an element in names. As well as the village name itself, there is also Finsthwaite House and Finsthwaite Heights. Finsyke is now the name of a house, but in the seventeenth and eighteenth centuries often applied to the whole group of houses at Lower Finsthwaite. A syke is a stream and one flows round the edge of the field which lies just in front of the house called Finsyke. It is possible that this is the earliest place of settlement in the village, a cleared area of pasture, near both a water supply and the fell grazing. Slightly east of this, we think that the old arable field Pigeon Croft is the croft or field next to Fin's Shaw (shaw means a wood). We have also found Finsknott in the Pedder archive,

A Herdwick ewe at Finsyke

which is The Knott, or Great Knott; the name crops up many times as either Finsknott or The Knott at Finsthwaite. Mentioned in association with Finsknott is Finscarr, which we think is likely to be the steeply sloping edge of the Knott coming downhill from Finsthwaite Tower towards Newby Bridge. Both are named together as sites for 'cropping and lopping' of wood in 1606. It seems fitting that we can find *Finnr's* name associated, if tentatively, with all the areas that are characteristic of the village: fields, fell, woodland, and houses.

Working the woods

All the people mentioned in the greenhew rent list from the court of 1537 are called Taylor. If this is an occupational name, it should be emphasised that they are not making clothes; they are cutters and workers of wood, not fabric. Paying greenhew rents, of 4d per person, gave each household the right to cut and work the wood. At this time, woodland would have been valuable, probably more so than the agricultural land. Most families were occupied in making both domestic wares out of wood (plates, dishes, buckets, barrels, and spoons) and a wide range of other products, like pack-horse saddles, hoops, baskets, and the most significant product of all: charcoal for the Furness iron-makers.

The greenhew rent list names each person, or rather we know the names of the men who were either living and paying monies or had died and left behind a widow who was continuing to engage in working the woodlands.

Those living at Lower Finsthwaite or 'Fyncethwayt Inferior' were:

>Christopher Taylor
>Widow of James Taylor
>Thomas Taylor
>Widow of John Taylor
>Brian Taylor
>Roland Taylor
>Sons of William Taylor
>Richard Taylor

Those at Outer Finsthwaite, or 'Fyncethwayt Exterior' were:

>Widow of Richard Taylor
>Widow of Thomas Taylor
>Roger Taylor
>John Taylor
>Christopher Taylor
>George Taylor
>Robert Taylor the elder

Working the woodland took its place alongside agriculture, and indeed it is likely that the farming that the Taylors were doing was little more than subsistence. One of the signatories of the first document in Box 26 of the Pedder archive, John Taylor, is a 'dish-throwler', making wooden platters and presumably other turned wooden objects for household and other uses. A man fined for cutting too much bark, one Brian Taylor, is a bast-rope maker. Bast-rope uses the inner fibrous bark of lime trees (*Tilia cordata*) which grow in local woods to this day. The outer bark of species other than lime (oak was particularly popular) was dried and used to tan leather.

Rusland's woodland was exploited for centuries to make charcoal for iron smelting. Although some of the charcoal was shipped out to other bloomsmithies, there was also local iron working. This shows up in some of our survey names, at houses like Sinderhill and in field names like Bloomer Ridding near Backbarrow, which we think was an iron-working site, and Thompson Loop, an area of woodland near Waterside. A 'loop' is the name given to a piece of pig iron at the stage when it is going to be hammered to get rid of impurities in the metal. The demand for charcoal led to intensive coppicing of woodland, when trees are cut so that multiple stems grow back. These can be harvested at various stages of growth: slim for hoops for swill baskets, thicker ones for bobbins and for charcoal.

Swill basket making at Plum Green yard, Finsthwaite, in 1891.

As well as the all-important charcoal, a wealth of other objects and products were made from wood. Different types of trees in the mixed woodlands around the village would each have had their specific purposes. Traditionally, ash was used for charcoal although oak charcoal was especially prized in certain circumstances and juniper wood charcoal was favoured in gunpowder making. Oak, being exceptionally hard, was used for beams and axles, ash was used for tool handles and broomsticks, birch for bobbins (and their twiggy tops for besoms), swill baskets were made of woven strips of oak or birch suspended from hooped hazel branches. Other woods would have been valued for hurdles, clog soles, fence posts, sticks, furniture, carts, gates – and even firewood, although it would have been 'loppings and toppings' that were used to start kitchen fires that would mainly have burned peat. When Clement Taylor sells timber from his estate in the early eighteenth century, he is careful to specify that some trees are excluded from the sale: the crab apple trees (perhaps for their fruit, but also because they are a useful pollinator), holly (for fodder) and ash, perhaps because of its value in charcoal making, although ash leaves were sometimes used as spring fodder. In modern times, when timber was sold from Summersides and from Cotesteads Coppice, many crab apple trees avoided the clearance. The felled timber was being sold for pit props and so crab apple wood would have no doubt been unsuitable, but the trees are noticeable survivals on the fellside. Vanessa Champion has mapped over 60 crab apple trees dotted over Finsthwaite Heights.

Eking out a living

We found names for the entire patchwork of fields and woods in the village, something which itself bears witness to the intensity with which the natural environment of valley, fell and wood was worked. In agricultural terms, the land can best be described as marginal, and it is interesting to reflect on the extent of cereal and vegetable growing in the past. The will of Jennet Taylor in 1605, for example, mentions 4s worth of 'bigg corne' (barley) while that of Edward Taylor mentions 'corne in the ground'; he died in June 1610, just before the harvest. Many inventories note ploughs, which would have been worked by manpower or ox-power; very few horses are recorded. Fields once used for arable are now entirely grass pasture and hay meadow. We found, however, that what we identified as once being arable fields are now often of slightly better fertility, with thicker soils, and are cropped for hay and silage. The fellside is used as it has always been: to graze sheep (Herdwick, Rough Fell and some slightly more mixed species) and some cattle, in the summer. The fell above Chapman House farm, Summersides, is first mentioned in 1599, in the will of Edward Taylor, which lists 'a close called Somersyde'.

Fines issued during the courts of the 1530s and 1540s show people being penalised for exceeding the agreed limits for farming and working the woodlands. Brian Taylor and others paid 1s or 2s each for having cut more bark than they should. Several people were fined for keeping pigs 'on the common pasture beyond the agreed stint', at a rate of 3d per animal. The penalty for excess bark stripping was higher, as were those for 'elyng of ashes' (producing kiln-dried wood and ash for lead smelting and for lye) and coopering (barrel making) perhaps because of the need to safeguard the woodland resources. There was a general agreement that no-one should make new intakes, which might mean fields or woodland plots, without special licence 'according to the late agreement made between the abbot and the tenants'.

Stephen Kellett of Chapman House Farm at Cartmel Show 1950

As a slight aside, Brian Taylor, the over-eager bast rope maker, is fined again at a court of the 1540s, this time for drunkenness, alongside a Richard Taylor. Their fines, 2s each, are twice the level of those who were fined for selling ale and coopering (making barrels).

An emphasis on living and working within agreed limits so as not to exhaust the land continued into later centuries. In 1760, an agreement with a tenant of Town End Farm stipulates that fields could be ploughed, but not for longer than three years at a time, presumably so as not to overwork the thin soils. Thomas Dickinson, husbandman, a tenant of Town End Farm, is bound not 'to crop ash trees', perhaps to preserve them for charcoal or fodder, nor to 'turn cows into Little Butts'. This field is also earmarked in another tenancy agreement as one that may be grazed by sheep or horses, but not cattle. Thomas Dickinson is further enjoined not to 'commit waste' and must 'manure all parts as he shall plough according to the usual course of husbandry at Finsthwaite'. When Town End Farm is let again a few decades later, to a Thomas Braithwaite, he may not 'sell hay, straw, manure or peat from the estate', and must not plough for more than three years running.

The tone of these agreements underscores the careful juggling and bartering that went along with eking out a living on the land. As tenant farming increased in the eighteenth and nineteenth centuries, there is careful specification of what has been negotiated. In the tenancy agreement with Thomas Braithwaite, Edward Taylor his landlord says he will buy manure from Town End Farm at 6d a load, although he specifies that for 6d it must be a load in a cart that can be drawn by one horse, just in case there is any monkey business about what a load is. Another tenant of Town End, Thomas Huddleston, 'is to have Peslands this year, but John Benson is to have the price deducted from (his) rent', suggesting that tenants and landlords worked out agreements as they went along to some extent, perhaps depending on decisions about how land was to be used each season.

By 1813, we have the first occasion on which a farmer seems to find nuisance-value in trees growing in the fields. When Jolliver Tree farm is let, for £58 per year for 7 years, to a John Burns, it is stipulated once again that the tenant may not sell any hay, straw or manure off the land, but is to 'spread and bestow' manure 'on the premises'. So far, so familiar. He has 17 acres of arable and pasture land, but the timber and wood rights are 'excepted' (excluded; the woods are retained by the landlord). He is warned 'not to cut or damage the timber', but may grub up 'part of a wood lying within the fields' and when it is 'grubbed up, trenched, drained and fenced' he is to pay 'the same rent as for the rest of the land'. Mr Burns presumably regarded the work as improvement. The practice of clearing trees from fields continued throughout the nineteenth century. Although much woodland remains, it is more clearly demarcated than in the past.

Scattered holdings and boundary disputes

Most of the Finsthwaite farmers have holdings scattered across the valley. From the earliest times, the farms of Lower Finsthwaite in particular have lands, mainly meadows and arable, on Rusland Pool. Throughout the late sixteenth century, documents in the Pedder archive make references to fields like Broad Meadow 'at Pulle' or 'Powesyd'. The fields in question lie between Ealinghearth Moss and Border Moss Wood, to the east side of Rusland Pool. Within the village, there is also evidence for farms having holdings that are not confined to lands immediately by the farmhouse. Instead, holdings are made up of half-shares and plots spread around the valley and fellside. All the farms hold a range of arable land, fell grazing and woodland that would have been essential elements in the farming mix.

Clement Taylor's account book gives examples of valuations of farms, like Waterside, which includes fields across the parish from Newland Head, Tarn Potts and Haggscar (near Newby Bridge), the Dales and a share of Pincher Croft (arable fields at Lower Finsthwaite) and land at Rusland Pool. Similarly Tom Crag Farm in 1756 holds 'Wood Moss and Meadow, and Rough Moss, Will Bridge End Wood' (near Ealinghearth) together with part of the Dales adjoining Whitestone, Great Hagg and Little Hagg, Becking (at Lower Finsthwaite), Tarn Haw (on the fell near Boretree), Little Butt and a share of Great Meadow (which could be any of several but is likely to be by Finsthwaite House). Parts of the Pedder archive are concerned with consolidation of land to some extent and, in the case of Finsthwaite House, a gradual enlarging of the estate from the mid-eighteenth century onwards.

When Henry Taylor was married in the early 1720s, his marriage settlement included his father's farm at 'Plumb Green' (the house there that is now Rose Cottage) incorporating fields at Stott Park called Cowper Ridding and Water Meadow, as well as closes called The Field and Head of the Field (now Finsthwaite Field) and other land at Plum Green like Burn Knotts, Great, Little and Low Intake, and Parrock of the Height.

The practice of farming on common or shared land was not without problems. This state of affairs was in itself helpful to our research, because it often led to a legal resolution of the conflict and, in the case of the Taylors, another archive in the collection. Disagreements, and some hot disputes, occurred and had to be sorted out by neighbours who acted as 'umpires'. In 1593, dissension arose 'about a close called Tarn Potts between Peter Taylor of Waterside, a blacksmith, Richard Sands and John Taylor'. Agreement was reached, adjudicated by five neighbours from Finsthwaite and another man from Stott Park. Rights to work the field were agreed, with Peter Taylor getting the 'over end' or northern part, John Taylor getting the middle and Richard Taylor the 'nether' or southern end. Restrictions are set out in the document covering when any of the parties can go in and cut wood, presumably because the trees grew across the field and cutting and carting it could interfere with another man's arable work. Furthermore, the parties are bound over to be on better behaviour in future, and are said to have been 'bookesworne to be lovers and friends as Christians ought'.

In 1670, a row broke out between Richard Taylor and George Taylor, both yeomen of Finsthwaite. Each man's rights were carefully stipulated: for example, that each had their own 'bracken dales' (shares to cut bracken for animal bedding), each must maintain walls, hedges and fences and, in future, go about their business 'quietly on the common height'. The argument had not been confined to Finsthwaite Heights however. The agreement spells out that Richard has the right to carry goods from Wright Bridge End through George's close called Corn Moss, 'except when the corn is growing', when he must drive his cattle further south so as not to damage crops. Equally, at Finsthwaite, George has 'leave of way from Hagg to Whitestones through Richard's dale of Peaselands except when the corn is growing' when he must go through Little Nook – and must himself 'uphold sufficient yeats (gates) and rails for the said way'. Several outside parties adjudicated the decision; they were from further afield than Finsthwaite, so the dispute was perhaps particularly heated and locally notorious.

No argument between neighbours was as devastating as that between Roland Taylor and John Taylor, which resulted in the latter's murder. We know of it only because, in 1529, a man called Thomas Kendall, who was a leather seller from London, complained that the abbot of Furness had encouraged Roland and fomented the row between the two men, who were arguing over which of them should be the Abbey's under-bailiff for the area. Roland is said to have killed John Taylor with his own 'cropping axe' when he was up a tree cutting holly for his sheep, pulling him down from the tree and 'smiting him' about the legs and, fatally, his head. Thomas Kendall's connection to the area and to the parties involved is unknown, although his information is graphic. The abbot stoutly denied any involvement, Roland Taylor said it had all been settled, and the eagle-eyed reader may have noticed that in the list of residents of Finsthwaite in 1537 are one Roland Taylor and a 'widow of John Taylor', but whether these are the same people ten years on is not absolutely clear.

Finsthwaite today

Later farms like Chapman House, Jolliver Tree, Sinderhill and Finsthwaite House are founded in a line along the lane that runs under the fellside along the valley, and do not show the same pattern of clustering as is seen at Lower Finsthwaite and Plum Green. Town End Farm is also later and marks the southern end of the village. Of these, only two are still working farms today. To the north, Finsthwaite borders Low Stott Park, on the road to Hawkshead. The village was originally part of Dalton parish, and later Hawkshead. After the creation of Colton parish, in 1676, some villagers continued to be buried with their ancestors at Hawkshead, but Colton became Finsthwaite's parish church. In 1724, Finsthwaite built its own church. The original chapel was later rebuilt by Paley and Austin in 1875. At the end of the nineteenth century the population was around 440 (1901 census), today it numbers 70 permanent residents.

Today our farmers keep sheep, with Chapman House also having some cattle. Woodland still offers a source of income but is by no means the resource it once was. There are caravans on Summersides on the Chapman House farm, but tourism has made relatively little impact in comparison with some Lake District villages. A number of houses are let to visitors, and some are second homes. The greatest change in farming is that there is no longer arable land; neither cereals nor vegetables have been grown since the Second World War. Even then, there was no ploughing or harvesting machinery: it had to be provided by the War Agricultural Executive Committee, WAEC. Labour was imported too, in the form of a local conscientious objector, Arthur Duxbury. Chapman House had dairy cattle until 1987, and a local milk round. Direct sales of farm produce now include very free-range eggs (Rosie and Stevie Watson) and Charlotte Chaplin Tweed (from the Finsthwaite House Herdwicks).

Rosie Watson with Chapman House sheep on the fell

Newby Bridge and the Knott

The bridge, which marks the point at which Windermere ceases to be a lake and becomes the River Leven, appears as 'the new bridge' on John Speed's map of 1577. The first reference to Newby Bridge appears in 1659, and Diana Whaley suggests that there is an association with a local family called Newby. Edward Taylor of Plum Green, in his will of 1599, left 12d for 'repair to Newby Bridge'. He is unlikely to have been responsible for damage to it; the donation was made for general upkeep of a useful facility. As with the fords at Landing, it is a convenient crossing point giving access to the main road to Kendal and Lancaster, and a landing area for transport of goods. Wharf Field next to the Swan Hotel suggests that a pier for unloading industrial produce, probably charcoal, was established. The Swan Hotel itself is a typical piece of infrastructure for travellers, at what became a hub for transport of various kinds. The Furness Railway shows on the Finsthwaite House estate plan in 1851, as being under construction. A branch line from Ulverston came through to Haverthwaite, with a station at Newby Bridge Halt. In 1868 the line was extended to Lakeside.

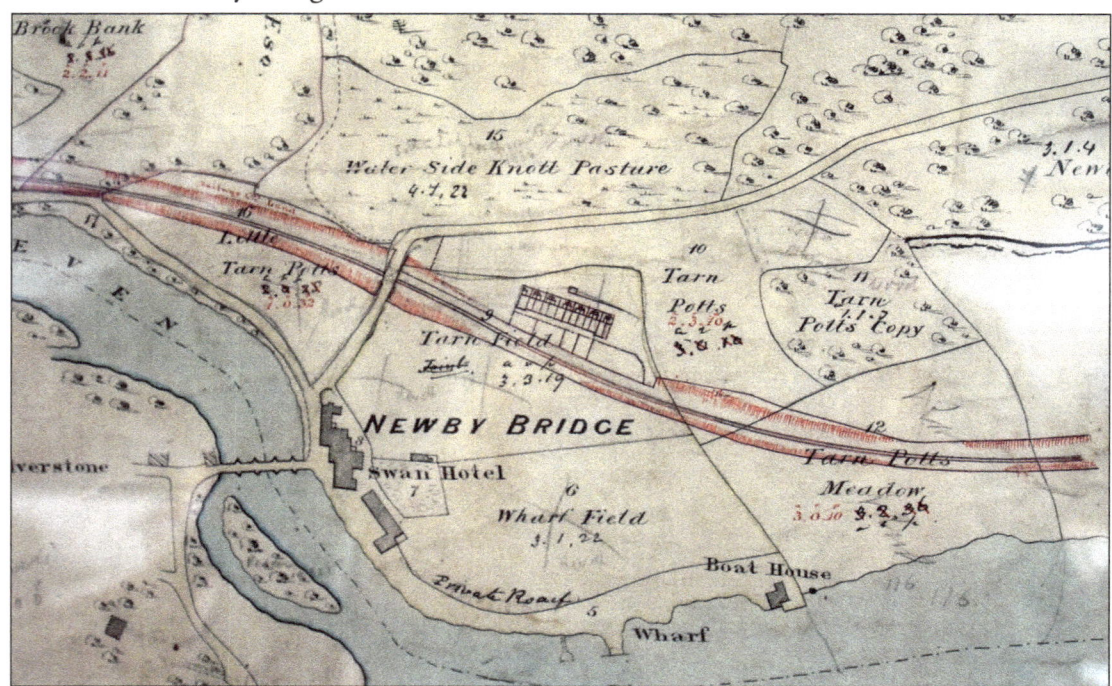

Newby Bridge on the Finsthwaite House estate plan 1851

The main settlement of Newby Bridge, together with a second hotel, lies over the river, and was outside the Mapped Histories area. The farm within our survey, Waterside, was farmed by a branch of the Taylor family from at least the late sixteenth century, and was later absorbed into the Finsthwaite House estate. Early references to Waterside farm begin in the 1590s, when Peter Taylor, a blacksmith of Waterside, was involved in a dispute about land at Tarn Potts, a field at the back of the Swan Hotel which he shared with two others. The argument was about rights of access and the nuisance caused by conflicting uses of the land. In the agreement which was eventually thrashed out between them, the owners of the field are bound to do any wood cutting on their various dales by 'St James's Day'. Unfortunately there are three saints: St James, St James the Great and St James the Less who have varying feast days, and it is unclear which saint is indicated. The idea would be that any wood-carting or timber felling does not interfere with ploughing or harvesting. There is no provision made for setting out clear ways through the plots, only an exhortation that 'none shall be a nuisance daily fetching and carrying goods'.

A little later, in a will of 1625, another blacksmith of Waterside, Richard Taylor, leaves to his son Peter 'smythy bellows and all the work toyles thereto belonging'. It seems likely that these same tools had come down from Peter's grandfather and namesake, who had the dispute at Tarn Potts in the 1590s. In the eighteenth century, the farm was owned by Clement Taylor's brother-in-law, Richard Robinson. He had no children and on his death the farm was absorbed into the Finsthwaite House estate and was let to tenants. Waterside land is still part of the Finsthwaite House farm.

Three fields between the river and the railway line have seen some change in their boundaries. There is now only one long strip of meadow, called Waterside Meadow, but in the past it was three fields: Great Field, Little Field (which was smaller) and a field called Grubbin – a name which implies that it was cleared of tree roots and stones to make a small additional pasture. A further change, wrought directly by the railway, is revealed in a document in the Pedder archive from 1869, which refers to 'the garden part of Great Field'. This would appear to be map plot 800 or 800a and the wording suggests that there was still a sense of the land having been sliced through by the railway, leaving this part cut off from the main field.

The Knott, a craggy hill which separates Finsthwaite from Newby Bridge and Lakeside, is first named in 1552, when a parcel of land in the 'Knott at Finsthwaite' was traded between Robert Taylor of 'Plomgreen', a yeoman and Edward Taylor son of John, a 'dish-thrower'. A little later, in 1587, John Taylor of Plum Green and Myles Taylor of Landing How have dealings over 'a dale of wood in Myles's tenement in the Knoot'. Plots on the Knott are valued by craftsmen like the dish-thrower (a wood-turner in modern parlance) but they would also have been coppiced by charcoal burners. On the 1843 map of the Landing estate there is a small plot called Knot

Pasture near the summit of the hill. It has fewer trees on it than the surrounding plots and was used for sheep or cattle grazing, illustrating the way in which farming and wood-working co-existed. The number of plots on The Knott, divided by dry stone walls, suggests that this, like Finsthwaite Heights, was a resource shared amongst various farming neighbours. Waterside farm certainly had land there (a large plot is called Waterside Knott) as did Landing (Landing Knott).

The Knott's association with *Finnr* and Finsthwaite is interesting. Not only is it described in sixteenth and seventeenth century documents as being 'the Knott at Finsthwaite' or Finsknott, it is also likely to be the site of Finscarr, a now unused name. However, it is one which we think applies to the very steep slope that descends from Summer House Knott, at the south-west end of the hill, to Newby Bridge.

View of Landing / Lakeside and The Knott with Finsthwaite visible top right.

Landing and Lakeside

Visitors to Lakeside, and it attracts many, can be forgiven for supposing that it is a village that has always been here, but almost the entire settlement has grown up since the railway first came in 1868. Given the centuries-old villages we have surveyed during Mapped Histories it is surprising to learn that this place is the product of development over a relatively short time. Even the 1850 OS map shows only two main houses on the site, and one of them, Quay House, now the Lakeside Hotel, was then a relatively new one.

The old settlement of Landing

One of those houses, Landing, is of ancient foundation. The name, usually spelt Lendin, is associated with a crossing point on the lake, and a place for loading and unloading goods, most particularly charcoal being moved from the woods further north to bloomsmithies elsewhere in Furness. A modern house called Landing How still occupies this old site, and takes its name from the small, round promontory that sticks out into the lake. Windermere is very narrow at this point and there were at least two fords here where people and carts could cross, the water being usually only about two feet deep. The fords are known to date back to mediaeval times and were used until the sixteenth-century bridge at Newby Bridge became the preferred way of crossing the lake at its southern end. Cowper's *History of Hawkshead* recorded the name of the crossing at Landing as Tinklers Ford. He also notes that both fords had long since fallen out of use at the time of his writing in the late 1890s.

There is a little less scope for cultivation at Lakeside than at Finsthwaite, where the valley is wider than the strip available between the lake shore and the Knott (which blocks the sun, especially on winter afternoons). We have noted fewer arable field names here than at Finsthwaite. A branch of the Taylor clan lived here in the sixteenth century and it supported one farm. These Taylors also appear on the list of those paying greenhew rents (for working the woodland) and, as at Finsthwaite and Stott Park, people are fined for cutting too much bark, bast-rope making and coopering beyond the allowances for these activities, at the courts of the 1530s and 1540s. George Taylor, who made a will in 1685, held land on the same scattered basis as we have found at other places in our survey, in his case with fields at Plum Green

(Finsthwaite), Landing itself and woods in Breakbank (near Waterside). This family also owned the farm at Sinderhill. George Taylor had fell pasture near Boretree tarn, together with 'liberty of gait or way' to it.

The Taylors of Landing sometimes let part of the house to tenants, including a James Fleming 'gentleman' who was living there when he made a will in 1715, because he was 'now going abroad to venture my life in the service of my king and country from whence, perhaps, I shall never returne againe'. He made legacies to various relations in Langdale and ordered that the value of a debt, owed by John Taylor of Lending, should be paid to John's daughter Ann 'in respect of her cair over me att several times when I was very much indisposed here'. An inventory of James's property, drawn up in 1720, lists sources of income, and property which suggests a man on campaign: a horse, saddles, bridles, some furniture including a large dressing box, a musket, a gun and bayonet, a case of pistols, holsters, an old sword, belts, cartridges and cases. He also owned rings, glasses, combs and brushes, and some books, valued at £1 6s 3d.

Landing was held by the Taylors until 1734, when Henry Taylor went bankrupt owing over £1,400. Ten years earlier, he had been one of the primary movers behind the foundation of Finsthwaite chapel, and he provided land for the site of the church and churchyard, taken from Little Field at Plum Green. His money problems were not attributable to this cause, but are uncertain. His schedule of debts, to 23 creditors, included some £70 owed to the landlady of the Newby Bridge hotel.

The estate was bought by the Harrisons who farmed at Low Stott Park farm and this family held the Landing estate until the last parts of it were finally sold off in 1920. In 1843, preparations were made to sell – again because of debt. A survey was made (both a working copy and a printed version exist at Kendal Record Office) which yielded more than 70 field and woodland names; one of our richest archive finds. The sales particulars offer a most beguiling picture of the property. They describe the mansion house (remodelled in 1830, by the Kendal architect George Webster), the 'beautifully wooded' estate and the lake frontage. The property is said to offer 'ample gratification in fishing and shooting, several packs of hounds are kept in the neighbourhood'. The auction poster goes on to flatter the neighbours by concluding that it would be a splendid purchase 'to a family desirous of a permanent country residence in the vicinity of good society'.

Despite such allurements, the proposed sale never went ahead. Questions were raised about whether the recently deceased owner, John Harrison, had been of sound mind. The Westmorland Gazette report in 1846, of a hearing to dispute the will, gives a vivid account of his behaviour, drinking, and decline from a 'careful, prudent man' to one who 'became addicted to wine and at one time was a very intemperate' one. Susan Sharp, his servant at Landing for 6 years, reported: 'I used to think him a nice, gentlemanly man but then afterwards he got into a very low way....he used to lie in bed in the day time...and he would come and sit by the kitchen fire half-dressed and then go back through the lobby talking to himself. When he was in that high way he would purchase pots and carpets, little trumpery pictures and articles which did not appear to be at all necessary'. John Harrison had been treated at The Retreat at York, an enlightened mental health facility established by the Quakers, which was said to have restored his capacities. The case was abandoned and his brother bought the estate, settled John's debts and honoured the legacies in his will, keeping the estate in Harrison hands.

In 1822 Dorothy Harrison left the entire property to her eldest son, and specified in her will that she should be buried at 'the chapel of Finsthwaite, without funeral pomp or any unnecessary expense whatever'. The last of the Harrisons, Thomas Newby Wilson, inherited Landing from his grandmother Elizabeth who died in 1867. He was a noted breeder of Dalmatian dogs. With neither wife nor children to leave the property to, and after a prolonged search for heirs after his death in 1915, the Harrison estate was sold and broken up in 1920. The house at Landing continued as a private house and for a short period was a hotel. It fell into disrepair gradually; the modern building on the site was a new build in the 1990s. It uses the same building footprint and the gardens include surviving ornamental tree-planting from the late nineteenth century.

The new community of Lakeside

The 1850 OS map shows only one house besides Landing at what would become Lakeside: Quay House, which was probably built by the Harrisons as a farmhouse for the tenant or manager of their farmland. Quay House was sold in 1871 to the Kellett family who had been the Harrisons' last tenants at Low Stott Park farm, and it became an inn and public house and later the Lakeside Hotel. Significant house building at Lakeside did not begin until the railway branch line came through from Newby Bridge in 1868. Pleasure boats had already begun to ply a trade on the lake, originally with a makeshift pier in the form of an old cart driven into the water with planks on top; it was soon replaced by a more appropriate structure. Catering for tourists, visitors and incomers looking for a country house rapidly became attractive business. Thomas Newby Wilson took the opportunity to sell land for villas, and so began a process which would, over the next few decades, completely transform the area and bring Lakeside into being.

Thomas Newby Wilson had to take a case to the Chancery Court for permission to sell off some of the 'settled estate'. He seems not to have resented but rather to have encouraged the influx of new people, taking full advantage of the opportunity to sell building plots and small parcels of land for cottages for his own gardeners, estate workers and farm bailiff, as well as for villas and houses for incomers. The process began in 1869 and he continued through the 1880s to sell building lots. He made the case rather oddly to modern ears, downplaying the value of his own Webster house saying: 'the mansion at Landing is a plain old fashioned structure of no architectural pretension with small rooms and low ceilings'. He went on to explain: '...it stood in a low position and looks onto a marshy pool...That the said extension of the (railway) line passed within about 100 yards of the house and cut off the grounds from the lake frontage (the Furness Railway company provided him with a beautifully-made iron bridge to reconnect his grounds to Landing How, but he glosses over that fact) and the value of the said residence had been thereby considerably depreciated and building in the neighbourhood would not further injure it.'

Local authority records for North Lonsdale District Council show multiple plans for houses at Lakeside from the late nineteenth and early twentieth centuries. The Lakeside Hotel was an inn by the 1870s and applications were made for extensions, remodelling of the premises, and in 1890 for pigsties. Once started, the building of villas and cottages proceeded apace, followed by applications to make alterations and improvements to buildings with the addition of greenhouses, washhouses, stables, and so on. At Buck Yeats an application was made for building a gardener's cottage in 1890. A lodge was added to Fern Ville, the first of Lakeside's new villas. The Landing estate accounts include payments for large water tanks to supply various houses and the hotel, with monies paid to 'John Brown of Ambleside for the building of great tanks in Great Knott'. Several such structures, now ruined, can still be seen in the wood.

Near Buck Yeats, maps show a powder magazine by the pier (at Magazine wood on the lake shore). At first we wondered whether this might have been a place where gunpowder was shipped out, although we had nothing to suggest any local gunpowder making. It then became obvious that it was for bringing gunpowder in to the area, to assist with blasting rock for water tanks and for house building. The new houses at Lakeside all look to have used local stone; quarries are marked on the 1890 OS map.

In 1887 the Jubilee Institute, a public hall for the education and entertainment of the growing population, was built by Thomas Newby Wilson on a piece of land that had once been Bull Copy Wood. The census records show the great diversity of the resident population: manufacturers and industrialists, vicars, retirees, widows, carters, publicans, a keeper of horse-drawn carriages (including one 20-seater charabanc drawn by four horses), a dancing instructor, pleasure boat proprietors, a steamboat captain, as well as the servants and nursemaids and other domestic staff, and ladies' companions, who came to work in the new Lakeside houses. It attracted returnees too: the 1911 census records John Machell, 'lately returned from the United States', living at Fern Ville with four children under the age of 12, who were all born in California.

The first of the many new buildings at Lakeside is the villa called Fern Ville (in the early twentieth century it changed its name to the current Ridding Bay). Later came Buck Yeats, Crag Wood, The Knoll and other houses. Fern Ville was built by a Manchester tin plate manufacturer who owned other land and property locally, including at Hawkshead. People interested in country sports like hunting, shooting and fishing, were attracted to the new houses. Sporting rights and landing rights for boating are often specified in tenancy agreements for villas and the immensely desirable lake frontage is frequently mentioned, and boathouses built.

William Kellett with rowing boats at Lakeside

Of the amenities for visitors the pleasure boats, which arrived first, are still there in the form of the Windermere steamers and other smaller craft, along with the guest houses and the Lakeside Hotel. The resource which started it all, the railway, is there too: it is now a heritage line run by steam enthusiasts for the delight of visitors, who can have little idea of the transformation it once wrought.

Stott Park

Farming families

Stott Park was founded as an outlying farm of Furness Abbey; Abbots Reading to the south west of Finsthwaite was another Abbey property. Its name first appears in documents of the 1530s but it may well have been established earlier, to raise cattle, or possibly horses (a 'stot' can mean either a bullock or a horse) for the abbot. The land is good for livestock rearing, with access to fell grazing on Stott Park Heights, and lakeshore fields for hay for winter fodder. Three farms developed on the site: Low Stott Park (associated with the Harrison family), High Stott Park (farmed by a branch of the Taylors, who were also the builders of the later High Stott Park House), and a now demolished farm called Stock Park (which had a long association with the Braithwaite family).

The farming resources are typical of the area, with fell grazing, peat mosses, arable lands at the lower level, and woods which were exploited for charcoal making and the production of other wood products. Whilst the resources may be typical, the value of the land seems to have been considerable. The 1670 will of Robert Taylor includes an inventory of his possessions that stands out for their value: he had £47 16s 8d in 'beasts' (cattle), £39 of sheep and lambs, stores of 'bigg' (barley) worth £8 15s, and hay, straw and, unusually, horses – worth £5.

In the 1530s, there were four holdings at Stott Park with two families living there: the Ashburners and the Blumers (or Bloomers) suggesting that industry had taken over from cattle or horse rearing, or at least has taken its place alongside agriculture. Once again it was the prolific woodland which offered opportunities for craft and industry and which attracted fines for over-working the woods; both families are charged 'for exercising the art of the smith'. The Ashburner name implies a family involved in charcoal-making; ash is a favourite wood for charcoal for iron smelting, although their name may also refer to potash making (using bracken for lye, to make soap used for cleaning wool). The Blumer name is more straightforwardly one for people making iron and running bloomsmithies. A bloomsmithy, or bloomery, is a small scale iron-making site which would have been common all over the area. The hill above Low Stott Park is Smithy Haw or Smithy Hall, which may mean it was an iron working site, although a will of 1643, of a man in Plum Green bequeathing blacksmithing tools and equipment, may identify the owner of the wood.

The Ashburner family were clearly involved in agriculture too. Edward Ashburner left a will in 1576 (the earliest will preserved in the archives for anyone in our survey area) which mentions leaving 'a lamb to each godchild', a typical gift to godchildren. The inventory that went with the will of John Ashburner in 1586 mentions ploughs and plough gear. William Ashburner in 1619 made a 'nuncupative' will (meaning that it was dictated to the witnesses) and the inventory which accompanied it mentions the value of 'pease sown', and later of 'meal, malt, hemp and yarn', and plough gear and a harrow. He also, as would be typical of all the residents of the area, had many 'wooden objects of all sorts', valued at 10s, and charcoal: 'coolle in pytte', valued at 6s. Less typically he also possessed a sword and dagger, valued at 21s.

The family names of Ashburner and Bloomer had died out by the mid-seventeenth century and the land became associated with new owners, although one field named in the Braithwaite archive as 'Water Meadow or Bloomer Meadow' is likely to have been called that after the Bloomer family who sold it. One of the Ashburners was also a cooper and may have given a name to Cowper Ridding, further south on the lake shore.

Low Stott Park

The family who came to Low Stott Park farm in the mid-seventeenth century were called Harrison. A member of the family, Myles Harrison, bought the Landing estate in 1734 when Henry Taylor went bankrupt. The first Harrison, Laurence, was a cooper – a craftsman making barrels and casks. He married three times, and lived to be over 90. In 1835 the family founded the bobbin mill at Stott Park, on a triangle of land opposite the Low Stott Park farmhouse which seems previously to have been orchards.

Stott Park bobbin mill.

Three orchards are mentioned in a description of the farm in 1769. We can identify the site of one from a later map, and in the 1769 list another is referred to as being the 'nethermost orchard' adjoining Underside (a plot we know from an 1843 map) placing it in the area later used for the mill.

The site was ideal for a bobbin mill, having a stream to provide water power. High Dam was also created in the 1830s to provide a head of water for the mill, when an area of springs and peat mosses was dammed. On the enclosure map in the Pedder archive from 1771, there is no large body of water at that site, but it was part of 'Mr Harrison's property', in a plot then called Broad Oak. The mill also benefited from its proximity to an ample supply of coppice wood for the bobbins themselves. The 30-lathe mill was leased from the 1850s to the Coward family, who bought it in 1920 when the Harrison estate was sold after the death of Thomas Newby Wilson. It stayed open until the early 1970s when, by good fortune, it was acquired by English Heritage, who run it as a fascinating industrial museum. It is the very last of what were once hundreds of such mills in this area.

The Low Stott Park farm was last tenanted by a William Kellett. His descendants later bought another property from his landlords, Quay House at Lakeside, which was turned into a public house and inn; it would later become the Lakeside Hotel. His son, also William, made the first pier at the pub by driving an old cart into the water and covering it in planks – although this rustic ingenuity was later replaced by a more orthodox structure. William Kellett's move to Lakeside ended farming at Low Stott Park, which became purely the industrial bobbin mill site. The old farmhouse was put to house mill workers, alongside the mill lessees and their families and servants. It must have been very crowded; there were 11 millworkers, many in their teens, in the house in 1841, 16 in 1861, and 11 in 1891. The house was later divided into cottages.

High Stott Park

At High Stott Park there were two farms: High Stott Park farm and another on the east side of the lane, which was later called Stock Park. The old farmhouse at High Stott Park was rebuilt in 1712 by a Robert Taylor, and this building in turn was later remodelled by Robert's great-grandson Roger to create the elegant High Stott Park House. Money had come to the Taylors from their farming, from

Ruins of a bark peeler's hut on Height Lane above High Stott Park

iron-working (via a judicious marriage to a woman from an iron-master's family), and from commerce. One of the Taylors established a mercer's business in Manchester and had property in Ulverston. At their new country house at High Stott Park a vinery was added, and a new orchard behind the house in 1815. The farm land was let to tenants and a large new barn built. A sketch of the barn was drawn in Roger Taylor's account book, which survives in the Pedder archive.

Stott Park Heights was the scene of a dispute in 1673 between George Braithwaite and Edward Taylor of Stott Park and Thomas Chapman of Plum Green. In the agreement eventually struck by the second umpire, who had been called in after the failure of an earlier arbitration, Thomas Chapman was allowed a day's peat cutting in the moss in the pasture on Stott Park Heights. His Stott Park neighbours, Taylor and Braithwaite, could 'cut peat at pleasure'. Thomas Chapman's grazing rights were curtailed too. He was restricted to summer grazing only, and could keep 14 sheep, 1 horse and 1 cow – or an additional 10 sheep instead of the cow. George Braithwaite and Edward Taylor could put up to 120 sheep each onto the fell grazing, and 3 horses or mares. The surviving agreement, kept in the Pedder archive, explains that the pasture belongs to Stott Park and had been 'enclosed and severed from the pasture of Plum Green'. Thomas Chapman, who gave his name to Chapman House farm, was choosing to assert his rights to at least this limited use of the resources on Stott Park Height.

In 1751 another dispute was resolved, this time involving only Stott Park neighbours, a Robert Taylor and his neighbour William Braithwaite. The agreement which they struck details the ways the land was to be divided between them, the value of each man's share, and a compensation payment of £60 payable by William Braithwaite because his stint is more valuable than Robert Taylor's. Each also had access rights across each other's shares, and they agreed which walls must be repaired, or built, for future clarity on the subject. It is not possible to determine after all this time whether there was a main culprit, but it is specified that Robert Taylor must 'repair and uphold the wall, and a way through Brows Gate or Yeat' so that William can 'at all times and forever hereafter quietly and peacefully have, hold, use and enjoy' his rights 'without any let, stop, suit, molestation, interruption, claim, demand or disturbance whatsoever' by Robert. It is tempting to interpret that one way. A map of 1794, in the opening pages of Roger Taylor's account book, shows the Taylors' High Stott Park holdings, the fences for which he is responsible, and Mr Braithwaite's land running next to his own in alternate strips down the fell. It illustrates how closely enmeshed neighbours could be in their work, and how one broken-down wall might lead to such trouble.

In 1821, Roger Taylor of High Stott Park inherited Finsthwaite House from James King. The will names Roger as 'my relation' but the exact nature of the connection is vague; however Roger became the last of the long line of Taylors to own Finsthwaite House. After his death, his own heirs to the Stott Park properties were the children of one of his surviving sisters, Margaret Lewthwaite. She and her husband John lived at Stott Park after John's bankruptcy and dismissal from his post as town clerk of Lancaster for mismanagement of town funds. Margaret is remembered at Peggy Taylor's Well on Fearing Brow (a minor landscape feature marked on the Ealinghearth map section). The Lewthwaite children and their descendants lived at Stott Park and refurbished and gentrified a cottage up the hill at Burrow Croft. Robert Taylor's will of 1670 mentions land at Stott Park he had 'lately bought' of a John Borrow. Janet Martin pondered in her notes whether this was a name which may remain linked to the land around Burrow Croft and the nearby field Burrow Newlands.

Many of our field and wood names from High Stott Park come from a map of 1890, beautifully set out, with a key, acreages and colour coding which came from the Lewthwaite family papers – a dream find in our early days of researching names. This archive gave us information which lay just to the north of one of our sheets of map, but has been included in the map section to complete the picture of the High Stott Park farm estate.

A tenant of High Stott Park farm in 1920 was a William Scales whose wife Jane was a noted keeper and doctor of pigs. She was also a friend of Beatrix Potter and her skill with sick pigs was woven into Potter's story *The Fairy Caravan*. When Paddy Pig eats a raw potato his friends at the circus send for Mrs Scales's cat Mary Ellen to administer her owner's 'valuable prescription for sick pigs'. Pony Billy goes by night to fetch her, waiting while she finds the rue and other herbs for the medicinal 'pig powders', and then brings her back to Stott Park when the treatment has been successfully given.

Stock Park

The hamlet contains another house, the Stock Park Mansion, which was built by the Braithwaites in c1865, just to the north-east of their earlier farmhouse and making use of the same 'pleasure gardens'. The OS 1850 map shows a summer house in the curve of a small wood which was later planted as an arboretum. The OS map also shows surrounding land as parkland, suggesting a degree of landscaping. However, the open pasture may be much older than the eighteenth or nineteenth century. A description of the position of Water Meadow says that it is bounded to the east by Windermere, to the south by a close called Cowper Ridding and to the north by Low Parks suggesting that the land between the lake and High Stott Park was always open and not divided into smaller fields. It may even be a field landscape which dates back to what might be described as the ranching origins of the Stott Park farm when the Abbey founded it. This area of meadow grazing was probably shared between the different Stott Park farmers. A 2019 find at Barrow Archives of an estate plan for Stock

Park in 1850, shows the whole of Low Parks was then held by the Braithwaites. Yet this may have included a relatively recent addition to the estate; one of the divisions is called New Lands. The name Low Parks is also that of the woods to the north of this grazing; to the north of that is Parks Wood.

The oldest field names at Stott Park came from the Braithwaite family papers at Barrow Record Office, where they are part of the huge Hart Jackson collection. These include names which date back to the late sixteenth and seventeenth centuries. It was the Braithwaites who used the name Stock Park for their farm. One document in the collection is annotated on the outside by George Braithwaite in 1746, saying that the deed inside is for 'half of Longdale and Harrison Land bought of (from) Richard Taylor of Stott Park by old George Braithwaite', the writer's grandfather. He notes that that purchase was dated 1636 and the land was bought 'by my Granfather (sic) old George Braithwaite who died in the year 1688 and was buried in the Quaker sepulchre at Colthouse near Hawkshead: a gracious good man'.

The Braithwaite family held the Stock Park farm for over 300 years until 1895. The Stock Park Mansion which exists now on the site was built in 1865, and was let before the death of the last Braithwaite, passing through various owners and tenants. Tenants included the Hoylands, who helped organise the war memorial clock at Finsthwaite church in 1919 in memory of 11 parishioners killed in the First World War. One of them was their own son John, who died at Thiepval in 1916. The Stock Park estate passed to Col Dixon, who sold some of the land in 1939 to the YMCA. After his death in 1958 the mansion passed again through various hands until its conversion to flats in the late twentieth century. The agricultural land is owned by a farmer from Lancashire. The flat owners' association has recently repurchased woodland and farmland near the house and residents are pursuing various environmental projects like pond-building.

Ealinghearth

Origins

Ealinghearth is a settlement which bears the name of an activity which would have been widespread in the area: the 'elyng of ashes' or burning wood in a kiln to produce a dried product, kilnwood, that was used to smelt lead and also, if the dried wood disintegrates, ashes. The wood ashes were used to produce lye for soap, used for cleaning wool. Lye can also be made by burning bracken, another common activity locally, but less likely to earn the name of 'hearth'. In the sixteenth century the demand for kilnwood for lead and silver smelting rose strongly. At Graythwaite licenses for kilnwood hearths were granted to a Miles Sawrey, and permission to use 'broken wood and sticks there'. The hearth at this hamlet would have been a similarly licensed site and elyng of ashes was probably an activity overseen and sanctioned by Furness Abbey. Janet Martin found a reference in the Duchy of Lancaster records at the Public Record Office (now the National Archives) to a Thomas Rawlinson 'cutting wood and exercising the art of Elyng of ashes' in 1537. It is unclear exactly where he was working but the entry is alongside others for Finsthwaite and Stott Park within the bailiwick of Haverthwaite; so it is possible that Thomas Rawlinson set up the hearth at Ealinghearth. Rawlinson is later the name of the family at Rusland Hall and it is common locally. Both the 'hearth' element of the name and *aeling*, meaning 'burning', have Old English origins.

The settlement at Ealinghearth later had three farms, two at the foot of Yewbarrow and another, up the lane towards Finsthwaite, called Hill Top. At this settlement, as at others we surveyed, farming and woodland industry co-existed. Yewbarrow, the steep hill slope at the west end of Finsthwaite Heights, dominates the hamlet. Elsewhere in Cumbria the name would be taken to mean the barrow (hill) where ewes graze and the word is sometimes spelled 'Ewbarrow' in the seventeenth century. However, the very large numbers of yew trees which grow on the west-facing slope of the hill are more likely to have given it the name. The stream which flows down the slope is referred to as Yew Beck in the late eighteenth century enclosure award. The yews are a magnificent feature of the hill.

Residents

Ealinghearth as a place name appears in various spellings, the most distorted being 'Elmlath'; Elmlath Moss appears on the OS maps. The settlement is called 'Elenharth' in the 1851 census. In 1841 the occupants were all farmers but in the 1891 census there were also a hoop-maker and a man, with a son and a daughter in their teens, who all worked at the gunpowder works at Black Beck, just along the causeway road towards Bouth. In 1901, one of the inhabitants was a gamekeeper. Even in this tiny hamlet the census reveals a variety of occupations across the range of agriculture and industry.

In the will of James Walker of Ealinghearth in 1729 we see a glimpse of the value of woodland and the intensity with which it was worked as part of the farm. James had two sons and a daughter and he leaves instruction about the wood for the inheritor to 'have the standing wood...to peel, fall, cut, work, cole (make charcoal), and carry away within two years'. In his inventory of property, as well as a clock and its case, furniture and three hives of bees, valued at 10s, he also leaves 'oak and ash timber £4, cole wood (charcoal) 10s, and a 'cropp on the ground' valued at £2 7s.

A branch of the Taylor family lived here, although they also had land at Finsyke in Lower Finsthwaite in the seventeenth century. One George Taylor, baptised at Colton church in 1644, bought a farm at Ealinghearth. George himself and other members of the family were Baptists, but he was a churchwarden at Colton and his wife and daughter were buried there. A later member of the clan, Thomas Taylor, made a will in 1803 which gave us several field names for Ealinghearth and detailed how many years' growth the 'spring woods' or coppice woodland had. This will identified the land immediately in front of the farm as Great Ealinghearth and Little Ealinghearth, fields which we had previously not been able to name. When we had asked Miles Saunders,

Ealinghearth with Yewbarrow behind

who still rents the field and whose grandfather farmed it, if it had a name he thought for a long time and then said 'It's just Ealinghearth really'. Seeing the list of fields in the 1803 will, and recognising that we had not fully made use of the information we had been given, made us realise that taking information from oral sources is a skilled business. We had not thought to note Ealinghearth as the name of the field, despite knowing that the field in front of the church in Finsthwaite has become known as Finsthwaite Field – and that too is hardly the only field in the village.

The last Thomas Taylor to own land at Ealinghearth had been a vicar in south-west England, after graduating from Cambridge. His land, inherited from his grandfather, was sold after his death at the end of nineteenth century and the auction notice included a map giving several field names. We later found an earlier map which pushed dates back to the beginning of the nineteenth century, while most of the names stayed the same. Thomas Taylor was an active manager of his property in Ealinghearth; there is correspondence from him in the Pedder archive about the woodlands he owned and how they should be worked.

To the north of Ealinghearth, by the road that runs to Rusland Hall, are lands which have been traditionally owned by Finsthwaite landowners, especially Finsthwaite House and the Lower Finsthwaite farms. Fields on the Finsthwaite House estate plan in 1851, the Pool Meadows, are part of that estate and others, running down towards Elmlath Moss, are identified by John Chaplin as part of the holdings of Tom Crag, Cobby House and Charley Crag. In the 1750s land belonging to Jolliver Tree farm is listed as including, as well as the holding at Finsthwaite, 'all the netherfields at Pull Side and Yewbarrow'. Fields by Rusland Pool tended to be slightly larger than some of the Finsthwaite fields, and would have been better for arable crops and perhaps also for fattening sheep after a summer living on the sparse grazing of the fell.

Ealinghearth farmers also had holdings in the area around Rusland Pool. The map that went with the sale of Thomas Taylor's land after his death shows his own holdings and a mix of names of other neighbours from Finsthwaite and Rusland who had fields there. This was the area where George and Richard Taylor argued over access to their shares of arable land near Will Bridge End in 1670. In 1624 a Robert Taylor leaves his son Robert a 'rood of meadow at the Pow' (a common early spelling; documents in the Pedder archive also refer to the 'Powsyd'). Robert leaves his son all his clothes; these may have been relatively new, or good quality garments, and therefore not to be wasted. Particular items of clothing are frequently left to family members in early wills, although later they tend to be subsumed in inventories under an entry headed 'purse and apparel'.

Hill Top, Fearing Brow and the Ealinghearth Dobby

Hill Top farm stands near the top of the hill above Ealinghearth on the lane that runs north towards Finsthwaite. We found names for Hill Top's fields from an early nineteenth century map (which also covered Abbots Reading farm and land at Bouth including Old Hall Farm) as well as from some early twentieth century sales particulars. Hill Top was lived in by Arthur Ransome, the journalist and children's author, with his wife Evgenia in the late 1950s, first as tenants and later as owners.

Just north of Hill Top a lane runs down the back of Ealinghearth hill, down a slope called Fearing Brow. Fearing is a dialect name for a ghost or evil spirit. The first reference to the hill being called Fearing Brow is in the Pedder archive in 1564, suggesting that the road has been thought to be haunted for many centuries. It is locally known as the terrain of the 'Ealinghearth Dobby', who is a still active spirit if Sophia and Pat's experiences are anything to go by. Cowper's *History of Hawkshead* records the story that she haunted the road, dressed in white and that a 'strange waffling sound' in the trees heralded her arrival. She caused alarm by hitching a lift on passing carts. It was to avoid an encounter with the Dobby that caused poor Christopher Cloudsdale to walk back from Rusland to Stott Park via Finsthwaite Heights in 1849; he froze to death on the tops after getting lost in snow. This ghost story was associated with Margaret Taylor, 'The Maid of Ealinghearth', who drowned in Rusland Pool in 1787 and was said to haunt the road by the Rusland Beeches. A nineteenth century poem by Mary Gregson, the daughter of the vicar of Rusland, described Margaret's ghost desperately searching for her cruel and heartless father, a carrier. However, as Cowper observed, dobbies and ghosts have long been associated with hillside roads like Fearing Brow, and they traditionally have a tendency to hitch lifts on carts, and to walk along with foot travellers. Dobbies also have a domestic manifestation, hiding property and doing occasional chores.

The Dobby's habit of interfering with travellers has found a modern manifestation. Sophia and Pat, while checking field boundaries at Border Moss wood, picked up a pair of lost walkers who, once they were in the car and being taken back to Newby Bridge, said that they had missed the turning up Fearing Brow because their mobile phone GPS had mysteriously stopped working at just that point. They had set off along the lane towards the Beeches instead of turning up Fearing Brow and making east. It seemed quite clear to us who was to blame.

Peggy Taylor's well on Fearing Brow lane memorialises a different Margaret, one Margaret Lewthwaite, née Taylor (see Stott Park history) who used to let her horse drink from the Yew Beck stream part way up the lane. Her brother Roger was the last of the Taylor clan to own Finsthwaite House. He died in 1849, passing the estate on to the Pedder family and Margaret herself died in 1854. Not everyone locally would know or use this name for the well (it is a name preserved in the Chaplin family) but our survey included searching for names of minor landscape features and this is a good example both of a naming that memorialises a local person, something they habitually did or were known for, and a glimpse of the past that would otherwise be lost.

The Maps

Our map illustrations use the 6" 1890 OS map. OS plot numbers appear in brackets by each plot we have named. The reader can use these to refer to the map and the associated text.

In the case of plots with more than one name, which is most common with fields, we give first the name which it had at the time of the OS survey. We give alternative or later names in date order finishing with the modern name. Dates given refer to the archive source used and are either specific, eg 1552, or broad, eg 'early nineteenth century' when only an indication of date is known. If a name is in modern or current usage we use these phrases. When oral tradition or memory is the source of a name we mention either the individual or family who told us, or say 'local people' if it is generally known.

Minor landscape features are indicated with a symbol: ⚑ and the plot number in which it appears will be given, where possible, in the text.

Archives are given their Record Office catalogue numbers. All documents from Lancashire or Cumbria Archive Services are available to the public. The collections are truly inspiring.

DDPd 26 refers to Box 26 of the Pedder archive which contains over 400 documents relating to Finsthwaite. The Pedder family inherited Finsthwaite House from the Taylors who had lived at Finsthwaite since at least the sixteenth century. They added to the archive they inherited with the estate and later deposited the papers at Lancashire Record Office. We have also referred to DDTy, also held at Preston, from the Townley family who once owned Jolliver Tree at Finsthwaite.

WDAG refers to documents held at Kendal Record Office in the collection from Arnold Greenwood, solicitors. Boxes 17, 19 and 64/4 were our chief source of documents about the Harrisons of Low Stott Park and later Landing and Lakeside. BDHJ refers to the large and varied collection from Hart Jackson, solicitors, held at Barrow. The Hart Jackson archive at Barrow provided field names from our entire survey area, but particularly for Ealinghearth and High Stott Park.

We also refer to privately held archives: FHEP is the Finsthwaite House estate plan of 1851. Janet Martin studied documents about Plum Green held by a one-time resident of Finsthwaite, Derek Sodo.

When we reference Clement Taylor's account book we have used Janet Martin's 1997 edition of *The Account Book of Clement Taylor of Finsthwaite, 1712-1753*. We also used Wright's *Dialect Dictionary* (1902-6), Angus Winchester's *Lake District Field Names* (2017) and Diana Whaley's *Lake District Place Names* (2006).

• Section 1 •

Plum Green

Plum Green seems like the centre of Finsthwaite village to the modern eye, and it is the place where house building took place in the nineteenth and twentieth centuries. This area is called Outer Finsthwaite in 1537; the name Plum Green dates back to 1561. It was the site of Finsthwaite's first church, in 1724, and its replacement in 1874. The 1874 school is now the village hall.

The 'plum' element of the name refers to damson or bullace plum trees which presumably grew here. The name survives in that of two cottages and the Plum Green yard, a gravelled area in front of a row of cottages with a public footpath running through it. The houses here are sometimes also called Tanyard Cottages because of the yard's brief life as a tannery in the nineteenth century. If there was once a green on this site then it would mirror the situation at Lower Finsthwaite with a cluster of old farmsteads, around a green, with a beck running through it (at Plum Green this is now culverted under the ground). Fields were cleared working outwards around this centre and, just as at Lower Finsthwaite, some of these had names which suggest they were open (shared) fields in the past. There were three farms at Plum Green, which are now all private houses, the land being part of Chapman House farm. Several barns also survive and have been converted into houses.

As well as the farms there has been a rich life of industry and craft in Plum Green. One of the barns of the Rose Cottage farm later housed a besom making business (brooms made of birch tops with a central handle, the classic witches' broomstick, although it had a more innocent function as a domestic broom and many industrial uses). Plum Green yard was the site of a long-running and successful 'swilling' business which made swill baskets, one of the most useful carrying devices ever invented, and still in use at the bobbin mill museum. Devonshire House was a shop and post office until the late twentieth century, and for a time from the mid nineteenth century it was an inn, the Devonshire Arms. In 2018 retail began again when Kim Hooper started to sell ice cream.

Finsthwaite Field (496): the field that St Peter's church looks onto, so to the modern eye it appears to be at the heart of the village. The name is recorded on an undated list of the Chapman House fields which names plot 496 Finsthwaite Field (WD/AG Box 17). The Kelletts occasionally still use a family name, the **Bull Field**, but Finsthwaite Field would be more common. This plot is called the **Meadow behind the Barn** on maps in 1843 (WDB/135/3/4) and in 1868 (WD/AG Box 19). This name is also self explanatory if viewed from its original farm: the meadow lies behind one of the two barns for Plum Green farm (Rose Cottage). This name appears as early as 1778 (DDTy2/2/2) but the farm is much older, being documented in the late 1590s. This plot is probably the one called **The Field** in 1694 (in DDTy 2/2/1 which lists parcels of land in a marriage settlement that included this farm). We have found that such a simple name is common for a field right by a farmhouse. The list also mentions **The Head of the Field** which we have associated with the steeply sloping north-east edge of the plot. Finsthwaite Field had become part of the holdings of Chapman House by the late 19th century (WD/AG Box 17), and is described as 'old pasture' in 1920 (BDHJ/11/19).

The Shilla (497): this is now the church car park and is surfaced with tarmac, but the name The Shilla was common in the village in the 20th century among local people. 'Shilla' is a dialect name for the small, rough pebbles that were used to surface the area. The name is still in use – in defiance of tarmac – mainly in the expression **the Church Shilla**.

Paradise (499): this small triangular patch of ground is Paradise on a map of 1843 (WDB 135/3/4) and lies next to the churchyard. It was part of the land granted to the church in 1724 when the first Finsthwaite Chapel was built, but remained unused until a school was erected next to the new church in 1874. Wall lines suggest that it, and the church yard, were separated off from Little Field (465); the land was given by Henry Taylor of Landing. Rent was paid by an Anthony Hewartson for Parradise Parrock between 1853 and 1856 at a rate of £2 5s per year (Janet Martin's notes of the Harrison papers). It seems unlikely that this could be an appropriate level of rent for plot 499 itself which is tiny and so it is more likely the rent for plot 465. He also paid £3 4s 6d rent annually for Plum Green Parrock which may therefore refer to plot 438.

The Parrock (490): this plot next to an old farmhouse (now Rose Cottage) was divided into several sections of garden and field plots. Like 487 nearby it is simply named The Parrock in 1924 (BDHJ/122/3/11), a document which mentions the informal use by various cottagers in Plum Green as allotments. The plot still includes gardens for Rose Cottage and its neighbour High End House. The most westerly section was called the **Vacant Lot** in the1970s, by which time the allotments had been abandoned. It was later acquired by the owners of High End House and incorporated into their garden. In 1694 (DDTy 2/2/1) it is the probable site of **The Parrock and the Little Parrock** indicating that it was several plots even then.

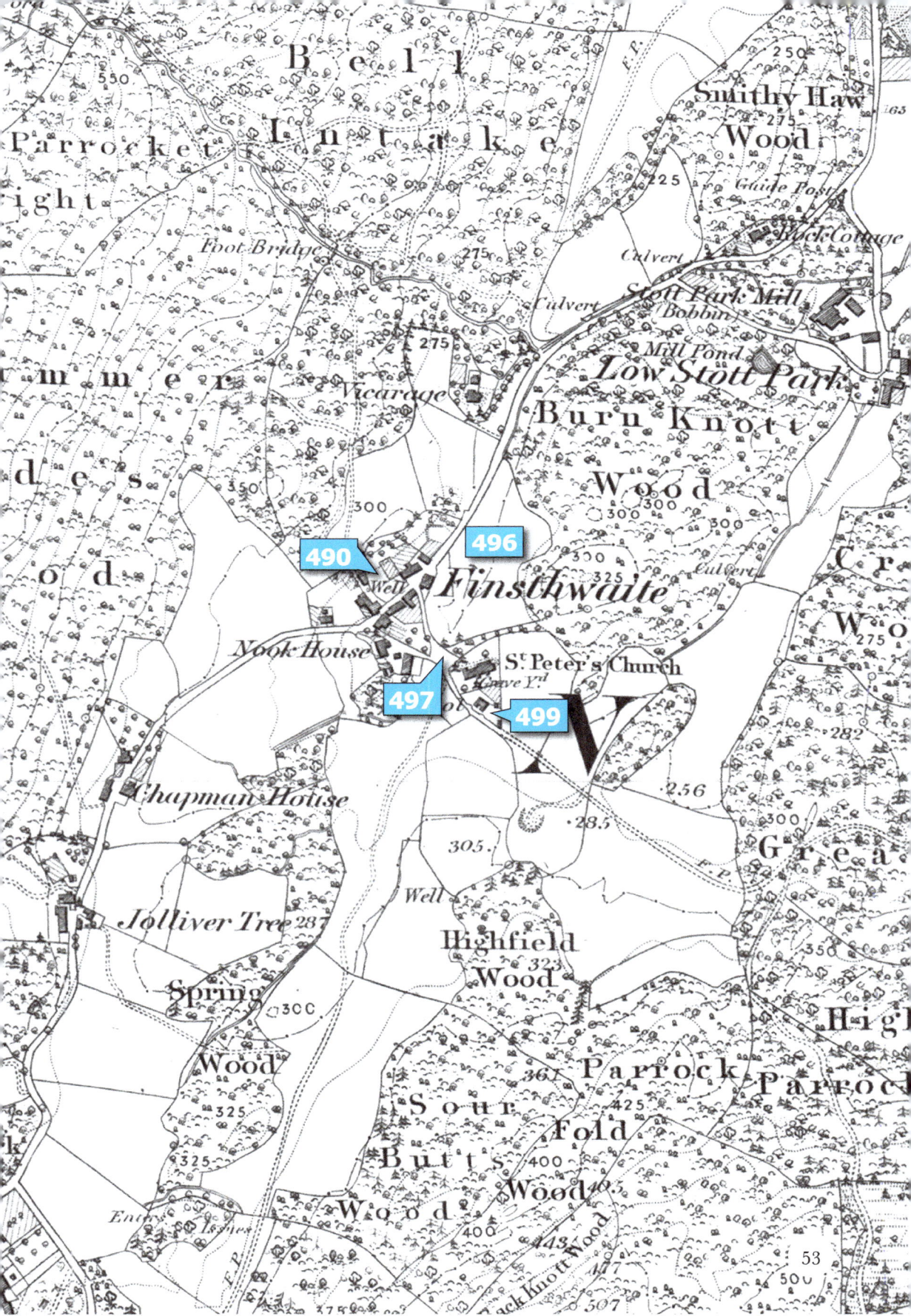

Little Field (465): not notably smaller (especially if the acreage given over to the church and to Paradise is added back in) than its neighbour Great Field (438), so a sense of fun may be involved in the pairing of the names Little and Great Field in this instance. The earliest reference to this field is as **Little Intake** in 1694 (DDTy 2/2/1) when it is part of Plum Green farm (Rose Cottage). In 1802 (Janet Martin's notes of Derek Sodo's Plum Green deeds) it has become Little Field, and is named so on the map of 1868 (WD/AG Box 19). Current usage is **Sandholes** or **Sandhole Field**, in reference to a gravel extraction site in the south corner. The name Sandhole is used on an undated list of Chapman House fields (WD/AG Box 17) which uses the 1890 plot numbers, so the gravel extraction must have occurred by then. It is described as 'old pasture' in 1920 (BDHJ/100/19). The field may have been called **Parradise Parrock** in the 1850s when Anthony Hewartson paid rent for it, and named so because of the little neighbouring plot called Paradise (499).

Little Busk (436): a small oblong of woodland or bushes east of Little Field. This is still, just, a wooded area. The name derives from Old Norse *buskr*, a group of bushes or small wood. The plot is named Little Busk on a map in 1868 (WD/AG Box 19).

Great Field Busk: a small area of woodland (Old Norse *buskr*) within the greater area of Great Knott Wood at the edge of Great Field. Identified as Great Field Busk on a map in 1868 (WD/AG Box 19) although it does not have its own plot number and other maps do not differentiate it. An example of an area of woodland which would have been held by the same person who held Great Field (438) although by the time of OS mapping it had perhaps been sold off to the owner of the larger Great Knott Wood and so lost its separate name. (FLAG 01)

Great Field (438): a large field, if only marginally bigger than its neighbour Little Field (465). The plot is named as Great Field on an 1868 map (WD/AG Box 19) but an earlier reference to this, as **Great Intake**, appears in 1694 (DDTy 2/2/1). Great fields also exist at Waterside and in Lakeside, and 'great' is more often used in the past to describe a large field. The modern name is **The Big Field.** On the undated list of holdings of Chapman House in WD/AG Box 17 which uses OS plot numbers (so it postdates 1890), it is called **Foot Road Field** and it has a footpath running through it which leads into Great Knott Wood and over to Lakeside. The footpath contrasts with the cart track in Little Field (465) which stops at the gate between the two. This field may also have been called **Plum Green Parrock** when Anthony Hewartson paid rent for it, along with Parradise Parrock (see notes on 499 and 465).

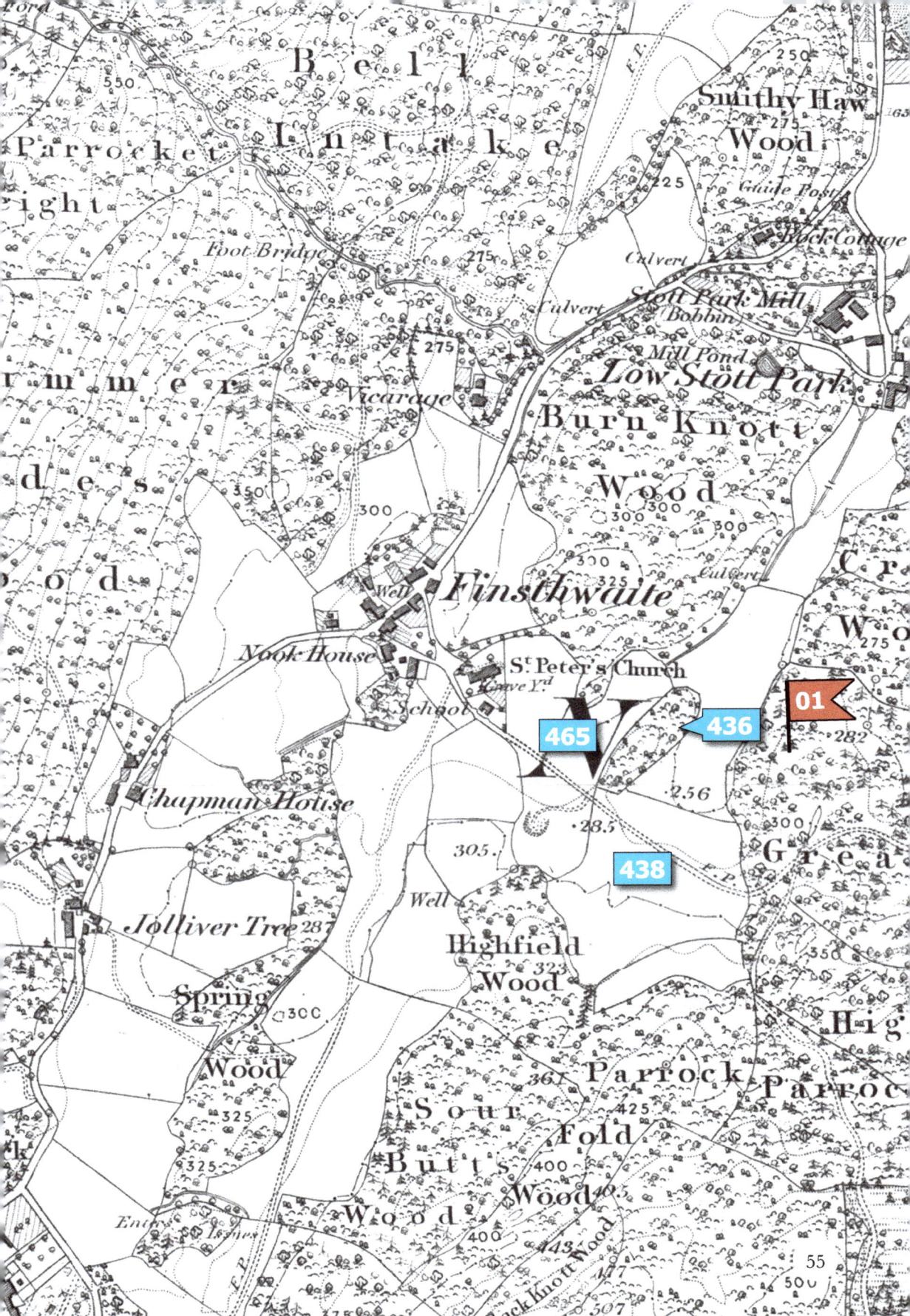

Burn Knott Wood (435): a small hill (knott), with a stream or 'burn' running along the foot of it by the lane side. Diana Whaley gives the meaning as the stream, although the word 'beck' is usually preferred for a stream locally. Other Burn Knotts occur in Colton parish, and the meaning may be more to do with charcoal burning in the woods here. This wood is one of the traditional holdings of Plum Green farm (Rose Cottage), the earliest reference being in the will of John Taylor in 1612 which mentions **Burne Knotts**. It is marked on a map of 1843 as **Bur Knott** (WDB 135/3/4) and on OS 1850 and 1890 as Burn Knott Wood. The local name for this is **Diana's Wood**, after its late owner Diana Stokes. We are slowly adapting to calling it **Richard's Wood**, after her son, but Diana's Wood persists.

Pigeon Parrock Coppice (part of **435**, Burn Knott Wood): the 1843 map (WDB 135/3/4) identifies this little area of coppice wood on the southern tip of Burn Knott Wood as Pigeon Parrock Coppice. It was presumably a wood where pigeons nested. **(Flag 02)**

Piet Holes (437): a low-lying field where magpies once nested or gathered: piet is a dialect word for the magpie. Named Piet Holes on a map of 1868 (WD/AG Box 19), the earlier spelling is 'Pyotthole' (in Janet Martin's notes of Derek Sodo's Plum Green deeds, 1802). The magpies are no longer in residence, but the name is still used. In 1694 this is called **Low Intake** (DDTy 2/2/1) because of its low-lying character. Also named **Peat Moss field** in 1878 (Janet Martin's notes of the management of the Landing Estate after the death of Elizabeth Harrison).

Parrock Folds (439): a small field that may have been used as a fold or place to pen or gather animals. It lies at the top of the slope above Great Field (438) and may have been a convenient place to hold animals when they came out of the wood beyond and needed to be kept out of an arable crop growing there. The name first appears in 1694 (DDTy 2/2/1) and on an 1868 map (WD/AG Box 19). It is mentioned in Clement Taylor's account book as **Parrack Fould** in 1734, although whether this refers to the field or the woodland (456) is unclear and it may mean both. It is now called **The Little Top Field** because it is small and is at the top of the slope above Great Field.

Parrock Fold Coppice (456): the coppice woods next to Parrock Folds Field (439); this paired combination is one of many examples of a field and adjacent woodland sharing a name. In this case the name seems to attach to the field first, then the woodland nearby because of the reference to the animal fold. The name Parrock Fold occurs in 1694 (DDTy 2/2/1). It is marked on the map in WD/AG Box 19 in 1868, and referred to as part of the holdings of Chapman House in a schedule of 1878 in Janet Martin's notes (the field 439 is not included on that list, only the woodland). OS 1850 and 1890 record the same patch of woodland as **Parrock Fold Wood**. It may be referred to, along with field 439, in Clement Taylor's account book in 1734 as **Parrack Fould**, when he records the sale of land following the bankruptcy of Henry Taylor of Landing.

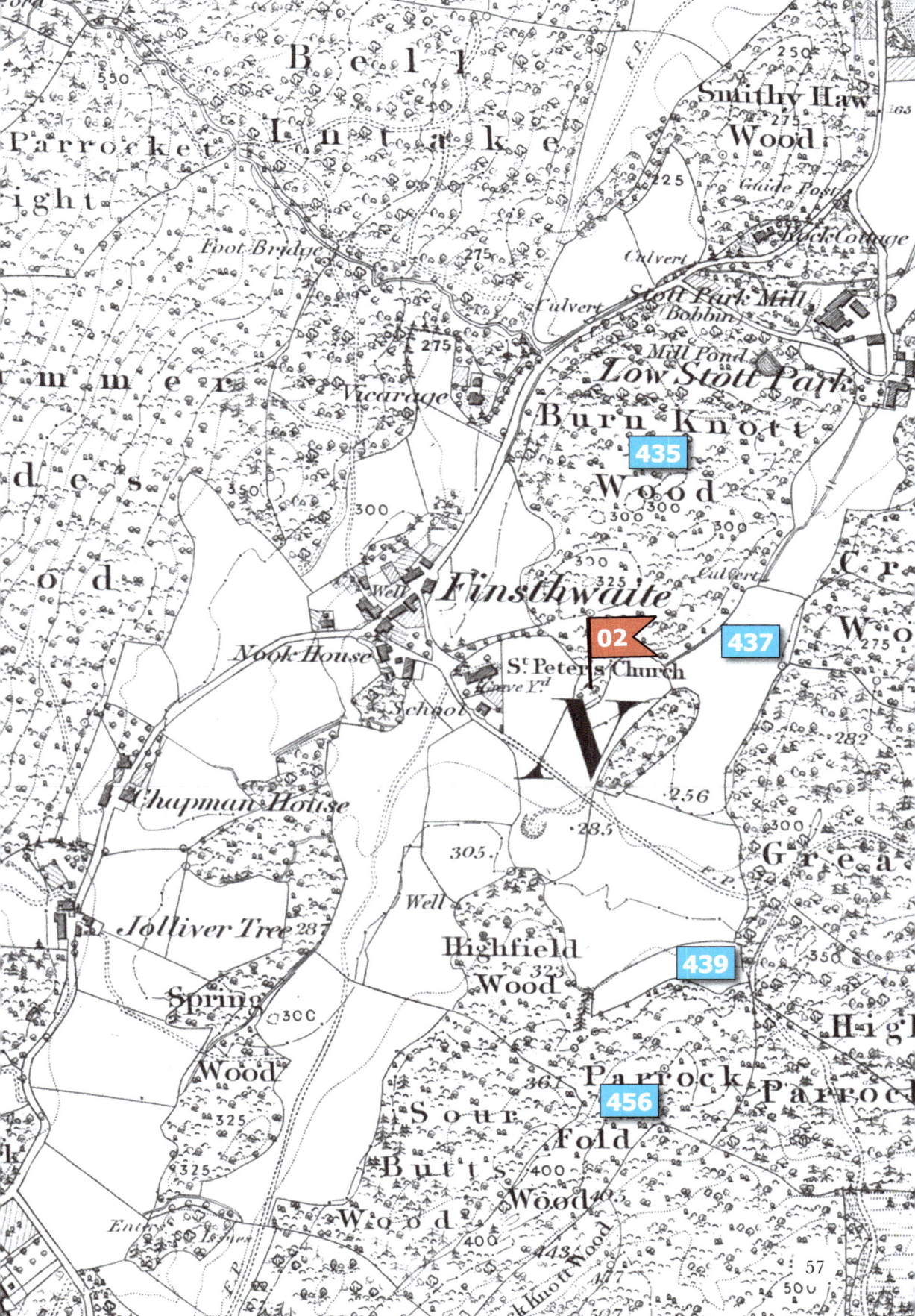

Low Brow Dales (500): a field on a slope (brow) lower down the hill than its neighbour 501. The name Brow Dales suggests that this field and the neighbouring 501 may have been open fields in the past both because of their sequences of names (low and high) and because of the name Dales (which means a 'share' – see also The Dales, plot 733, and Low, Middle Far and Great Hagg). It is named Low Brow Dales on a map of 1868 (DDPd 26/427). The plot is now known as **Scales's Bottom Field** after John Scales of Devonshire House. He died in 1965, but his fields (500, 501, 502 and 503) were acquired by Chapman House farm before his death. This field is now used as a silage/hayfield, like other old arable fields. Iain Kellett recalls it being used for vegetable growing during the Second World War. 1850 OS map shows a fence line running down this field, but this is not apparent on OS 1890, or now.

High Brow Dale (501): a field on a slope (brow) higher up the hill than its neighbour 500. Previously an open field: *dael* in Old English means a share, hence a field where people had shared rights. It is named High Brow Dale on a map of 1868 (DDPd 26/427). Now known as **Scales's Middle Field** (see note on plot 500), and like 500 and 503 is used as a silage/hayfield.

High Field (503): a field at the top of the slope below which are Low and High Brow Dales. Appears on the map of 1868 (DDPd 26/427). This field gives its name to Highfield Wood (456). Now known as **Scales's Top Field** (see note on plot 500 and 501).

High Field Wood (456): the name High Field wood shows on OS 1850. This wood takes its name from High Field (503) a field on the top of sloping ground. It is one of many examples of a wood and a field sharing a name. On the map of 1868 (DDPd 26/427) it is simply called **High Wood**. It shares a plot number with Parrock Fold Wood.

Long Field (502): a long narrow meadow running along the bottom of the valley, it is called Long Field on a map of 1868 (DDPd 26/427). The name is descriptive of the shape of the field. Now known as **Scales's Big Meadow** (see note on 500 above). Although called a meadow now this field is no longer cut for hay, but was when John Scales farmed it (up to mid 20th century). Old photographs show a small parrock was once fenced off at the north end of this field by the church, and this is shown on OS 1890 as a separate plot, **489**. On the 1868 map in the Pedder archive a square shaped plot, perhaps slightly larger than 489, is called **Little Meadow**. The field is shown at full length as it exists now on OS 1850.

Paddock (487): a small enclosure next to the farmhouse at the Nook (now Whitegates), shown on a map of 1868 (DDPd 26/427). This is a typical name for a small field next to a farmhouse (another example is 490). In the early 20th century this plot was used by people from neighbouring cottages to hang out washing and to keep hens (activities which can be seen on some early postcards of the village). In the 1970s the site was sold for housing and now contains the Lowside bungalows which take their name from the adjacent field (486).

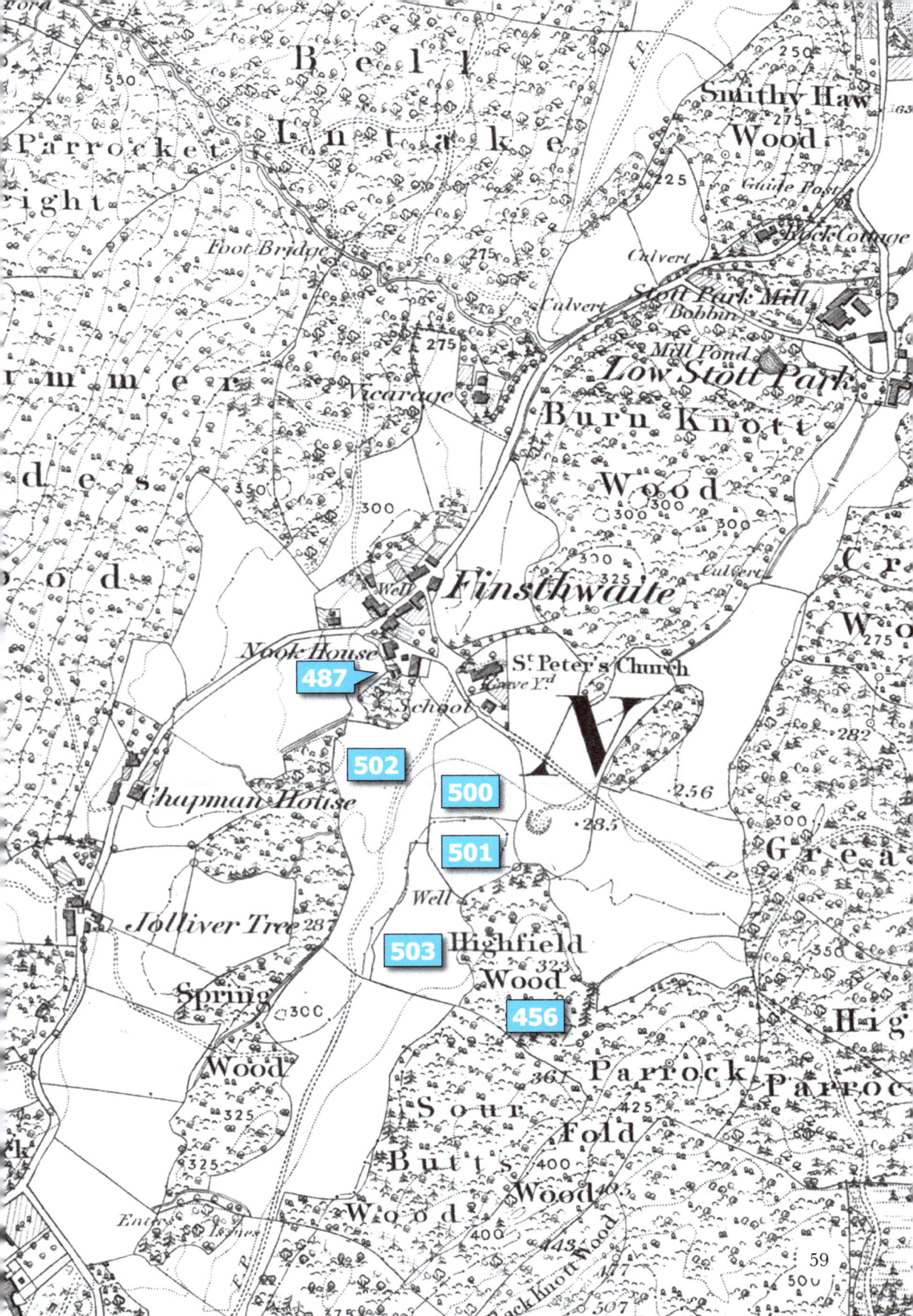

The Hill Orchard (488): an orchard for the Nook farm (now a private house called Whitegates). The hill element of the name is explained by the large outcrop of rock at the edge of this enclosure. The OS 1850 map shows orchard trees. It is named the Hill Orchard in 1868 (DDPd 26/427).

Orchard (489): a plot marked as an orchard in 1868 (DDPd 26/427), this is now a garden and site of a late twentieth century bungalow. The orchard is likely to have been more extensive in the past. Church View Cottage (Janet Martin's house) which stands on part of the site only dates to 1740 or 1750 and may have been built on part of an orchard or small busk.

Cotesteads (491): a field with animal housing, or a cote, in it (now vanished). Old Norse *stadr* means a stead, the site of a building. This field was called Cotesteads on a map of 1868 (WD/AG Box 19). As such it shares a name with Cotesteads Coppice (492), but this field is also known as **Old Laithe** by the Kelletts who farm it now, and Old Laith was the name in 1802 (Janet Martin's notes of Derek Sodo's deeds of Plum Green). Laith is a dialect word from Old Norse *hlada* which Diana Whaley notes is usually a barn for storing grain. The field was described as arable meadow in 1920 (DDHJ/100/19) and it was used as a hay meadow in living memory (Calvert family). A public footpath runs through this field, from the Plum Green yard, up through Cotesteads Coppice (492) and joins the path in Bell Intake (466) to High Dam.

Cotesteads Coppice (492): shares a name with its neighbour Cotesteads (field), this wood is called Cotesteads Coppice in 1868 (WD/AG Box 19) and OS 1890. On OS 1850 it is simply part of the larger Summer Sides Wood. It is now cleared of trees (the timber was sold for pit props in the 1930s). It was bought by the Kelletts in the 1920s when it was known as **The Coatsteads**. The land remains mainly cleared of trees except for crab apples, one fine beech and some oak and is used as pasture. When Thomas Kellett bought The Coatsteads from the bobbin mill owner John Coward, he secured an agreement to access the stream in Bell Intake to wash sheep, on condition that the stream must not be diverted permanently or used in a way that damaged the flow of water down to the mill at Stott Park. On the western edge of this plot is a small enclosure which was referred to in 1802 as **the New Orchard** (Janet Martin's notes of Derek Sodo's deeds of Plum Green). The orchard trees, cherry and damson, have gone. (**Flag 03**).

M7 (in 483): a trackway built by Stephen Kellett of Chapman House farm; the M6 was under construction at Preston at the time and he named his handiwork the M7. (**Flag 04**).

The Khyber Pass: this steep track on the fell side was named by an earlier generation of the Kellett family, presumably making a topical reference to one of the Afghan wars of the late 19th century. (**Flag 05**).

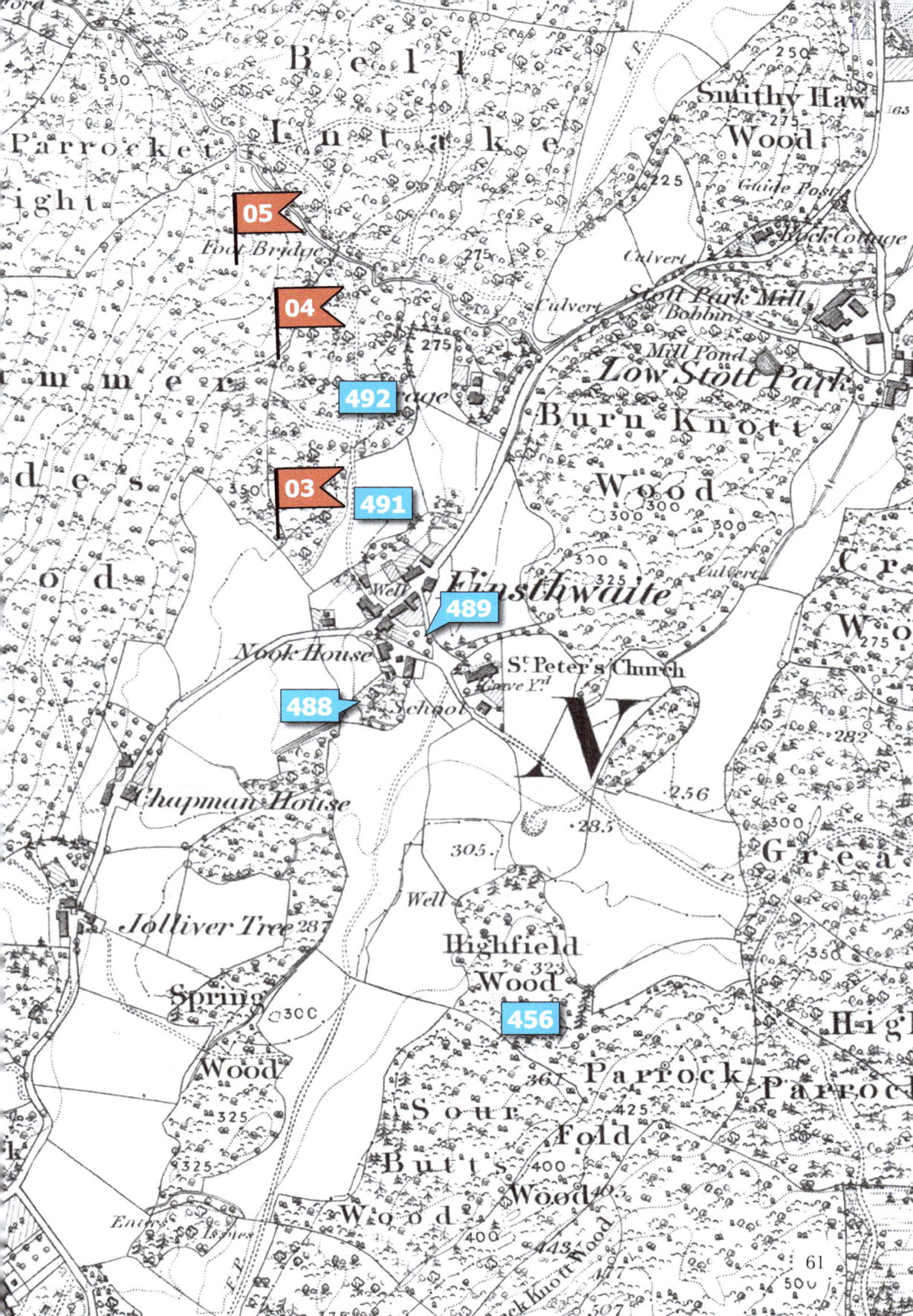

Netherside (495): a field furthest distant from the farm (at Rose Cottage), and on a slope (side). A map of 1868 (WD/AG Box 19) names this as Netherside. This may be a field called **Conythiehowe** (coney is a dialect term for a rabbit, and conyger for a warren, and the land is sloping and so might be described as a howe or hill) said to be on the 'Neddersydd of the way which doth goe from Plum Green to Stott Park'. It was traded in 1616 (WD/AG Box 64/4). The name Netherside lives on in the house built on part of this field in the 1930s, Nethercroft. 495a, a small area of woodland, is named **Netherside Busk (Flag 06)** in 1878 in a schedule of holdings of the Landing Estate (in Janet Martin's notes about the management of the estate following the death of Elizabeth Harrison). The upper part of the plot (ie not Nethercroft garden) is **Parson Field**, so called because it was next door to the 1870s vicarage and may have been let to the vicar.

Gill Beck Field (401): a field next to the stream (*bekkr* in Old Norse) which runs down from High Dam. The description 'gill' refers to the rocky ravine that this stream flows down. Diana Whaley quotes Machell noting that gill, like slack, is a name given to a field that is cleared of or free of stones but here 'Gill' seems to refer to the beck and not the field. The field, together with plot 402, is called **The Gillbeck** in the list of Laurence Harrison's holdings in 1769 (WD/AG Box 64/4) when it is listed as 'arable, meadow and woody'. The name Gill Beck Field is used in 1843 (WDB 135/3/4). Later in the 19th century (WD/AG Box 17) this plot is **Bell Intake Field** because of its proximity to the wood Bell Intake (plot 466). Current usage is **Beck Meadow**, and this name covers both 401 and 402. The current gate into the field is at the foot of the High Dam path, but another gate, now blocked up, is visible in the side of the lane which may date to a time when the two plots had separate entrances, or may have been the only access when the field was part of Low Stott Park farm. This positioning of the gate, further north, would then have been more convenient.

Gill Beck Meadow (402): see note on 401 above for an explanation of the name. This is identified as an area of meadow, as opposed to being simply a field, in 1843 (WDB135/3/4). In the later 19th century (WD/AG Box 17) it is called **Back of Beck Meadow** at a point when 401 is called Bell Intake Field, which implies that Beck Meadow, the modern name, had currency at the same time. Now this plot is combined with 401 and the whole is called Beck Meadow. Iain Kellett remembers the field being used for vegetable growing until the 1950s.

Bell Intake (466): is named because it is a more or less bell-shaped intake or enclosure. It was named **Bell Intack** on the 1843 map (WDB 135/3/4). In 1897 it is mentioned as a place where Scots Pine was planted, as it had been in the nearby Parrocket Height, to make a feature of 'a clear well determined line to the sky of dark green'.

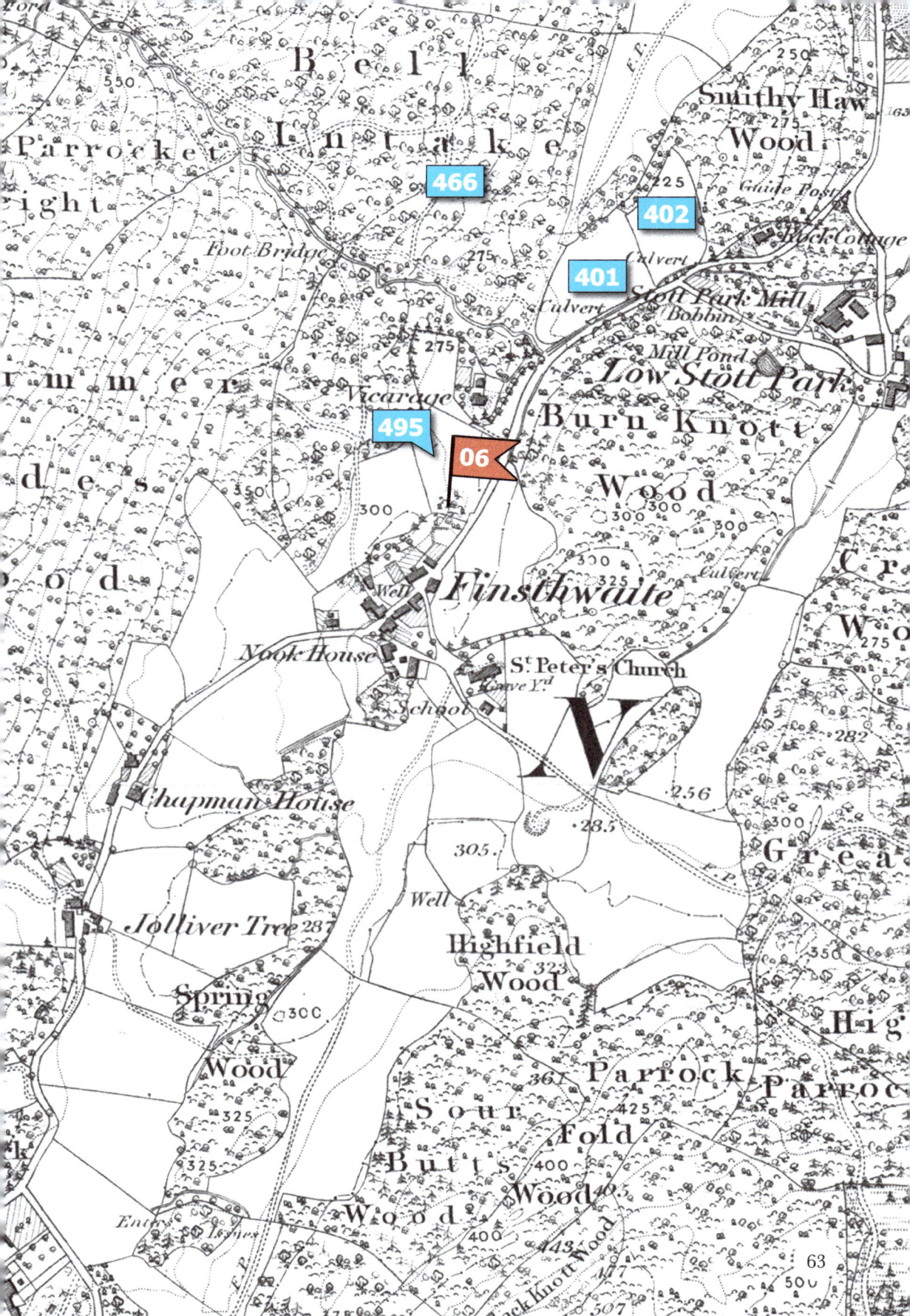

• Section 2 •

Chapman House and Jolliver Tree

Chapman House is still a working farm, one of two in Finsthwaite. It was bought by the Kellett family, who were already tenants there, in 1920 when the Harrison estate was sold off after the death of Thomas Newby Wilson. The farm probably existed in 1600 (DDPd 26/26) when Pedder archive documents mention the field name 'Barn Parrock'. In this area barns are usually built in proximity to a farmhouse; we have no cases of stand-alone field barns. The farm got its name after coming into the possession of Thomas Chapman in the mid-seventeenth century. He probably built the existing house (although the kitchen wing may be older). In the mid-eighteenth century it was owned by James Backhouse of Jolliver Tree, who added to its holdings of land. In 1801 it was bought by the Braithwaites of Stock Park, and in 1856 was sold to the Harrisons of Landing.

Field names have changed at Chapman House, a process which may have coincided with the tenancy and later ownership of the Kelletts. The names which we found on maps of 1843 (WDB 135/3/4) and 1868 (WD/AG Box 19) can be found also in earlier archives, but later nineteenth and twentieth century documents and oral information show changes.

Jolliver Tree (called July Flower Tree in Jane Penny's will of 1807 and in DDTy 3/1 in 1773) is the name of an old farm and a later 'new house' built by the owner of the farm, Mary Gurnell (née Taylor) in the late 1730s. The name Jolliver, first used in 1670, is unusual, and likely has its origins in the orchards next to the house, which may have grown a variety of apple tree, the Gilliflower, which has a clove-scented juice. It was the home of various members of the Taylor family, later coming into the possession of Mary Gurnell, who married her second husband James Backhouse in 1728. James outlived his wife, but on his own death in 1762, Jolliver reverted (indicating it was her property) to Mary's relations who lived at Crakeside near Penny Bridge. It was later owned by the Townley family. The land and both houses were let to tenants throughout the late eighteenth and nineteenth centuries, and the censuses show multiple occupation. Of three barns known at Jolliver Tree from photographs one has been demolished and the other two converted into houses.

No estate map exists for Jolliver Tree, but there are lists of holdings in both the Townley and Pedder archives from the mid- to late-eighteenth century. These include fields at a distance from the farm but others are described as being by the house, or on the opposite side of the lane. However, the field boundaries have also changed in such a way as to make it impossible to be entirely confident of where some fields were. This is the only place in the village where the earlier farming landscape is no longer visible. A clear change in field boundaries was made between the OS maps of 1850 and 1890, but even using the 1850 boundaries it is not straightforward to allocate the eighteenth century names, despite descriptions of their situation, and some old wall remnants. Barn Parrock and Barn Close have been allocated to fields we know had barns in them, but Sourbutts had a smaller acreage than now, and so must have changed its boundaries somewhat. Little Meadow and Christopher and George's field are even more speculative. Neither eighteenth century list mentions Spring Wood, which covers a long rocky strip of ground which may once have been incorporated into the fields.

Most of the land is now known as Mrs Doble's Fields, after a recent owner, and is let to the Kelletts of Chapman House. On this map section some of the land is part of Finsthwaite House estate.

Stevie Watson walking cattle near Jolliver Tree

Barn Parrock Meadow (486): a meadow next to a field called Barn Parrock (509). Marked on a map in 1868 (WD/AG box 19) and described in 1920 as 'old pasture' (BDHJ/100/19). The current name (Kellett family) is **Lowside** because it is on the lower slope below the lane (compare with Well Close/High Side, 485).

Barn Parrock Busk (508): a small wood (the name derives from Old Norse *buskr*) on a piece of rocky ground in Barn Parrock Meadow. Both OS 1850 and 1890 show this area of woodland, and it is named in 1868 (WD/AG Box 19) but it has now been grubbed up to extend the pasture in the field plot 486. The remains of the curving enclosing wall are still just visible.

Well Close (485): a field with a well in it – although the stream that feeds the well has been culverted and so is not a visible feature now. Named Well Close on a map of 1868 (WD/AG Box 19) and first mentioned in 1600 (DDPd 26/26). The field is now called **High Side** (Kellett family) as it lies on the slope on the upper side of the lane (compare with Lowside, 486). The track through Well Close/High Side to the houses on the top of the hill is known in the Kellett family as **The Professor's Drive**, or **Professor Scholes's Drive** after the man who built the Well Close bungalow in the early 1950s. Pleasingly the current occupant of one of the houses is also a professor – academics seem to have a homing instinct for the place. The fact that his name is John Taylor is another echo of Finsthwaite's past.

Barn Parrock (509): a field behind one of the barns at Chapman House. It is named Barn Parrock in 1868, (WD/AG Box 19) and the name appears in 1600 (DDPd 26/26). It was described as 'old pasture' in 1920 (BDHJ 100/19). It is now called the **Bull Field** (Kellett family).

Corn Parrock (484): not named on the map of 1868 (WD/AG Box 19) but mentioned as Corn Parrock in 1802 (Derek Sodo's Plum Green deeds) and simply as **Parrock** in an undated list of the holdings of Chapman House, which uses OS 1890 plot numbers (WD/AG Box 17). Named by the Kelletts as **Little Field** it is also now called **The Prison Field** (Kelletts, 21st century) because a wire fence has been erected inside the dry stone walls, which has so far baffled all but the most determined ovine escapees. This small field was again used during WW2 for growing arable crops. Stephen Watson has said he notices when walking it that it feels to have a better depth of soil. It was described in 1920 as 'old pasture' (BDHJ/100/19).

Orchard (511): an orchard on OS 1850 and named the **Crabtree Orchard** in 1802 (Derek Sodo's Plum Green deeds). On an undated list of the holdings of Chapman House which uses 1890 OS plot numbers it is called **Homestead** (because of its proximity to the farmhouse). One of so many orchards in our survey area, it is pleasing to note that this one keeps some apple trees – although they are no longer crab apples but include varieties like Scotch Bridget. Its current name is **The Orchard** (Kellett family).

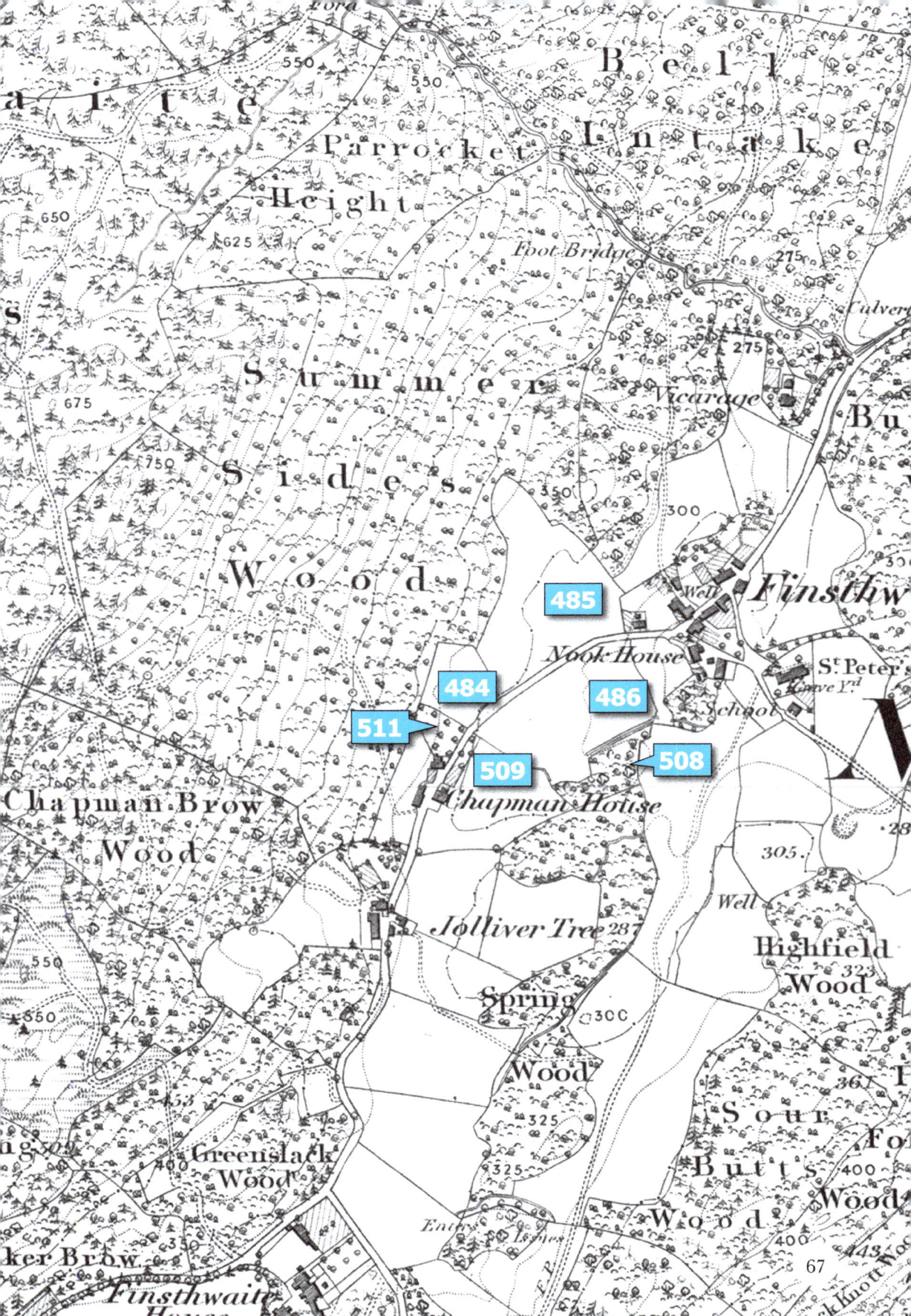

School Brow (512): a section of hillside (brow) named after the school house which was built in 1724 when the first church was built in Finsthwaite. John Taylor whose father had owned Jolliver Tree bequeathed money in 1723 for the 'building of a Free School… the said school to be erected as near Jollyvertree as can conveniently be'. An undated list of the holdings of Chapman House which uses the 1890 plot numbers (WD/AG Box 17) names it as School Brow. In 1730 (BDX 606/7) the plot was called **Chapman Brow** (after Thomas Chapman of Chapman House) and a section at the south-east end of it was granted to the church trustees in exchange for a pew in the church, with rights for the 'boys and scholars' to play on the hillside when they attended the school. 1920 sales particulars (BDHJ/100/19) describe it as 'old pasture'. The plot now includes the Chapman House yard and it houses various farm buildings including the old shippon (where the dairy cows were milked). At the western edge of the plot the Old School House still stands, and Stephen, Rosie and Stevie Watson live there.

Summersides (483): an extensive area of summer grazing on the fellside immediately above Chapman House. The name echoes a very old local farming practice and is derived from Old Norse *saetr*. In a schedule of the holdings of Chapman House in 1878 (in Janet Martin's notes about the management of the Landing Estate following the death of Elizabeth Harrison) it is divided into three parts: **South, Middle and North Summer Side**. The name **Summer Sides Wood** survives onto modern mapping and is used on 1850 and 1890 OS maps. The name is first mentioned in 1599 in the will of Edward Taylor: a 'close called **Somersyde**'. Cleared of trees in the 1930 and 40s but once as heavily wooded as the rest of the fellside.

Parrocket Height (469): a plot on the fell (height) named on OS 1850. Its earlier name suggests that the OS surveyors diligently wrote down exactly what they heard when they came up with this version of the name. In 1843 it is **Parrock 'eth Heights** (WDB 35/3/4) and on the enclosure map of 1771 (DDPd 26/336) it is **Parrick of Height**. Clement Taylor's account book records it in 1734 as **Parrack of Height**, one of the plots sold when Henry Taylor of Landing was bankrupted. In 1769 it is **Parrock oth Height**, one of the holdings of Laurence Harrison (WD/AG Box 64/4), and was let to William Danson of Cobby House, along with other land. The list notes 'woods in these closes are 4 and 6 year growths' meaning that in the 18th century there were coppice woodlands on the plot. The plot is mentioned in a letter of 1897 in the Landing archive (WD/AG Box 20) saying that Thomas Newby Wilson's grandfather, who had a taste for forestry, had planted Parrocket Height with Scots Pine to make a 'clear well determined line to the sky of dark green'. The name Parrocket Height is the current usage.

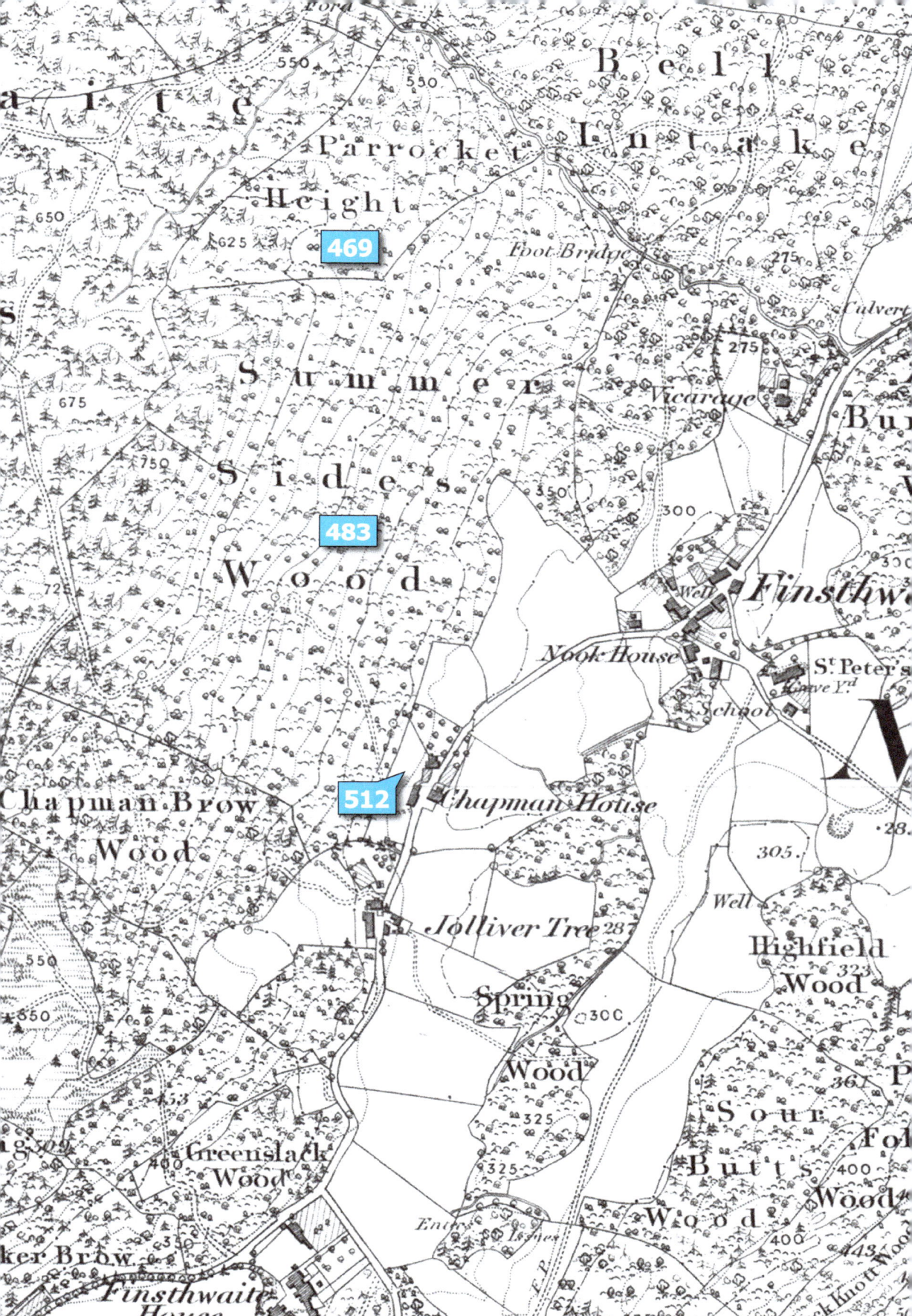

Spring Wood (506): a spring wood is often one which has been coppiced and has sprung back; archives often note '3 years' growth' or whatever. This wood is shown on OS 1850 but there is no mention of it in the lists of holdings of Jolliver Tree until the 19th century. It has a plantation of oak trees, best preserved at the southern end, and we speculate that it was created as a wood in the 19th century, perhaps when one of the tenants of Jolliver was allowed to clear trees from the fields (see Finsthwaite history) and would have been happy to lose this rocky plot from his arable land and let his landlord plant it with trees. There are also springs nearby and these may also have affected the name.

Sourbutts (504): a field where different neighbours' parcels of land 'butted up against each other' ie a common or open field. The 'sour' element in the name is derived from Old Norse *saur* which means muddy and there is a large reedy bog at the northern corner. The rest is gently sloping ground which would have made good arable plots; it is now a hayfield. The name is used to this day, and first appears in 1683 (DDTy 1/3/6) when it is spelt 'Sowerebutts' which may account for some locals pronouncing the name Sowerybutts. The 'value of Sowerbutts' was left to his daughter Elizabeth by Nicholas Taylor in his will of 1628.

Sourbutts Wood (546): a plot of woodland on the Great Knott adjacent to (east of) Sourbutts field – another example of a paired wood and field combination. It is named Sourbutts on OS 1850. In c1740 (DDPd 26/332) it is probably **Sourbuttsheads**, an area of turbury (peat moss) and wood said to be east of Sowerbutts (which was arable and meadow). The 'head' of the plot indicates that it is on a hill slope.

Barn Field (513): a field with a barn in it. The name is more obvious than the site, but old photographs show that this field used to have a barn, and Barn Field is the first on the c1740 list of holdings of Jolliver (DDPd 26/332) so we have speculated that this is the site of Barn Field. This plot is now known as one of **Mrs Doble's Fields**, after its previous owner Jill Doble.

Barn Parrock (507): Barn Parrock was said to lie east of Barn Field (DDPd 26/332) so we suggest this field is the historic Barn Parrock. Now it is one of **Mrs Doble's Fields** in the same way as 513.

(514): certainly another of **Mrs Doble's Fields** now. One name left to be allocated from the c1740 list is **Little Meadow**, which may have been part of this field (the eastern edge) as Little Meadow stood to the south of Barn Parrock. It is also possible that what was once Little Meadow is now part of Spring Wood. **(515)**, another of **Mrs Doble's Fields** now. When **Christopher and George's Field** existed that was south of Little Meadow, and may have been sited at the eastern edge of 515, again perhaps a section of what is now Spring Wood. **(515 and 516)**: 516 as a modern plot is also one of **Mrs Doble's Fields**. In the past we know that **Nether Field**, an area of 5 acres (one list also mentions **Nether Field Close**, a further half-acre plot) ran adjacent to the lane. The 1850 OS map shows a different field boundary, and the large Nether Field may have occupied this area, or at least the western half of both these plots.

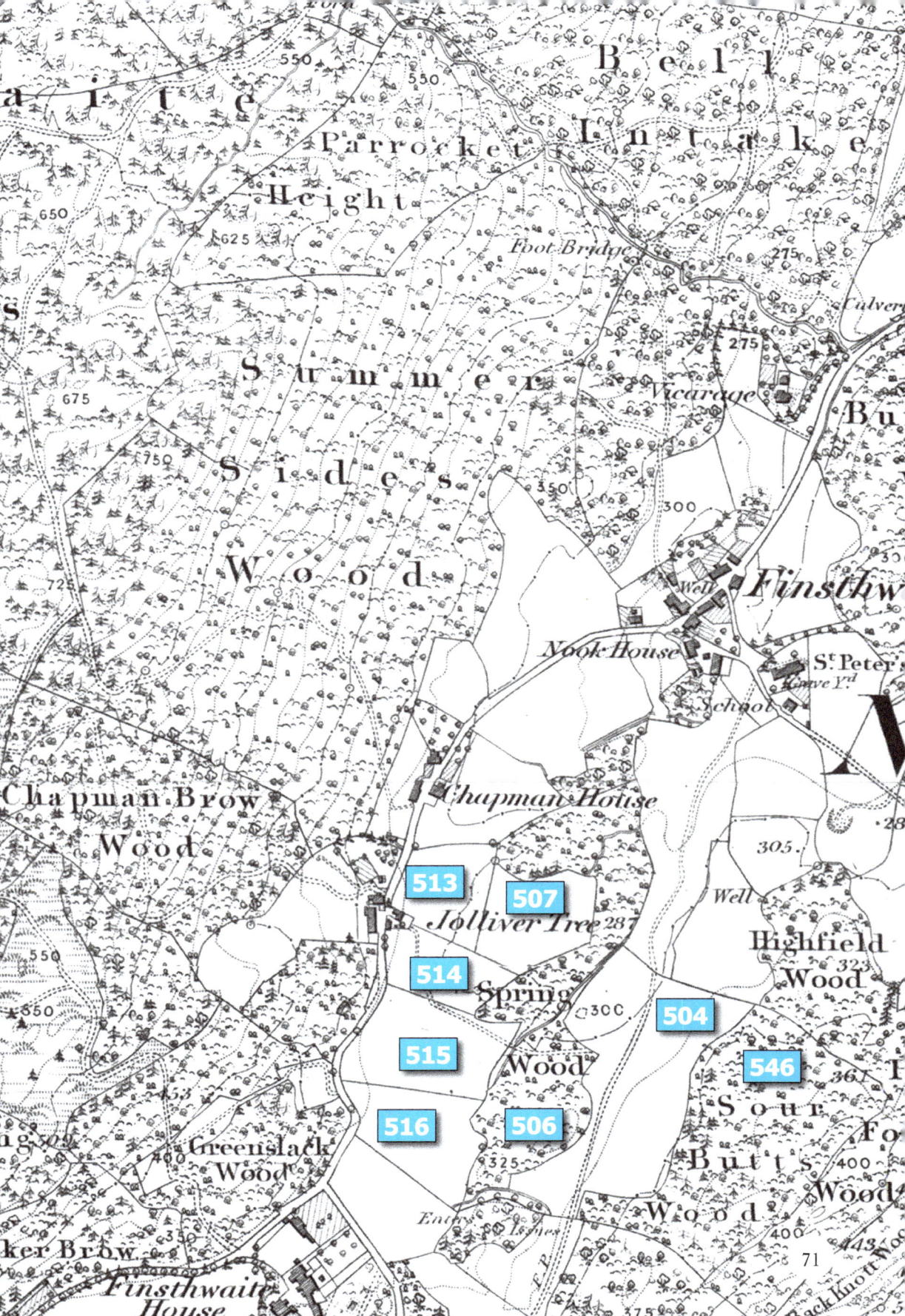

Swinebroach (516): a place where pigs were kept. Broach is a dialect word for a wide area and refers to both fields and nearby woods. A version of the Finsthwaite House estate plan shows this field being called Swinebroach (Janet Martin's notes). The nearby wood (519) is Swinebroach Wood and so we think the fields adjacent to it acquire the name by association. Now the name Swinebroach applies only to the small plot across the lane, 518, and the acreage of 516 is one of **Mrs Doble's Fields**.

Swinebroach (518): a field next to the wood called Swinebroach and so named after it, as a place where pigs were kept – although the pigs may have more often had the run of the wood (519). The field is named Swinebroach in 1851 (the Finsthwaite House estate plan) and the name is in current usage. The field is also **The Bus Shelter Field** because Dave Wilson says that the small building at the top of the slope looks like a bus shelter. In the absence of any public transport in the village this name is ironic.

Swinebroach Wood (519): OS 1850. This is one of two areas of woodland to have this name (see also 523), which means a wooded area where pigs were kept. Field plot 518 is also called Swinebroach, so this is a further example of a pairing of woods and fields. The name first appears in 1720 in the account book of Clement Taylor who was paying for walling in Swinebroach (at 7d per rood). This suggests that a wide area was being used for keeping pigs, and that Clement Taylor was beginning to break it up with walls into neater parcels of land. Broach is a dialect word for a wide area – again suggesting that at one time this (522, 515, 518) was a less structured and walled-in place. The name of this wood in 1892 (DDTy 3/37) is **Low Brow**: a woodland on a slope or brow, lower down the hill than High Brow Wood (522).

Orchard (520): shows as an orchard plantation on OS 1850. Orchards at Jolliver are listed in c1740 (DDPd 26/332). The plot has now lost its orchard trees.

High Brow (521): a plot on a high slope above the farmhouse. In c1740 (DDPd 26/332) and again in c1774-1790 (DDTy 3/1, a small book of planting plans and the acreages of various fields and woods) there is a plot of 'pasture, plowing and mowing' called High Brow which would seem to be this plot. The name is also associated with the wood, 522.

High Brow (522): a woodland plot higher up the hillside than the field of the same name, 521. This is named High Brow in 1892 (DDTy 3/37) on a map showing the woodlands of Jolliver Tree farm. OS 1850 and 1890 both call this **Chapman Brow Wood**, so it is a plot that has been associated with both Jolliver Tree farm and Thomas Chapman who owned Chapman House farm in the mid-17th century.

Swinebroach Wood (523): a field where pigs were kept. OS 1850 shows both this plot and 519 being called Swinebroach Wood. In 1851 (FHEP) it is **Intake Wood** a name denoting a plot which has been enclosed for cultivation from what was previously 'the waste' or open fellside. The whole area from this point west and north is called **The Intakes** now (see next map section).

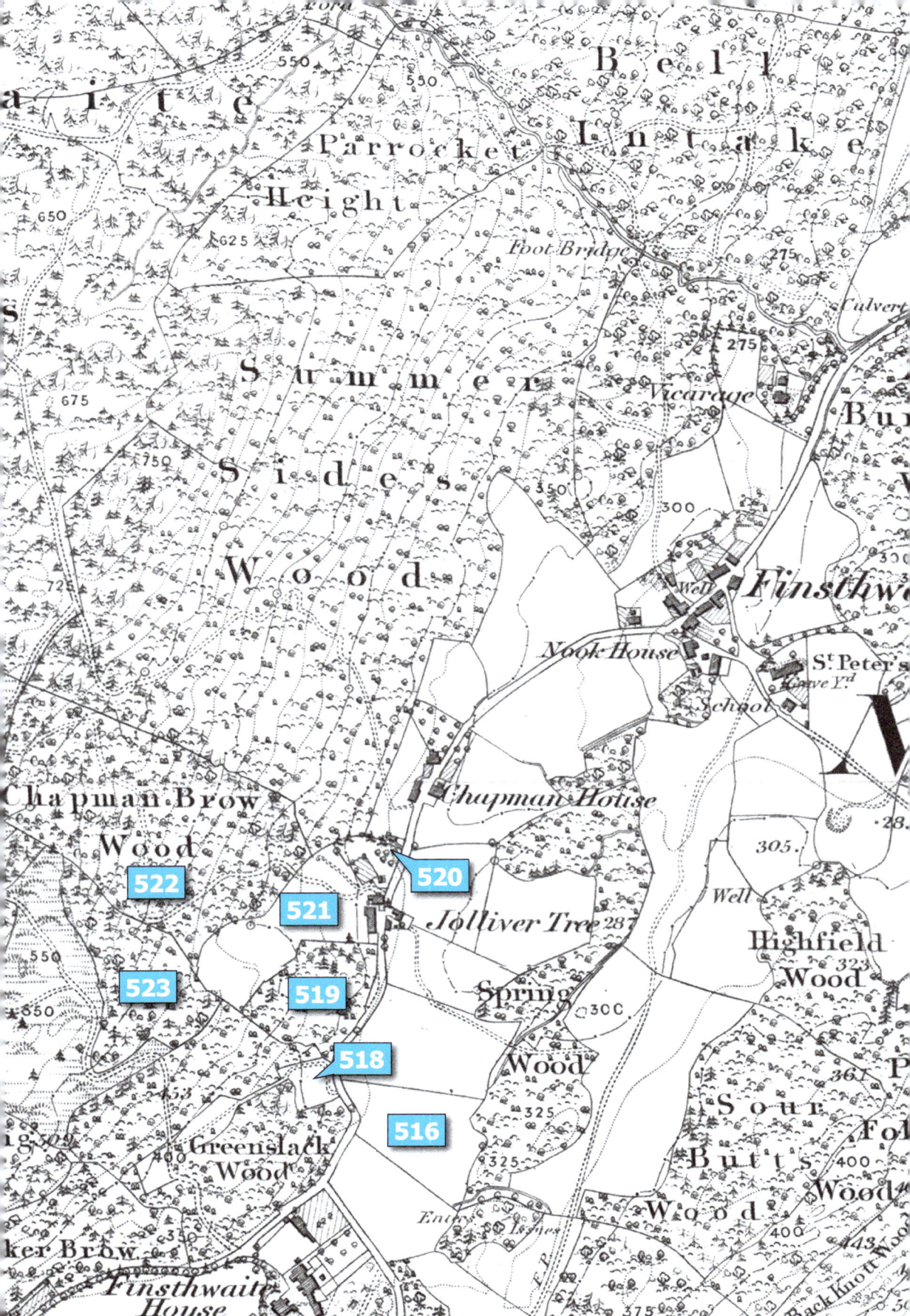

Nether End (517): this field is named on Finsthwaite House Estate Plan in 1851 as Nether End; it supports the case that 515 and 516 next to the lane (in their old boundaries) were Nether Field. This field, now part of Finsthwaite House estate, is known as **The Corner Field**, as it stands on the corner between the lane and the bridle path (The Nook) which runs up the side of the house and yard.

The Nook (517a): the Chaplin family name for the track which begins at this point and runs over the hill to Waterside House. **(Flag 01)**

Charlotte Dean in the Corner Field (517)

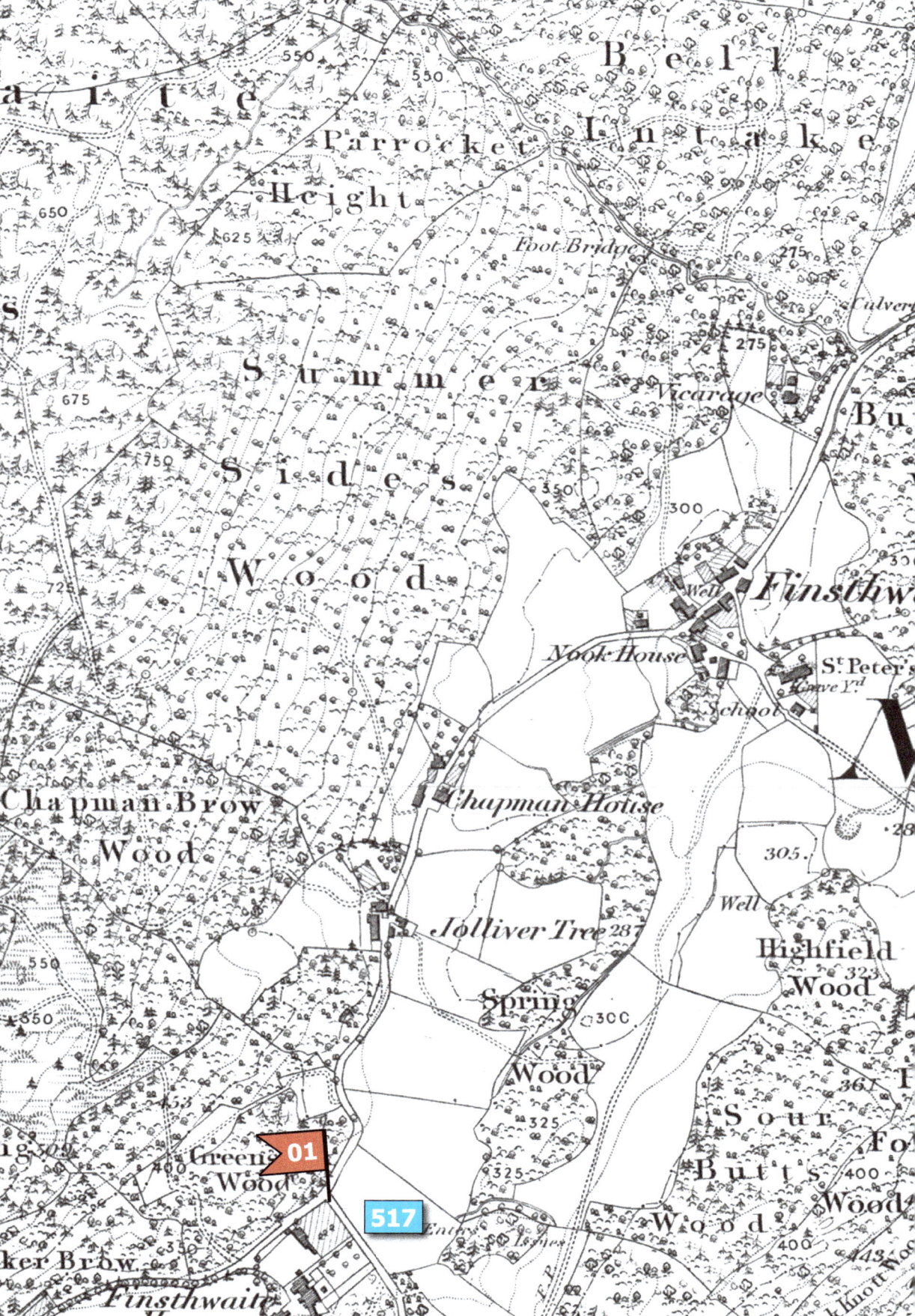

John Chaplin with part of the Finsthwaite House flock in Greenslack / The Intakes

• Section 3 •

Finsthwaite House

This section does not cover the whole of the Finsthwaite House estate, rather the house is a convenient feature on which to centre the map. The whole of the southern end of Finsthwaite is a working farm, with Herdwick sheep grazing the fell tops and lower level fields. The Chaplin family who own the estate are descended, with a couple of side-steps, from the Taylors who were living here in the 1530s. Finsthwaite House was built by Clement Taylor in 1724 and the house has been added to; in particular the front is the work of a later generation. The estate too has been built up by the gradual acquisition of land, as neighbours sold the tiny farms which had supported them in the sixteenth and seventeenth centuries and began to develop other occupations, or to become tenants. When the Pedder family inherited the estate after the death of Roger Taylor in 1849, they commissioned an estate plan, dated 1851, which has been a principal archive source for our work.

Clement Taylor's account book, edited by Janet Martin in 1997, is one of three which survive in the Pedder archive. Clement Taylor's is the most vivid, giving glimpses of the working estate and its tenants and neighbouring landowners. He recorded both domestic purchases (spices, food, clothes, dancing lessons for his children) as well as payments for land, monies to people who worked the woodlands, making charcoal and coppicing, and doing farm work like carting, harvesting, spreading manure. In a later generation Roger Taylor kept detailed accounts of woodland industry, listing all his woods at Finsthwaite and at Stott Park and when they were cut, and noting when coppice wood could be harvested again. These account books suggest that the names we have recorded here were current throughout the eighteenth and nineteenth centuries, and that coppicing the woodland continued to be a major economic activity. A house and adjacent cottages which have the name Sinderhill also appear on this map. The name suggests that there was a bloomsmithy site here in the past and that cinders or iron slag were visible, even if iron-working was not still going on; (Old English *sinder* or Old Norse *sindr* both mean slag). The name first appears in 1578 when a John Taylor 'of Sinderhill' witnessed a deed (DDPd 26/13). This was the home of John Walker, who sold plots of land in the 1630s, including some which still bore his name two centuries later: Walker Brow and Walker Parrock. Two houses at Sinderhill were owned in the eighteenth century by Mary Gurnell of Jolliver Tree. Later, Sinderhill passed to the trustees of the new church and school, and the surviving house was the home of the first Finsthwaite schoolmasters and vicars; the job was sometimes combined. Sinderhill was later bought by the Pedders of Finsthwaite House, until it was sold in the 1970s.

Slack (545 and 549): *slakki* is Old Norse for a hollow or low-lying piece of land, highly descriptive of this reedy and slightly marshy field. Diana Whaley notes that Machell says that the name Slack is often used for a field which has been cleared of stones – or is gratifyingly free of stones for this part of the world. The field is named Slack in 1851 (FHEP) but the name also appears in 1713 (DDPd 26/191) when Clement Taylor arranges extensive sales of timber with Slack, Reading (730) and Backside included in the list of fields from which wood was to be taken. He sold all the timber trees but made certain exceptions: ash, crabtrees, holly in Redding and Backside and oak trees in Slack. He also reserved all the loppings and toppings and bark. Slack is now known, with Reading, as **The Tower Fields** because they lie adjacent to the wood leading up to Finsthwaite Tower.

Slack Copy (505): a small wood (a copy can mean a small field or wood) next to the field called Slack (545, 549). It is named Slack Copy in 1851 (FHEP). This area of trees may have been left over from the general clearing of trees in Slack which was made by Clement Taylor in 1713 (see note on 545 and 549). The planting of the wood is quite different from the adjacent Spring Wood, with more underwood, bluebells and different tree species. The name is still current.

Reading (730): a 'redding' is a clearing – the name is derived from Middle English. Reading is the name in 1851 (FHEP) and, like its neighbour Slack, it is mentioned in 1713 (DDPd 26/191) as a site where Clement Taylor was selling timber. Along with Slack (545 and 549) this field is now known as one of **The Tower Fields** because of its proximity to Finsthwaite Tower).

Parting Tree Wood (548): a 'mere tree' or boundary tree may have marked some significant point in this wood. The name Parting Tree Wood appears on OS 1850, but FHEP calls it simply **Parting Tree**. Clement Taylor's account book refers to **Partintree** in 1734, so the name is older than the 19th century maps. Roger Taylor's account book (DDPd 26/341) records Parting Tree wood being coppiced in 1834. Chaplin family tradition has it that a tree split by lightning, or some other natural event, stood in this wood.

New Close Wood (550): a newly planted wood close to the back of Finsthwaite House. An early reference is given in Clement Taylor's account book in 1731. It may have been specially planted when the house was new. This plot is called New Close Wood on FHEP in 1851 and the OS map of 1850. On OS 1850 the name New Close Wood refers to both this plot and 551, although on the estate map and OS 1890 plot 551 is a wooded section of Finsthwaite House garden and not part of New Close Wood.

Backside: FHEP (1851) calls this plot Backside, as an inked-in addition to the map, the name meaning an area of land on the back side of the farm. This is now a concrete yard with sheep sheds, and an area of pasture, **The Kitchen Garden** (it was once a vegetable garden). Backside was wooded in 1713 (DDPd 26/191) when plans were made for extensive cutting of trees by Clement Taylor (see notes on Slack and Reading). It was also mentioned in Clement Taylor's account book in 1720 as a place where walling was being done. OS 1890 shows orchard planting. (**Flag 01**)

Copy Field (553): this large field is named Copy Field on the estate map in 1851. A copy is usually a small field and this, at 20 acres, is by far the largest field in the village and has presumably been landscaped to off-set the view of the house (it is shown as parkland on OS 1850). The name copy refers to the hill slope that is the dominant feature of this field (Old English *cop* is a hill or summit). In c1740 there is a reference to 'Clement Taylor's close called **Coppy**' (DDPd 26/332) which bordered Wintering Park, and so lay at the top of the hill. In the same document **Walker Parrock (Flag 02)** was said to lie at the edge of the lane opposite Sinderhill house. It was a 3-acre field 'bordering Mr Taylor's **Great Field**' which suggests that 553 contained one large plot called Great Field, and that Coppy was further up the slope. The early twentieth century diary of Barbara Sneyd, *Riding High*, mentions haymaking in the **Great Meadow**, which suggests that Copy Field had been renamed. The current name is **the Big Meadow**; it now has a fence across it reserving the top part for silage and the lower half for pasture, and the principal sheep-maternity field.

Walker Brow (543): this substantial wood on the brow or hill slope above Sinderhill is named after John Walker who sold it, and several other land holdings, in the 1630s. This is the oldest example in our survey of a plot being named after its vendor. John Walker's name was remembered until the plot was named on the estate plan for Finsthwaite House in 1851, over 200 years later and it also appears on OS 1890. On OS 1850 it was called **Fir Wood**, and the whole plot is shown as a conifer plantation. Viewed from the bridle path to the south-east a small remnant area of fir trees still stands at the top of the slope. In the mid-eighteenth century (DDPd 26/332) a field called **Hempland** was listed as being 'on the back of the house' at Sinderhill. Its location is unclear.

Greenslack (525): this is a field in a hollow (*slakki* is Old Norse for a hollow or little valley) and is named in 1851 (FHEP). This field lies between two areas of wood called Greenslack Wood (544 and 524) another pairing of field and wood names. This area is now called **The Intakes**, with this field being also more specifically **the Bottom Intakes**.

Greenslack Wood (524 and 544): these two areas of wood sandwich the field called Greenslack (525); the name means a wood in a green valley. Plot 544 is also named Greenslack wood on OS 1850 and 1890, but they name 524 as part of Swinebroach Wood. It is the other way around on the Finsthwaite House plan (1851) which names the more northerly wood 524 as Greenslack Wood, and leaves the southern plot unnamed. Clement Taylor mentions Greenslack wood in his account book in April 1724: 'wood bought of John Atkinson in Green Slack'.

Intack Wood (523): a wood by The Intakes; intake is the local name for pasture on the lower fellside. This is named in 1851 (FHEP) as Intack Wood. (See also map section 2 where this is named as part of the Swinebroach area.)

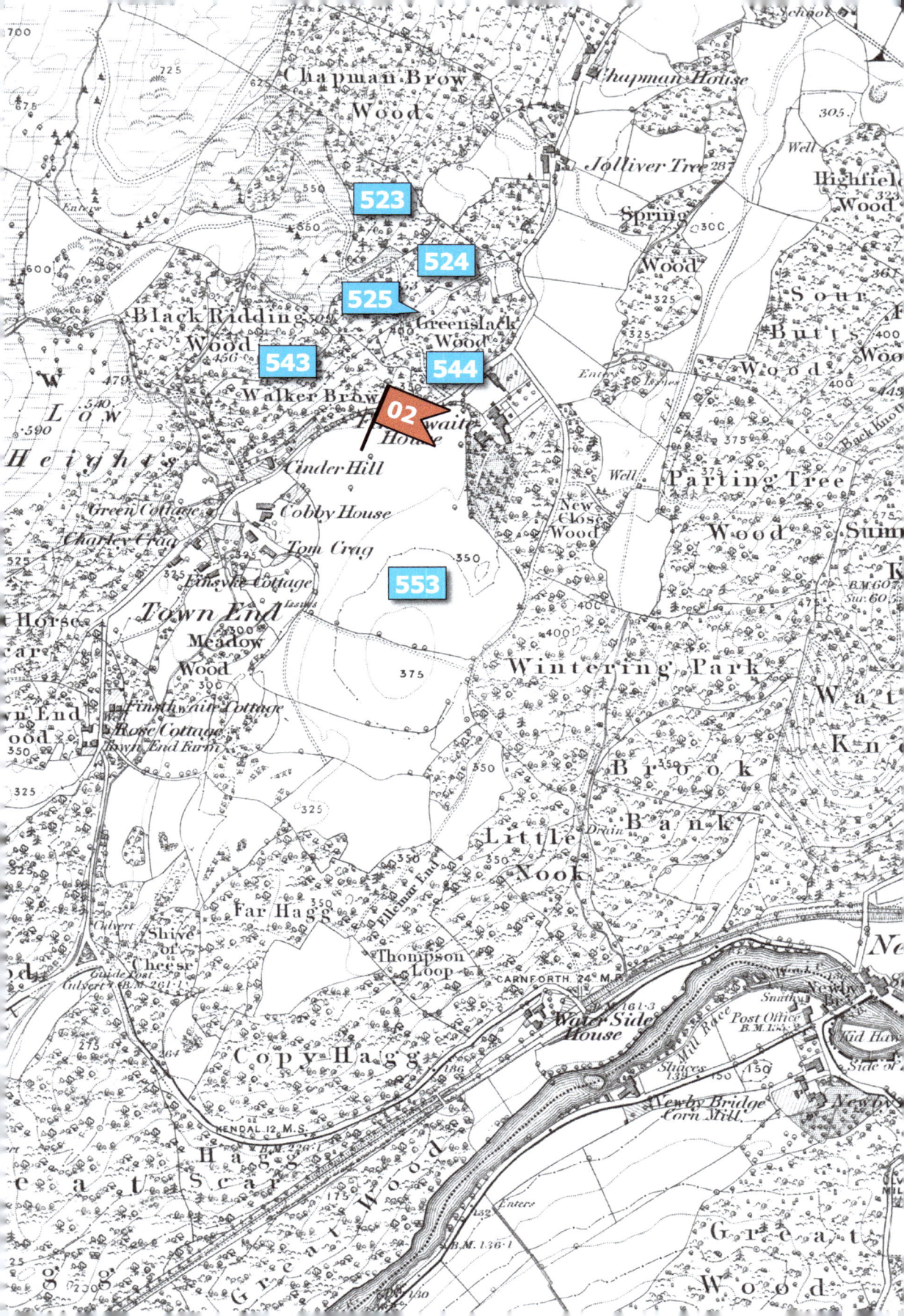

Lower Intake (527): a field, lower down the fell than Higher Intake (530). The 'intake' element of the name refers to the act of enclosing land on the lower fell slopes. This is named in 1851 (FHEP) and is still called **The Intakes** (Chaplin family).

Higher Intake (530): a field, or intake, higher up the fell than Lower Intake (527). Named Higher Intake in 1851 (FHEP) and now known as part of **The Intakes** by the Chaplins (see 527).

Intake Bushes (528 and 529): two small areas of wood (Old Norse *buskr*) in The Intakes. These are marked as Intake Bushes in 1851 (FHEP). The whole area is now known as **The Intakes** (Chaplin family).

Gate Cote (531): this field is named Gate Cote in 1851 (FHEP). The 'cote' element refers to a, now no longer visible, animal barn (but it is marked on OS maps and FHEP). The Old Norse word *gata,* is the origin of 'gate' (Diana Whaley) and means a track – and there is a path running through the field up the fell. Whaley also notes that the Old Norse word also means 'pasturage rights or permitted grazing land' and it is in this area (plus the Lower and Higher Intakes 527 and 530) that various villagers re-asserted their rights to the fell grazing around Boretree Tarn, and their rights of 'gait or way' to it, at various stages in the early and mid-18th century. Such rights were old. Gate Cote appears as a name for the first time in the Pedder archive in 1583 (DDPd 26/17). There is a reservoir tank, left over from the days when Boretree Tarn supplied water to Finsthwaite, which gives this plot its current name **The Water Tank Field** (Chaplin family).

Black Ridding Wood (526 and 532): these two plots are called Black Ridding Wood on OS 1850. A 'ridding' is an area which has been cleared, and so this plot was felled and presumably replanted as woodland. The 'black' element in the name is straightforwardly the colour black – but what it refers to in this case is unclear (but see note on 534). In 1851 (FHEP), it was not part of the Pedders' holdings, but is identified as belonging to Philip Hartley. In pencil it is called 'Intack Wood', in ink as 'Black Ridding' and below Philip Hartley's name it is identified as having been purchased 'in 1867 by R Pedder'.

Black Reading (534): this small wood is not named on OS maps but is on FHEP in 1851 as Black Reading with two field plots, 535 and 533, on either side as High and Low Black Reading respectively. 'Reading', like 'ridding', means a plot which has been cleared, although plot 534 must have been re-planted with trees. Black in this case, as with Black Ridding Wood (526 and 532) means the colour, but we are not quite sure why this area of wood and fields attracts the adjective. A stream flows from Boretree Tarn down the fell on the southern side of the plots with this Black element in their name. Although it is not recorded as being called Black Beck this kind of peaty mountain stream often has the name (Diana Whaley). Boretree Tarn may be the fishery referred to in the 1530s by the name 'Dulas', a name of Celtic or Gaelic origin meaning Black Lake.

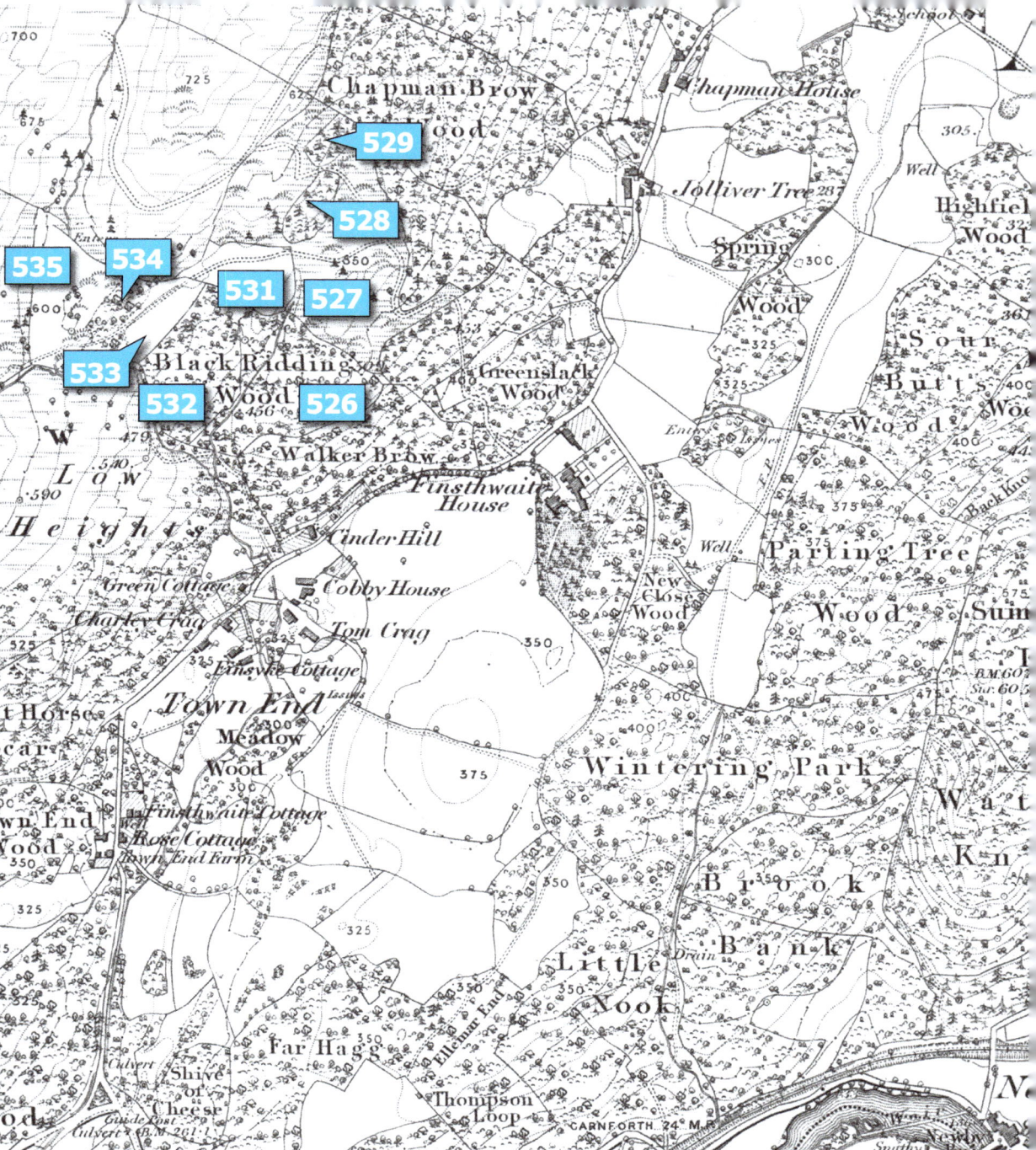

Low Black Reading (533): a clearing or reading near Black Reading (534) named in 1851 (FHEP). It is lower down the slope of the hill than High Black Reading.

High Black Reading (535): a clearing or ridding near Black Reading (534) which is higher up the hill than Low Black Reading.

Wintering Park (731): this 20-acre wood is first named in 1633 (DDPd 26/81). The park element is a contraction of the word parrock and means an enclosed area. Its name suggests it was a sheltered enclosure for over-wintering stock. It may always have had at least some trees in it, and the wood is recorded as being cut (coppiced) in Roger Taylor's account book in 1842 (DDPd 26/341), when it was co-owned with the Townley family. It is now wood pasture and has kept its name for nearly 400 years. FHEP also shows a section of wood which OS allocates to Little Nook (plot 791) as being 'part of Wintering Park'.(FLAG 03)

Brook Bank (796): a field on a steeply sloping bank which shares a name with a wood next to it (794 and 795). The brook element of the name is presumed to mean that badgers (dialect name 'brock') lived either in this field or the adjacent woods. This field plot is named in 1851 (FHEP) but the name is earlier and sometimes appears as **Break Bank**. The earliest reference uses this version of the name ('Breakebanke' a close of arable land) in 1633 (DDPd 26/77). In 1733 (BPR 17/M2/1-2 in Lancashire Record Office) **Two Brooklands**, presumably one being the field and the other the wood, are mentioned in a list of Henry Taylor's holdings. The 'lands' element, meaning a cultivated piece of either field or woodland, is rare in our survey area; it occurs a few times as 'Newlands'. The early name Breakbank could be derived from Old Norse *brecka*, a hillside, which would make the name a tautology (a bank on a hillside) but the steep nature of the field might have led to this double naming. The current name is **Brook Bank Field** (Chaplin family).

Brook Bank Wood (794 and 795): a wood which shares its name with the field 796, which it envelops. The pairing of wood and field names is very common across our survey area. Both plots are named as **Break Bank** on OS 1850 (using what is also the earlier spelling of the field name for 796) but as **Brook Bank** on OS 1890. On FHEP plot 795 is called **Brook Bank Wood** and was the only section of the wood which belonged at the time to the Pedders, the other being the property of William Townley. The will of George Taylor of Landing, in 1685, mentions his 'woods in Breakbank'.

Tom Crag and Cobby House in historical Lower Finsthwaite viewed from The Dales (733).

• Section 4 •

Lower Finsthwaite and Town End

In calling this map section Lower Finsthwaite we are using a name that has not survived into modern usage, but was the one given to this southern cluster of houses in the 1530s and this seems an opportunity to revive it. OS calls this small group of farms and cottages Town End, and some residents of the village would use this name. We are reserving Town End for the most southerly part of the village where Town End farmhouse (now a private house), two cottages and a barn conversion now stand. Lower Finsthwaite was called Finsyke in 1561. This name now only exists for a single house, but was current in the seventeenth and eighteenth centuries as a name for the area.

The settlement, with a cluster of farmsteads around a shared green with a stream running through it and with routes out to arable land to the south and up onto the fellside to the north, is one which is mirrored precisely at Outer Finsthwaite/Plum Green and has been described as characteristic of Irish-Norse settlement. There is a concentration of names associated with *Finnr* in this vicinity: Finsyke, Pigeon Croft (Fin's Shawe Croft), and further to the south-east Finsknott and Finscar.

The farm land is part of the Finsthwaite House estate, and the names listed here all come from the 1851 estate plan. One farm, Tom Crag, now a private house, was the last of the tenanted farms in Finsthwaite. It was sold in the late 1970s and the land reabsorbed into the main estate.

Butt Hills (739): the name Butt Hills is given in 1851 (FHEP). Place name convention suggests it would have been a place for practising archery, but militia records for Finsthwaite show no archers whatsoever. A local dialect word also exists, which describes a small piece of land cut off from a main field as a 'butt'. This plot, which is not particularly hilly itself, might have been all one with plot 737, which does have a rocky slope. This section may have acquired the name butt simply because it was cut off from field 553 as being a rocky plot that was best isolated from the main arable and meadow area. 739 was a common green in the eighteenth century (and Green Cottage opposite acquired its name in this way). Current usage is **Cobby House Paddock** (see 737).

Cobby House Paddock (737 and 739): a paddock or field next to Cobby House (Chaplin family current usage). The southern plot, 737, is not named on FHEP. 'Cobby' was a nickname meaning merry and brisk given to a 17th century John Taylor, perhaps to differentiate him from so many other John Taylors at the time. John Cobby Taylor's grandson sold the farmhouse in 1684, partly to pay off his father Christopher's debts. Cobby House was bought by Edward Taylor of what is now Finsthwaite House, and it has been part of the estate ever since.

The Dales (733): this large field would have been a shared or open field in the past, with various Lower Finsthwaite neighbours each having a dale of land to farm within it. The word dale is derived from Old English *dael* which means a share. The name is recorded in 1851 (FHEP) and is mentioned in 1754 (DDPd 26/285). It is still used today. The Dales is similar in size to the open fields Sourbutts and the Brow Dales. At the edge of the plot is an area called **Dales Meadow** on FHEP. (**Flag 01**) This may be an area known in the past as **The Miew**, a dialect word for a meadow or an allowance of hay (the *Dialect Dictionary* says it can mean the area that could be scythed in a day). The name occurs in 1609 as '**Dymewe** near Phinchawe Croft' (plot 788, DDPd 26/38) and as The Miew in 1754 (DDPd 26/285).

White Stone (787): a field which had outcrops of white stones in it, some of which still exist in the boundary wall. Named in 1851 (FHEP) and appears in the adjudication of the dispute between George and Richard Taylor in 1670 (DDPd 26/131) when George has 'leave of way from hagg to **Whitestones** through Richard Taylor's dales of Peaselands except when the corn is growing' when he must take his cattle round by way of Little Nook. The field has been absorbed into Pigeon Croft (788) in recent times.

Peslands (786): an arable field where peas were grown. Peslands is the spelling in 1851 (FHEP) but it is called **Pesse Landes** in 1609 (DDPd 26/38) and **Peaselands** in 1670 (DDPd 26/131). The name suggests that it was once an arable area on which peas were grown, although it will have had other uses over the years. 'Lands', meaning a cultivated area, is a relatively rare usage in our survey, where 'field' is much more common. FHEP and OS maps for 1850 and 1890 show it with wooded areas, suggesting its arable days were over by the 19th century.

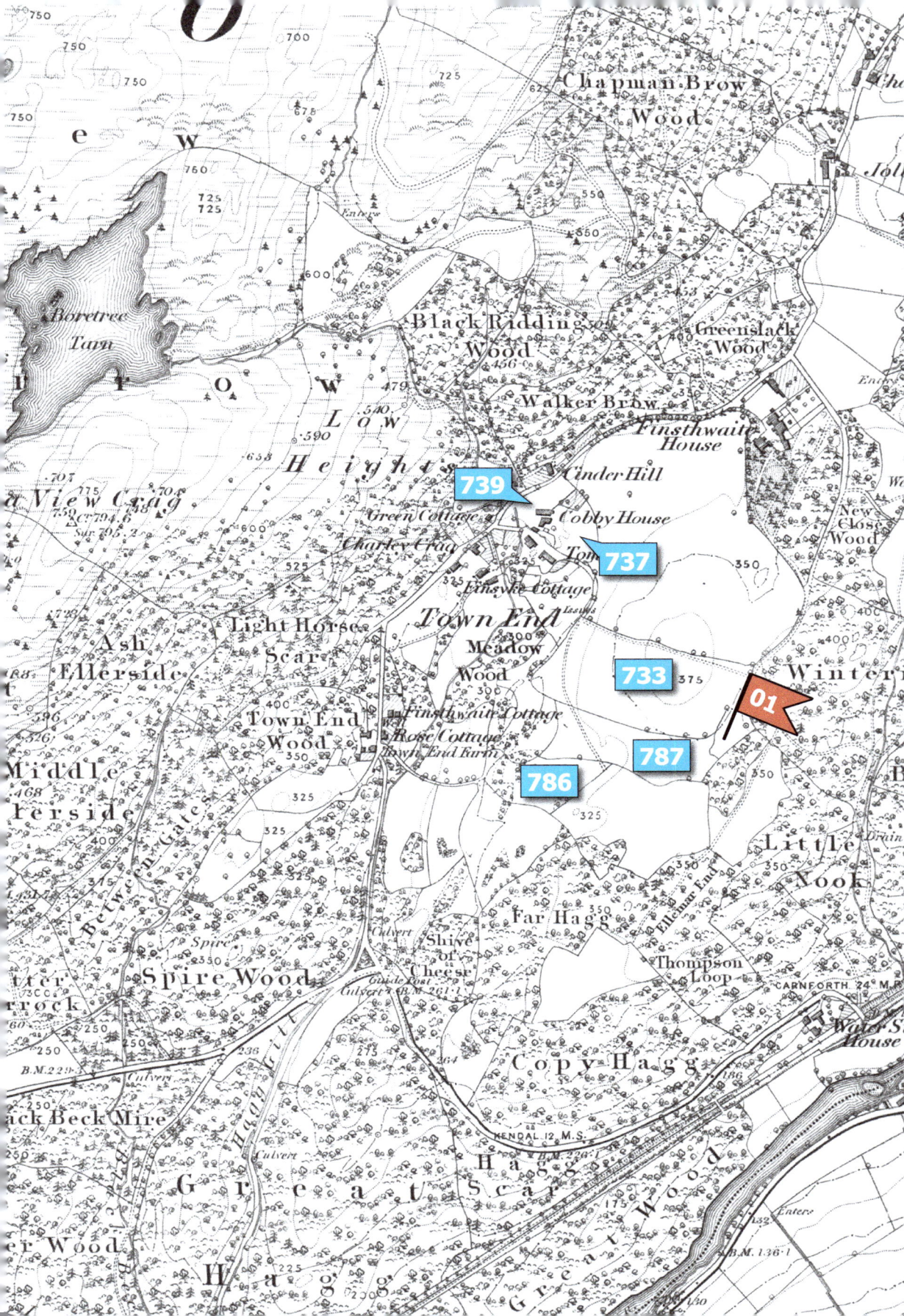

Pigeon Croft (788): the name 'Pidgeon Croft' appears in 1851 (FHEP) and first appears, spelled without the 'd', in 1719 (DDPd 26/208); it remains the modern name. It is not a field which has any association with pigeons. The 'croft' element is common to all the different versions, which Angus Winchester says is used for good quality land. The plot was ploughed and used for arable crops, and is notably smoother than the nearby Cow Pastures. Clement Taylor's account book notes Pigeon Croft being let for three years and that the tenant may 'plough it for two of the said years, to leave it in bigg (barley) stubble'. Earlier versions include: **Pynshowe Croft** (DDPd 26/15, 1582), **Phinchawe Crofte** (DDPd 26/38, 1609), **Pincher Croft** (DDPd 26/136, 1674) and then **Pinchway Croft** (DDPd 26/259, 1741) pops back up after Pigeon Croft was first used (in 1719). We believe the name is derived from Fin's Shaw (Fin's wood) where *Finnr* is the eponymous early settler of the village and his 'shaw' or wood was nearby. Shaw is a dialect word with both Old English and Old Norse origins. In 1564 there is a reference to a place 'known as the Shawe' (DDPd 26/4) which is in this area. In his discussion of Pigeon Croft, as an example of a 'Chinese whisper', Angus Winchester suggests that the first element of the name is 'Pin' and is obscure, but the authors want to fly the flag for *Finnr*.

Pidgeon Croft Bush (789): a wood lying next to the field called Pigeon Croft (788). The name bush is derived from Old Norse *buskr* which means a small wood or area of bushes. The name appears in 1851 (FHEP). Roger Taylor's account book (DDPd 26/341) records **Pincer Croft Bush** being coppiced in 1833.

Broad Moss (792): a broad field near a moss or bog, the Ellermire. Broad Moss is shown in 1851 (FHEP) but the earliest reference we have is 1660 (DDPD 26/116) when Broad Moss is described as 'peat moss and pasture south of Wintering Park'. It is now called **The Duck Pond Field** (Chaplin family) because it contains a pond used by wild ducks.

Little Broad Moss Wood (793) and **Big Broad Moss Wood (northern section of 791, Little Nook)**: two woods which share a name with the field Broad Moss (792), Little Broad Moss wood being to the north, and smaller, and Big Broad Moss Wood to the south of the field being a larger enclosure within the greater area of Little Nook (791). The names appear in 1851 (FHEP) only; OS records no name for plot 793 and gives the name Little Nook to the whole of 791. (FLAG 02)

Elmer End (784): a shortened form of the name **Ellermire** (a bog where alder trees grow); this name is given on OS 1850 for the larger western end of the plot, with the eastern end named **Far Hagg**. On OS 1890 and on FHEP in 1851 the whole plot is called Far Hagg. Although we cannot be sure of exactly which wood is meant, the Ellermire name appears as **Ellermire End** in 1741 (DDPd 26/259), and before that, in 1582, **Thellermy End** (DDPd 26/15).

Ellemar End: a track running between Broad Moss field (792) and Longmire (790), although FHEP in 1851 also shows a small strip of woodland south of the track having the name Ellemar End. By 1890 the name Elmer/Ellermire End, once a woodland plot 784, has become associated only with this trackway (OS 1890). In the modern era even this has disappeared into the mire, and the track to Longmire (the Hog House Field) has had to be re-routed further south. (FLAG 03)

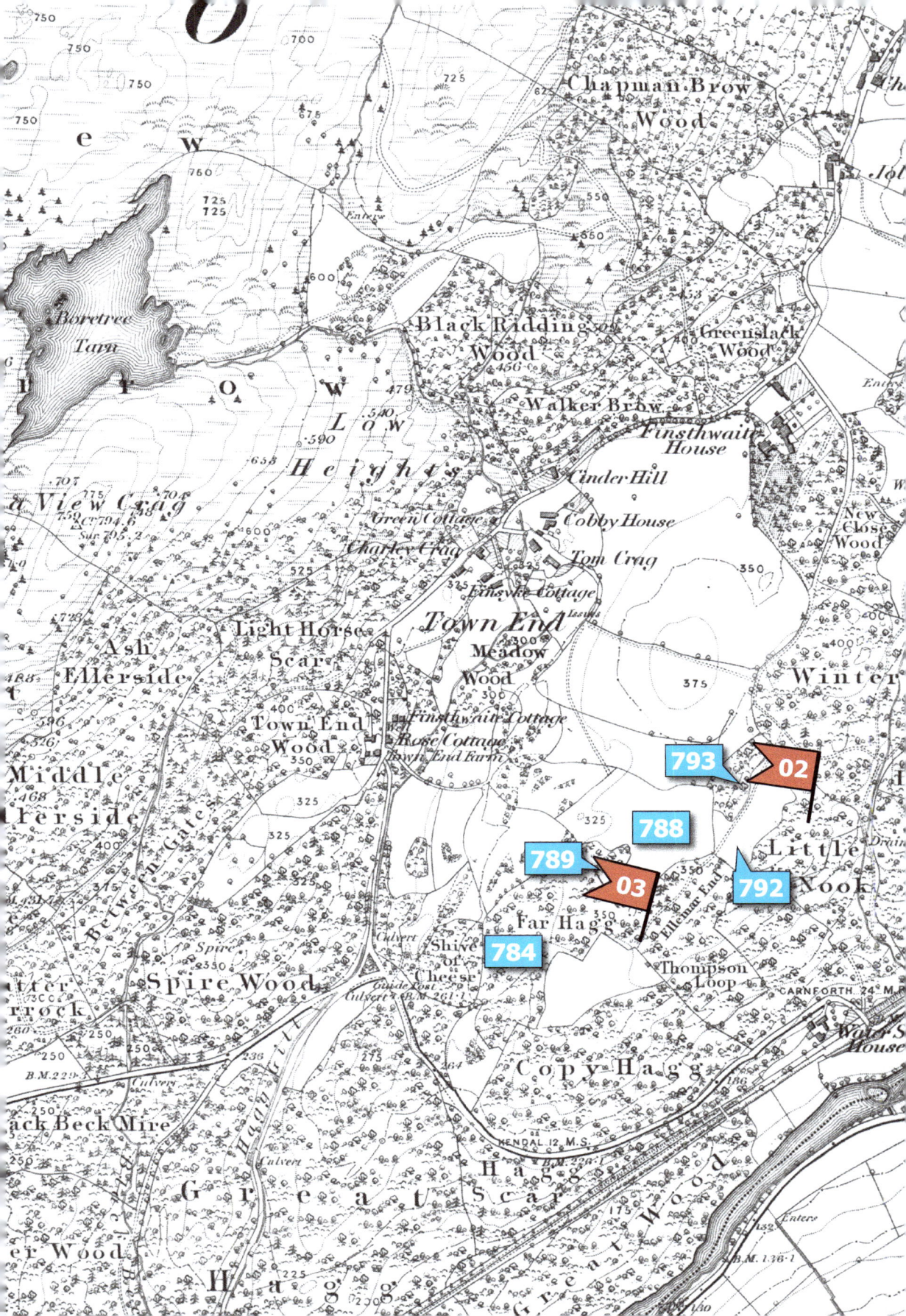

Long Mire (790): a long field next to the mire (the Ellermire, plot 784) is named in 1851 (FHEP). The current name is **Hog House Field** because of a sheep barn for 'hoggets', which are female sheep in the year before they begin bearing their own lambs, kept separate from the rest of the flock. The derelict remains of the hog house are visible and a square mark, and the name 'Hog House field', were pencilled onto the FHEP.

Little Meadow (736): a small meadow south of Tom Crag Farm. Named Little Meadow in 1851 (FHEP). A small division at the north end of plot 736 shows on the same map as **Croft** making this the only instance in our survey area of a field next to a farm being called Croft. All the others are called Parrock (see Plum Green for several examples and another at Low Stott Park.) Croft has now been absorbed into the garden at Tom Crag.

High Paddock (741): a field above the hill slope behind Green Cottage, this paddock is now wooded, but the boundary wall still exists. It is named in 1851 (FHEP) which also shows a pencil annotation of the word 'donkey' on this field – hence the modern name **The Donkey Paddock** (Chaplin family).

The Spout (FLAG 04): A place where villagers drew water before the water main was put in (Chaplin family). This may be the site of '**Waterefall Dub**' (DDPd26/47) in 1615. Dub is a dialect word for a pool, although this can no longer be seen.

Hard Hills (744): a very rocky field on a slope, typical of the thin-soiled field pasture available in Finsthwaite. Named in 1851 (FHEP) the plot extended down to **777, 777a** (777a was then a wood). The name **Hard How** is used in 1706 (DDPd 26/179) and in Clement Taylor's account book it is called **Hard Hall** (when he mentions it as a place where wood is to be cleared, although he reserves the 'crabtrees and holly'). How and Hill are synonyms, and locally (see Smithy Hall Wood at Low Stott Park) the name hall is sometimes substituted. The plot is now known as one of the **Charley Crag Fields** along with others in this area, because of their proximity to Charley Crag farmhouse (Chaplin family).

Meadow (745): a meadow in front of the house at Finsyke, with the simplest of names (we have other examples like 'Field' at Plum Green). The name is given in 1851 (FHEP). The name Finsyke may originate from the stream (Old Norse *sik*) which flows around Meadow. Its connection to *Finnr* may make this one of the earliest parcels of cultivated land in the village. Clement Taylor mentions Meadow in 1742 in his account book. The plot is now one of the **Charley Crag Fields** (Chaplin family).

Meadow Wood (735): a wood next to the field called Meadow 745 and therefore an example of a pairing of names where one plot has lost the name but the other one has kept it. It is named in 1851 (FHEP) and retains the name in modern usage.

Water Strands (746): a narrow strip of woodland, marked on FHEP in 1851 as Water Strands; the name is not entirely explicable. A strand means a ribbon or strip, and the ground is wet underfoot here, so there may have been a more evident stream in the past. The trees have all but disappeared and the plot is now effectively reabsorbed into plot 745.

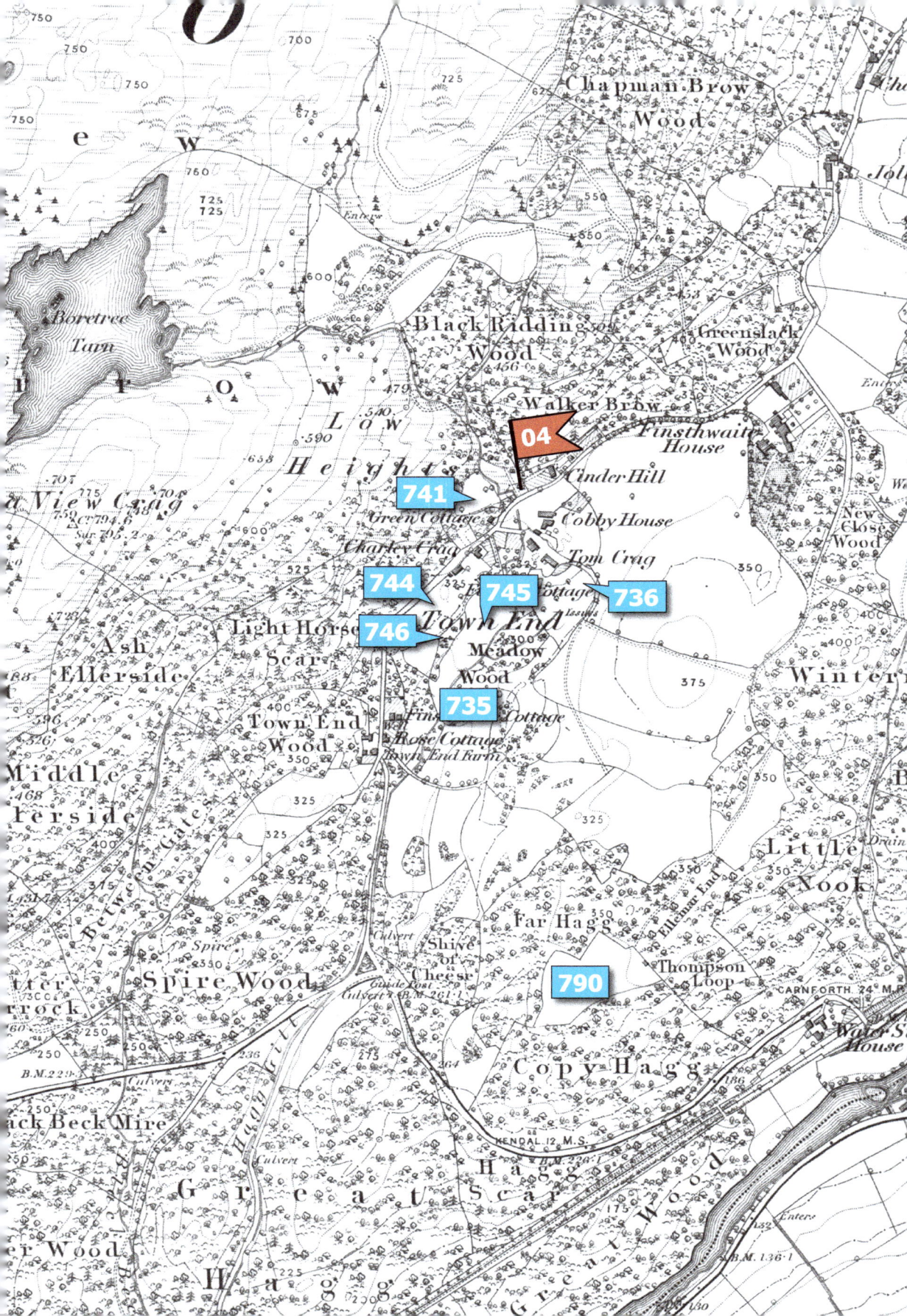

Grubbings (747): a small field separated out from the rest of Hard Hills and cleared of tree stumps and stones. It is named Grubbings in 1851 (FHEP) but is now one of the **Charley Crag Fields** in a group with 745, 744 etc. The walls that once separated this small field, which unlike the surrounding rocky pasture would have been a viable hay meadow or small arable plot, are still standing. The name Grubbing is mentioned in 1763 (DDPd 26/296) so it is at least an 18th century enclosure. Clement Taylor's account book mentions payments for 'grubbing' and carting of stones from fields.

Butts (734): the name may refer to a common field, with several individual plots abutting each other, although like Butt Hills at Cobby House (739) it is another rocky butt-end of land cut off from the main arable fields 733 and 787. It is named in 1851 (FHEP) and also in Clement Taylor's account book when it is subject to a restriction that it must be grazed only by sheep or horses (the same applies to Peaslands, plot 786).

Feather Bed (778): this field is named in 1851 (FHEP) as Feather Bed, a name which we thought was humorous as there is a large lump of bedrock here. The rock is topped by more pieces of stone, which may be field clearance. However the practice of 'feathering' (splitting) rock may have been carried out here, using the bedrock as a source of stone for walling and building. The name does not appear in the Pedder archive until the 1860s and seems not to have been used until the 19th century, which could support the idea that the plot is named after some contemporary stone-working activity. This is now known to Charlotte Dean as one of **Dulcie's Fields**, after Dulcie and Tom Curwen who lived at Rose Cottage nearby.

Low Becking Garth (FLAG 05): a small area of enclosed wood (a garth is generally smaller than a parrock) by a beck. The name Low Becking Garth appears in 1851 (FHEP) as do other plots near the same stream (see Higher Becking Garth, an area in Little Close, 771, and Lower Becking Garth part of plot 783). Clement Taylor's account book mentions Becking Garths so the name goes back to the mid-18th century.

Matthew Paddock (FLAG 06) (north end of **749**): a wood marked on FHEP in 1851 and named after Matthew Taylor a tenant farmer at Town End Farm between 1749 and 1761.

Light Horse Scar (749): a wood on a steep cliff or scar, named on FHEP in 1851 and OS 1850. The significance of Light Horse is elusive but must have associations with some military exploit. Roger Taylor's account book (DDPd 26/341) records the woods here being coppiced in 1842. The gate on the corner of the lane that leads into the wood is known as **Light Horse Gate** (Chaplin family).

Washhouse Hill (FLAG 07): the lane from Light Horse Gate (see 749) down the hill towards Town End is called Washhouse Hill after two sisters, Mary and Eleanor Croasdell who lived in a cottage ('The Washhouse', a name no longer used) at the foot of the hill. The sisters appear in the 1891 census as 'laundresses'. The washhouse name is a little disparaging; the Croasdell sisters had a reputation for fine laundry work, dealing with lace and other delicate fabrics. Washhouse Hill is still used by some locals, but the Croasdell sisters are largely forgotten.

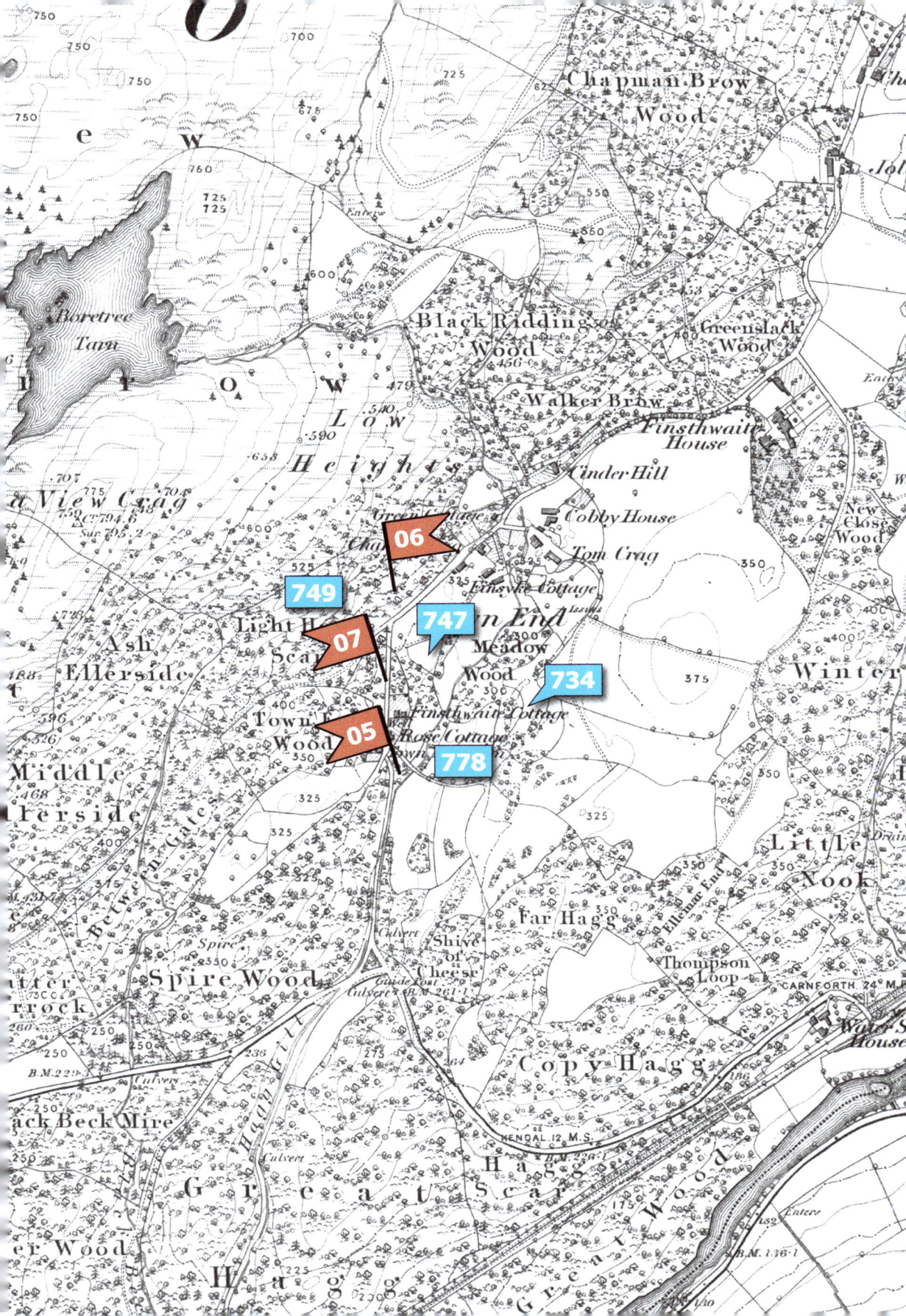

Town End Wood (774): a wood behind Town End Farm, named in 1851 (FHEP) and OS maps in 1850 and 1890.

Spire Wood (771): a wood that has a folly called The Spire (an obelisk) on a peak at the centre of the plot. It is named Spire Wood on OS 1890, although OS 1850 gives the wood the dual name of **Little Close or Spire Wood** and FHEP (1851) calls it Little Close with 'Spire Wood' added in ink alongside. The name Little Close is oldest, and appears in 1698 (DDPd 26/169). In 1729 the will of William Danson mentions a 'close of arable and wood called Little Close' which he leaves to his nephew. The current name for the wood and adjacent fields, is **The Spire**. On FHEP the north-east section of the plot is called **Higher Becking Garth** (FLAG 08) an area of woodland near a beck on the high side of the lane, opposite Low Becking Garth (777b). A track running through Spire Wood follows the line of the old lane, which was re-routed into its current line in 1829 and now passes south of Spire Wood, to Lane Ends and down Hagg Gill to Linsey Green.

Town End Paddock (773): a field or paddock by Town End Farm, as named in 1851 (FHEP). In 1706 (DDPd 26/178) it was called **Town End Meadow** and was said in the same document to be also known as **Great Meadow**, another example of 'great' for a large field. It appears to be **Bryan Way Parrock** in 1684 (DDPd 26/156) according to the description in the archive. There are various Brian Taylors among the Taylors of Finsthwaite.

Tarn Close (772 and 770): two fields or closes near a small pond or tarn. The tarn may be the **Horspots,** a drinking place for horses, mentioned in 1706 (DDPd 26/178). There is a marshy area on the edge of these fields, which in the past may have been a more substantial pond for livestock. The two Tarn Close fields are named in 1851 (FHEP) and are now known, with 773, as **The Town End Fields**.

Tarn Close Wood (in plot **771**): on FHEP a section of the west end of Little Close/Spire Wood is named **Tarn Close Wood.** It was walled separately, and ran from the end of the Tarn Close Field 770 in a curve round the end of Spire Wood until it met the top of plot 816. **(FLAG 09)**

Waterside Meadow

• Section 5 •

The Haggs and Waterside

We have treated this area as a specific section because of the prevalence of names incorporating the element 'hagg'. The word is derived from an Old Norse word for cutting or clearing, and comes to be associated with coppice woodland. It is also the origin of the name of a kind of grass pasture, grazing which would have been quite heavily treed, at least by modern standards. In this map section we have both types of hagg plot. The pasture plots are now largely cleared of the scatter of trees that were shown in 1851 (Finsthwaite House estate plan) and even OS 1890. Their names, Low, Middle and Great Hagg, suggest that they were once shared pasture used by a number of farmers (the sequence of names is given by Angus Winchester as evidence of this practice). The only trees that remain survive in separate garths, small walled enclosures, like Low Hag Bush.

The rest of this section is dominated by regular woodland, with old coppice and some modern planting. Parts of it were badly damaged by storms in 2005, when many trees were lost. Great Hagg, the biggest wood in our survey area, is over 50 acres and spans the 'new' road through Hagg Gill and at one time included a plot now cut off by the Furness Railway. This, and the smaller plots in this section, would have been the scene of regular intensive work by the residents of Finsthwaite making the plethora of wood products at which they excelled: barrels, laths, frames for packhorse saddles, hurdles, besoms, bark for bast rope and tanning, hoops for swill baskets, as well as a wealth of domestic wares, furniture and even firewood. Coppicing, where trees are cut down and allowed to re-grow until multiple slim trunks have developed, was crucial for producing poles which could be used for charcoal making and for bobbins, in mills like the one at Stott Park. Woodland is at the heart of the economic life of Finsthwaite from medieval times onwards. The very first document in the Pedder archive, DDPd 26/1 dated June 1552, mentions Haggscar, a plot on this map section. The signatories were two yeomen and a 'dish-throwler' (a wood turner in modern parlance).

Great Hagg (813, 808 and 860): a very large area of woodland, named on OS 1850 which shows it before plot 860 was cut off by the railway line. FHEP in 1851 names plot 813 on the other side of Hagg Gill as 'part of Great Hagg'. The combined acreage would have been just over 50 acres. A public footpath runs through Great Hagg, on the border between plot 813 and Turner Wood 814, which follows the line of the old road between Backbarrow and Finsthwaite which was re-routed through Hagg Gill in 1829. These woods are referred to in 1616 (DDPd 26/48) as 'the **Greathagge**'. Plot 860, on the other side of the railway line is now known as **Flat Hagg** (Chaplin family).

Higher Hagland (809): a field on the high side of the slope (and of the lane through Hagg Gill) at the northern tip of Great Hagg wood. In our survey area it is relatively unusual for 'land' to be used instead of 'field' for a cultivated area. The boundary walls of 809 and 811 suggest they were once one field, and pre-date the 1829 road. Higher Hagland is named in 1851 (FHEP), and is now known as **Long Field** because of its shape (Chaplin family).

Lower Hagland (811): a field on the lower side of the slope, and the lane, at the north end of Great Hagg, and may once have been joined to 809. It is named in 1851 (FHEP). This plot has the Hagg Gill stream running along its low edge by the lane and is now called **The Beck Field** (Chaplin family).

Hagg Gill (812): the site of a new road built in 1829 (DDPd 26/370) which takes its name from the stream, Hagg Gill, that runs through the wood called the Great Hagg between its main plot 808 and the western 813. The 'gill' element of the name refers to the ravine down which the stream runs. The stream is called 'Hagg Gill' on OS 1850 and 1890, but the name is not used now.

Lane Ends: a small triangular plot with trees, created at the junction of Finsthwaite Lane with lanes to Waterside and to Ealinghearth. Named in 1851 (FHEP), although Stephen Kellett used to call it **Ten Road Ends** which is the kind of brain teaser for which he was renowned. The Chaplin family call it **The Crossroads**. Some locals call it 'the Shive of Cheese' because of its *Dairylea* shape, but this is an error (see plot 783) (**Flag 01**).

Low Hag (779): an area of wooded pasture, or hagg, named in 1851 (FHEP). Low Hag is nearest to the lane, down a slope from Middle Hag, 781 and Great Hag 785. Angus Winchester identifies the name sequence (low, middle etc) as being evidence of this being common pasture in the past, used by multiple livestock owners for grazing.

Low Hag Bush (780): an area of bushes or a small wood within the pasture called Low Hag, 779. This section of wood has been walled off from the rest of the field, suggesting that the old pattern of quite heavily wooded pasture was gradually being cleared with some trees being preserved in a separate enclosure.

Middle Hag (781): an area of wooded pasture between Low Hag 779 and Great Hag 785. It is named in 1851 (FHEP) and mentioned in Clement Taylor's account book in 1720 as **Middlemost Hagg** (when Edward Danson of Cobby House was paid £1 for peeling bark there).

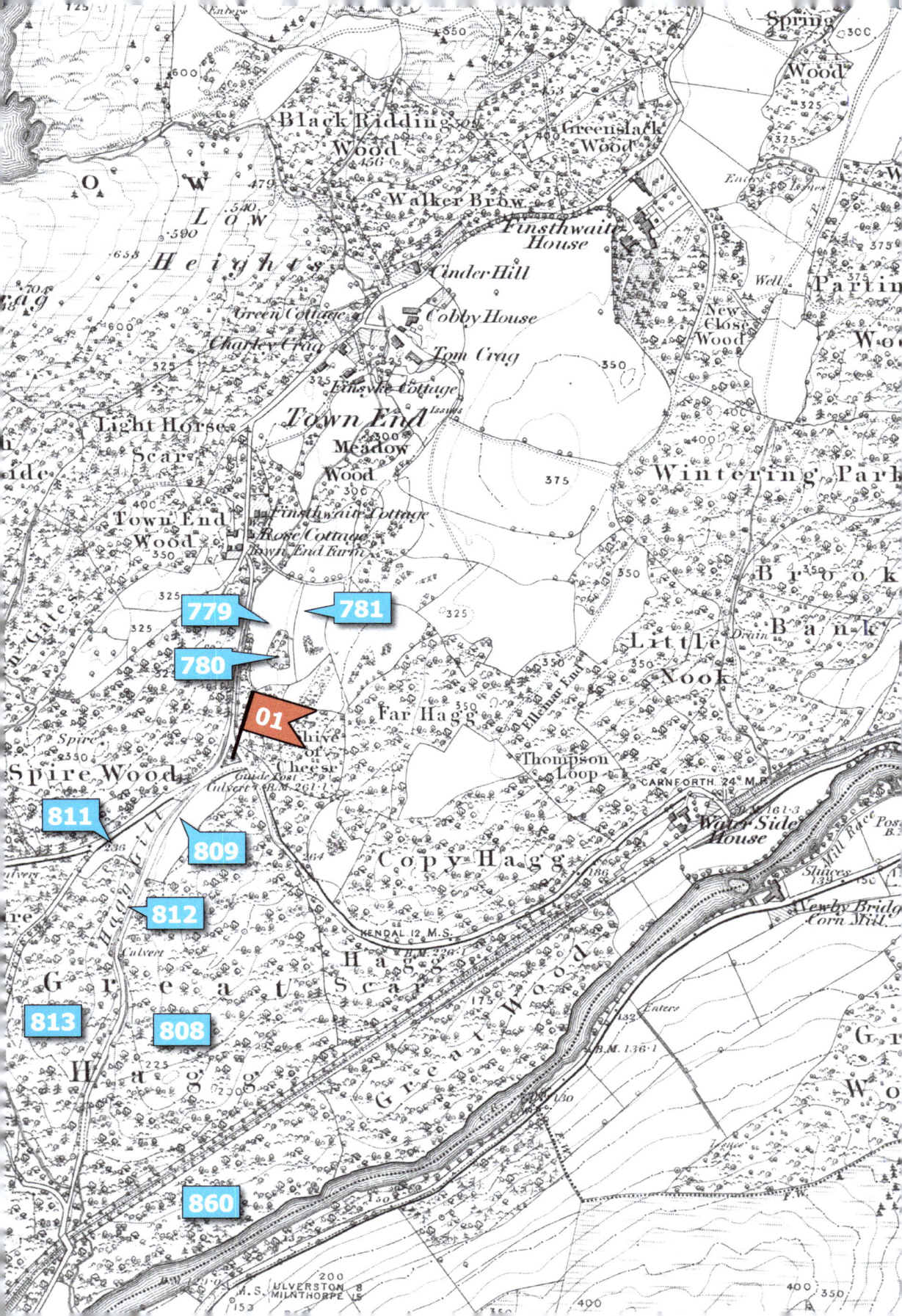

Great Hag (785): a wooded pasture on top of the slope above Low Hag and Middle Hag, and larger than the lower plots. The plot is named Great Hag (with one 'g' perhaps to differentiate it from the large wood Great Hagg nearby) and would have been wooded pasture like Low and Middle Hag. Its modern name is **The Cow Pastures**, which is annotated in pencil on the 1851 estate plan. The Cow Pastures is a name which is used for the whole of the area of grazing west of Town End (Chaplin family).

Far Hag (782): an area of wooded pasture at furthest distance from the farms at Lower Finsthwaite. It is named Far Hag in 1851 (FHEP) and is referred to in 1706 (DDPd 26/176) as 'a close called Farehagge adjoining the north side of the highway from Elinghearth Brow to Newby Bridge' (at which time because it is said to adjoin the highway it may have included part or all of plot 783).

Far Hagg (784): a woodland plot which shares a name with plot 782, where 782 would appear to be more of the pasture type of hagg and 784 to be fully wooded. OS 1850 calls most of this plot **Elmer End**, reserving the name Far Hagg for the eastern end (south of Pigeon Croft, 788). Both FHEP 1851, and OS 1890 call this plot, in its entirety, Far Hagg.

Lower Becking Garth (north section of **783**): an enclosure of woodland east of the lane with a stream or beck running through it. The plot is named in 1851 (FHEP) and forms part of a group (the others are Low Becking Garth, Higher Becking Garth, and Becking Garth) referred to in 1706 (DDPd 26/179). This section seems to be called 'lower' because it is south of two of the others (see Town End section). At the lane side is a very small triangle of land which is marked on FHEP as **Becking Garth**, making up the last of the quartet of enclosures by the beck (this local word for a stream is derived from Old Norse *bekkr*).

Shive of Cheese (783): an area of land marked on FHEP in 1851 as belonging to the Machell family. It was said to have been lost in a bet and was returned to the Pedder family in the 1950s as a wedding present for John Chaplin and Claire Mary Pedder. A 'shive' is a small slice or section, and is a word derived from Old Norse *skifa*. The name survives onto modern maps, although it is sometimes wrongly associated locally with the small triangle of wood at Lane Ends.

Robin Bush (807): an area of bushes or small wood named in 1851 (FHEP). We have not identified any Robin as a person, so it could be a place associated with the bird. It is listed in Roger Taylor's account book (DDPd 26/341) as having been coppiced in 1842.

Jenny Hagg (806): named in 1851 (FHEP) as Jenny Hagg this plot was once the property of Jane (Jennet) and her husband John Taylor, who farmed at Charley Crag Farm in Lower Finsthwaite in the 18th century. When Jennet Taylor was a widow, her financial affairs were managed for her by Clement Taylor who sold this plot to raise money to support her. She was over 90 years old when she died in 1728, so the survival of the name to 1851 is notable. The modern name for the field is **Haggscar** because it lies next to the head of Haggscar wood (plot 804).

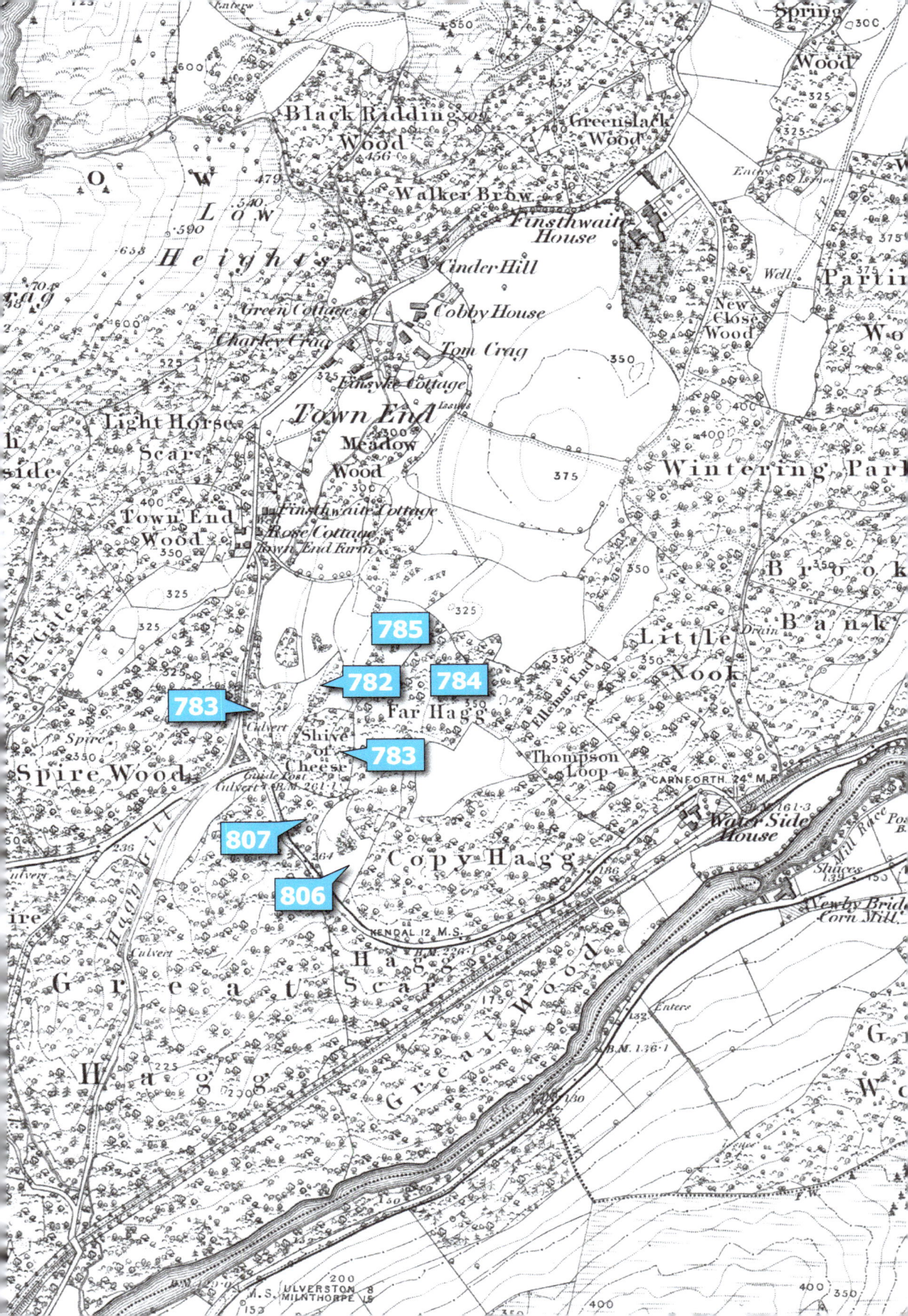

Haggscar (804): a steeply sloping wood on land running down towards the river Leven ('scar' means a cliff or very steep slope). The oldest documented name in our survey; the plot was sold in 1552 (DDPd 26/1). It also appears on OS 1850 and 1890, and FHEP, and still survives to modern times (in connection with this wood and the field 806).

Copy Hag (805): an area of coppice woodland, or hagg, on a hill (cop) or perhaps, despite the tautology, copy refers to coppice. It is named Copy Hag in 1851 (FHEP) but earlier versions of the name are **Cubby Hagg** in 1741 (DDPd 26/260 and 26/259) and **Covey Hagg** on OS 1850. Janet Martin suggests that 'copy' is a rationalisation of the name 'Cubby' and refers to Cuthbert Taylor who lived at Lower Finsthwaite in the early 17th century and was associated with this wood. The land is now absorbed into Thompson Loop (Chaplin family). On FHEP a strip of plot 805 by the lane edge is marked '**High Side Hag Scar**' suggesting that plot 804 may at one time have extended across the lane (**Flag 02**).

Little Nook and Thompson Loop (791): a wood in a secluded or corner spot. This plot is shown on OS 1850 with the smaller, north-east part of the plot called **Little Nook**, and **Thompson Loop** as the larger portion in the south-west section. We have not identified Thompson as a personal name, but it must have been. The name suggests the site was used for iron working; a 'loop' is the name given to a hot bloom of iron ready to be hammered to get the impurities out of it. On OS 1890 both names still exist, but Little Nook has become the larger portion and Thompson Loop confined to a square plot between Copy Hagg 805 and the rest of Little Nook. In 1851 (FHEP) the division is about the same as on OS 1850, but the north-east section is **Little Nook or Hatter Hag**. Hatter Hag probably has reference to it having been sold in the 18th century by William Braithwaite, a hatter, who gave his name to Hatter Parrock (plot 765 near Ealinghearth). Little Nook is named as early as 1633 (DDPd 26/79). It is also the site of the route which George Taylor agreed to use (DDPd 26/131) for his cattle if his neighbour was growing corn in Peaselands, which the animals would trample. He must then 'go round by Little Nook' and himself maintain the gates and fences for the route (presumably to stop his cows wandering at will in the wood). The agreement dates to 1670. A bridle path runs from Waterside House to Finsthwaite House starting in Little Nook and then following the border between this and Brook Bank (795); the Chaplin family call this path 'The Nook'. Both Little Nook and Thompson Loop survive as modern names for these woodland plots.

Great Wood (861): a large wood lying between the railway and the river Leven, named on OS 1890 and on FHEP (1851) but not named on OS 1850 (which does not show the railway line at all). The modern name for this wood is **Flat Hagg** (Chaplin family).

Grubbin (802): a field which has been cleared of trees and stones. Named in 1851 (FHEP). On OS 1850, before the railway came, this was a larger plot. Now absorbed into its neighbours 799 and 801, as the dividing walls between the plots have been taken down. The modern name is **Waterside Meadow**.

Little Field (801): a small field next door to Great Field 799, in this case in a logical pairing, unlike Great and Little Field at Plum Green which are nearly the same size. Named in 1851 (FHEP) and now part of one large field as the boundary walls have been taken down (see note on Grubbin, 802). OS 1850 shows that before the railway this field was larger, and extended to the west end of Waterside House. The modern name is **Waterside Meadow**.

Great Field (799): a large field next to Little Field 801. The plot has been, like 801 and 802, severed by the railway line. FHEP, 1851, shows it in its trimmed state, but OS 1850 shows it running up to the east side of Waterside House. Now one large field, joined with 802 and 801. The modern name is **Waterside Meadow**. In 1869 (DDPd 26/407) reference is made to '**the garden part of Great Field**' at Waterside House which refers to the plot at the east side of the house, suggesting that the memory of the shape of Great Field before the railway line came was still strong (**Flag 03**).

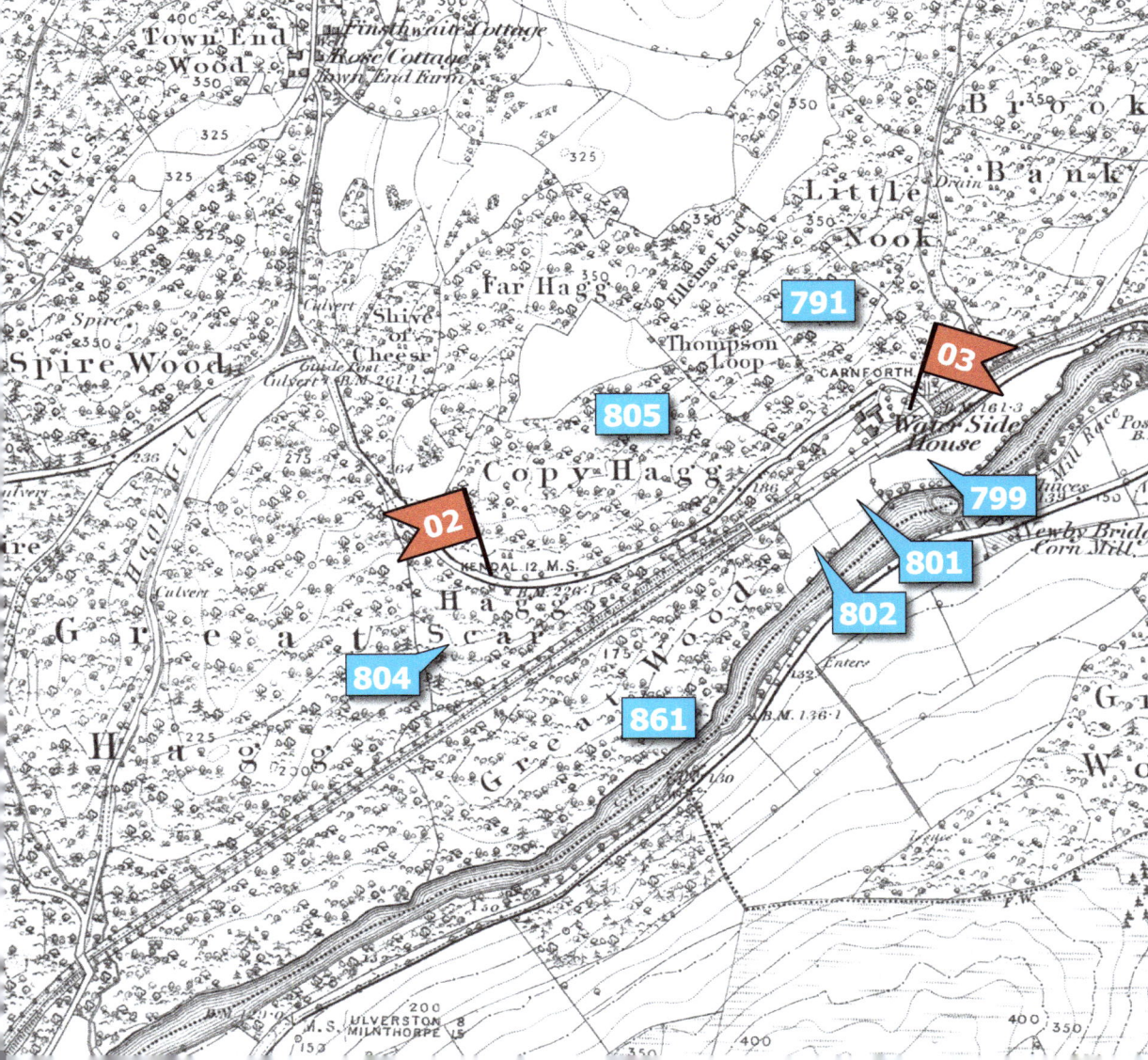

• Section 6 •

Finsthwaite Heights

Finsthwaite Heights is a large area of fell grazing, heath and mosses on the top of the hill which separates the village from the main area of the Rusland valley. The Heights was an important source of fresh water from Boretree Tarn and from the many streams which rise there. The fell is also home to bogs and mosses, which would have been cut for peat for fuel. It is still summer grazing for sheep, with ewes and lambs turned out onto the fell as they would always have been; although there is more emphasis on worming and anti-tick medication in the modern era. Finsthwaite farmers use the traditional name The Fell for their upland grazing.

The village houses are built along the lane which runs under the edge of the Heights, taking advantage of the source of fresh water. The summer grazing may have been what attracted the first settlers to the area, looking for a *saeter* for cattle and sheep. The Heights was described as 'common or waste' in the past, meaning that it was uncultivated and not enclosed, and would have been an area to which all villagers would have had some share of the resources like grazing and peat. Using the grazing was not undisputed however, as the argument between George and Richard Taylor in 1670 shows, (see Finsthwaite history) and it was sometimes bought and sold like any other land parcel. In 1734 Clement Taylor of Finsthwaite House, James Backhouse of Jolliver Tree and George Taylor of Stott Park bought 100 acres of 'pasture called Farr Height or Plumb Green Height and Ewbarrow Topp', an area which ran from the south-east corner of Great Greenhows (near what is now High Dam) over to 'the sheep wash at Intack Gate' (at the Intakes, on the fell above Sinderhill). The plot had come up for sale following the bankruptcy of Henry Taylor of Landing. The sale agreement, DDPd 26/241, notes that certain areas of peat moss and turbary are still 'in dispute'.

As well as peat mosses there are two main bodies of water on the Height. Boretree tarn is apparently mentioned, named Dulas, as a fresh water fishery in 1539; it attracted a tax of 20s. High Dam, at the northern end of the fell, was a couple of small tarns which were flooded to a greater depth by the building of a dam to provide a head of water for the bobbin mill at Stott Park in 1835. Low Dam was not created until later in the twentieth century; it does not appear on the 1913 OS map. There is another tiny tarn on Finsthwaite Heights which has no modern name, but on a list of holdings of Jolliver Tree farm in c1740 (DDPd 26/332) there is a reference to Hurleyhall Tarn at Little Ellerside. The *Dialect Dictionary* suggests that a 'hurley house' is a derelict or abandoned building. This was not the site of a dwelling house but it is possible that there was a hut there for a shepherd looking after flocks in the summer, with the tarn as a source of water. If the building was derelict in 1740 it may not have been very robust, or perhaps dated back to the sixteenth century or earlier.

The Heights were enclosed in the early 1770s when a group of landowners got together to identify a way in which the 300 acres of ground 'which was then of small profit' could be managed more productively. The agreement to enclose the area, both with an encircling wall and a dividing wall running from Chapman Brow across to Rusland Heights, was drawn up and the walls built between October 1771 and October 1773. Sheep were to graze the northern end and cattle the southern part. The dividing wall had to be built to a height which would prevent the sheep from jumping over; fell sheep are notorious wall climbers, then as now. Surprisingly there is mention in the enclosure award of the possibility of tillage plots, but it seems that better sense prevailed.

The dividing wall was robustly built and still stands, with capstones in place. The encircling wall is patchier, although still visible in places, especially at High Dam where we have noted where it may be seen. The enclosure map (DDPd 26/336) provided us with names for several landscape features, like Tup Haw and Dixon Hill, inside the enclosure.

The enclosure did not seem to disenfranchise villagers. The practice of grazing cattle and sheep on the fell continued but it was apparently already concentrated in the hands of the landowners who made the agreement. The enclosure wall had to have openings so that anyone who had 'ancient rights' to cut peat or 'loppings' of wood could exercise them. However in 1727 (DDPd 26/225 and 26/226) Jane Taylor and Margaret Sawrey both gave evidence of how they had, in earlier times, had pasture rights on the fell with 'liberty' to drive cattle through fields lower down the fell. Jane was aged 'upwards of 90 years' and Margaret was about 75, so their memories went back many years. They now objected to a gate having been put up by Clement Taylor's brother-in-law Richard Robinson, possibly in the area called Gate Cote, a name which implies access or a right of way, from Old Norse *gata*, a track. The gate prevented their neighbours, the Dansons of Cobby House, from reaching the pasture. The gate was duly taken down. The evidence of the two women is witnessed by the Dansons, who were tenants of Clement Taylor, and anxious to keep their grazing rights. Fifty years later, the enclosure wall was built without opposition.

Roger Height (184): an upland plot possibly named after Roger Taylor of High Stott Park, although we have no evidence that it was ever his property; as an alternative it may have acquired 'Roger' through its adjacency to Roger Intake (185 and 467) to the east. Roger Height and Roger Intake are names used by OS in 1850 and 1890. This plot is identified as Roger Height on an undated list of the holdings of Chapman House, which uses plot numbers from OS 1890 (WD/AG Box 17). In 1843 it is called **Near Fell** (WDB 135/3/4) and earlier still, in 1771 (DDPd 26/336) it is **Broad Oak** (on the enclosure map) and **Broad Oak Hill** (in the text of the enclosure award).

High Dam (183): a reservoir created in 1835 to provide a head of water to power the bobbin mill at Low Stott Park. The enclosure map (DDPd 26/336) shows only two small pools in the area in 1771 and so a substantial dam wall was built to enhance the natural body of water. It is named High Dam on both OS maps (1850 and 1890) and 'high' refers to its position at the top of the fell.

Low Dam (FLAG 01): south of High Dam an additional smaller reservoir was built sometime in the early twentieth century. It does not show on OS 1913, and so post-dates that mapping. In Janet Martin's notes about the management of the Landing estate after the death of Thomas Newby Wilson (WD/AG Box 19) reference is made to payments of 10s per year to Mr Jackson in compensation for land of his which was liable to damage by flooding when 'the tarn on the top of Finsthwaite Heights' was very full and overflowed. He makes a claim on the Landing estate in 1917 as these payments have fallen into arrears. The water had damaged Mr Jackson's land on the south side of High Dam, and had 'destroyed a larch plantation' there. Low Dam, when eventually constructed, is south of the High Dam reservoir wall on this low-lying spot and may have been a response to the flooding. A few large larches still grow here.

Holling Hill (470): a hill with holly trees (from 'hollin', a dialect word for holly), which overlooks High Dam on the west side. The name is given on the enclosure map in 1771 (DDPd 26/336). Holly trees were a valuable source of winter fodder in the past.

Plots 471 and 472: we have no name for these plots which lie east of Far Fell 182, but have found that they were bought by Thomas Kellett of Chapman House farm in 1919. Janet Martin found a note of the sale (in WD/AG Box 19) which took place after the death of Thomas Newby Wilson, in 1915, but before the sale of the rest of the Harrison estate in 1920. The '2 closes' are not otherwise named, but are identified by their OS 1890 plot numbers. 471 and 472 lie inside the enclosure wall in an area marked as mosses in 1771 (DDPd 26/336). A public footpath from High Dam to Crosslands runs along the north edge of 470 and 471; walkers can see the enclosure wall beside the path.

Far Fell (182): a fell plot further west on the Height than Near Fell 184, this area of grazing is named in 1843 (WDB135/3/4) as Far Fell. In the undated list of holdings of Chapman House farm it is **Peat Moss** (WD/AG Box 17).

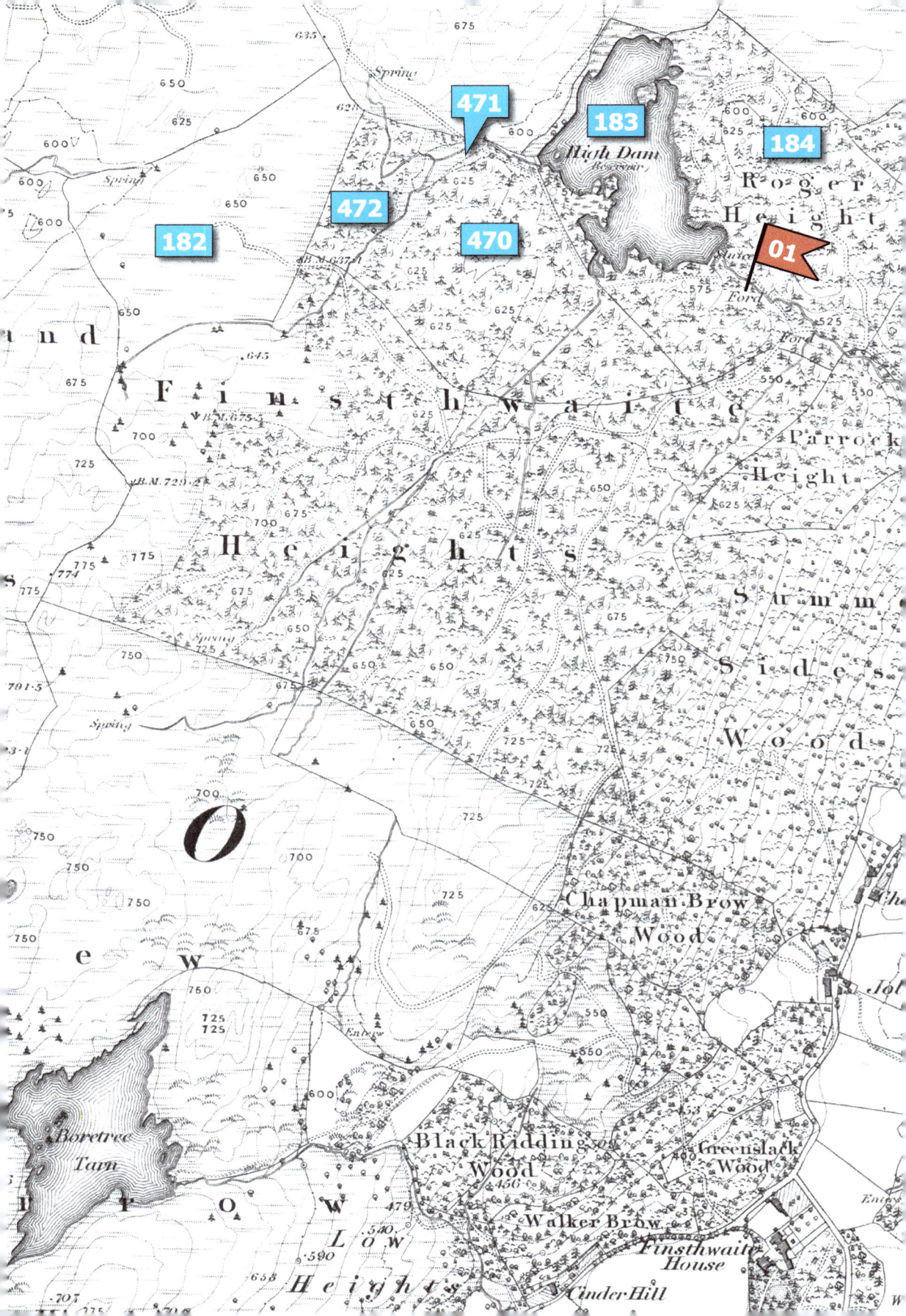

Finsthwaite Heights (482): the northern area of the Heights above Finsthwaite, in all about 90 acres, is called Finsthwaite Heights on OS 1850 and 1890. In 1734 (DDPd 26/241) this end of the fell was **Farr Height or Plumb Green Height**, although that plot is described as extending further south west towards Sinderhill. Plot 482 is called **The Intake** on an 1878 schedule of the holdings of Chapman House farm (in Janet Martin's notes of the management of the Landing estate after the death of Elizabeth Harrison). In 1734, before the enclosure, the plot is 'the height' a name which reflects its condition as 'common or waste' but 1878 it is called 'intake' as after the enclosure it is seen as cultivated land.

The enclosure map in 1771 (DDPd 26/336) notes three landscape features: **Dixon Hill (FLAG 02)**, **Tup Haw (FLAG 03)** and **Cros Walls (FLAG 04)**. Dixon Hill shows as open fell land on OS 1850 but is wooded on OS 1890. Janet Martin has notes of Dixon being a local name in Finsthwaite from the late-17th century. Tup Haw is the hill on which tups (rams) were kept when not with the rest of the flock. Cros walls is a plot on the far side of the enclosure, where the dividing wall meets the back wall.

Near here we have also marked the point on the enclosure where the boundary is a stream, not a dry stone wall **(FLAG 05)**. Information taken from the 1771 enclosure map (DDPd 26/336).

481 Jane Penny's Intack: this 13-acre plot of grazing belonged to Jane Penny, the only woman to own land in the enclosure. 'Mr Penny' is written on the oblong of land on the enclosure map (DDPd 26/336) and William and his daughter Jane were both signatories to the agreement. Jane inherited her father's land and holdings at Jolliver Tree by the time the enclosure was completed. It is named Intack in 1895 (BDHJ/398/4/10). The name **Jane Penny's Land** is modern usage.

High Fell (541): named High Fell in 1851 (FHEP) and was part of the Finsthwaite House estate when Edward Taylor was a signatory to the enclosure agreement in 1771 (the plot is marked 'Mr Taylor' on the enclosure map). The enclosure map also identifies two landscape features: **Winscarr (FLAG 06)**, a steeply sloping crag where whin (gorse) grows and **Windy Haws (FLAG 07)**, which may be a hill where whin grows. Given the terrain it may also mean a windy, exposed hill. In the evidence given by Jane Taylor in 1727, asserting ancient rights to fell pasture (DDPd 26/225) during a dispute with Clement Taylor and his brother-in-law, one of the areas she claims for cattle grazing is **Windhaws**. The earliest reference to Windhaws is 1631 (DDPd 26/76).

Tarn Haws (536): the hill by Boretree tarn, named in 1851 (FHEP). This plot is mentioned several times in Clement Taylor's account book when he built a reservoir wall, establishing that the name is older than the 19th century. It is mentioned even earlier in 1633 (DDPd 26/78) as a 'close of woods and pasture called Tarnehowe', and in connection with an enclosed plot 'Tarnhow Garth' in 1592 (LRO PR2850/6/2 No 8a), a wood that 'lieth in common pasture'.

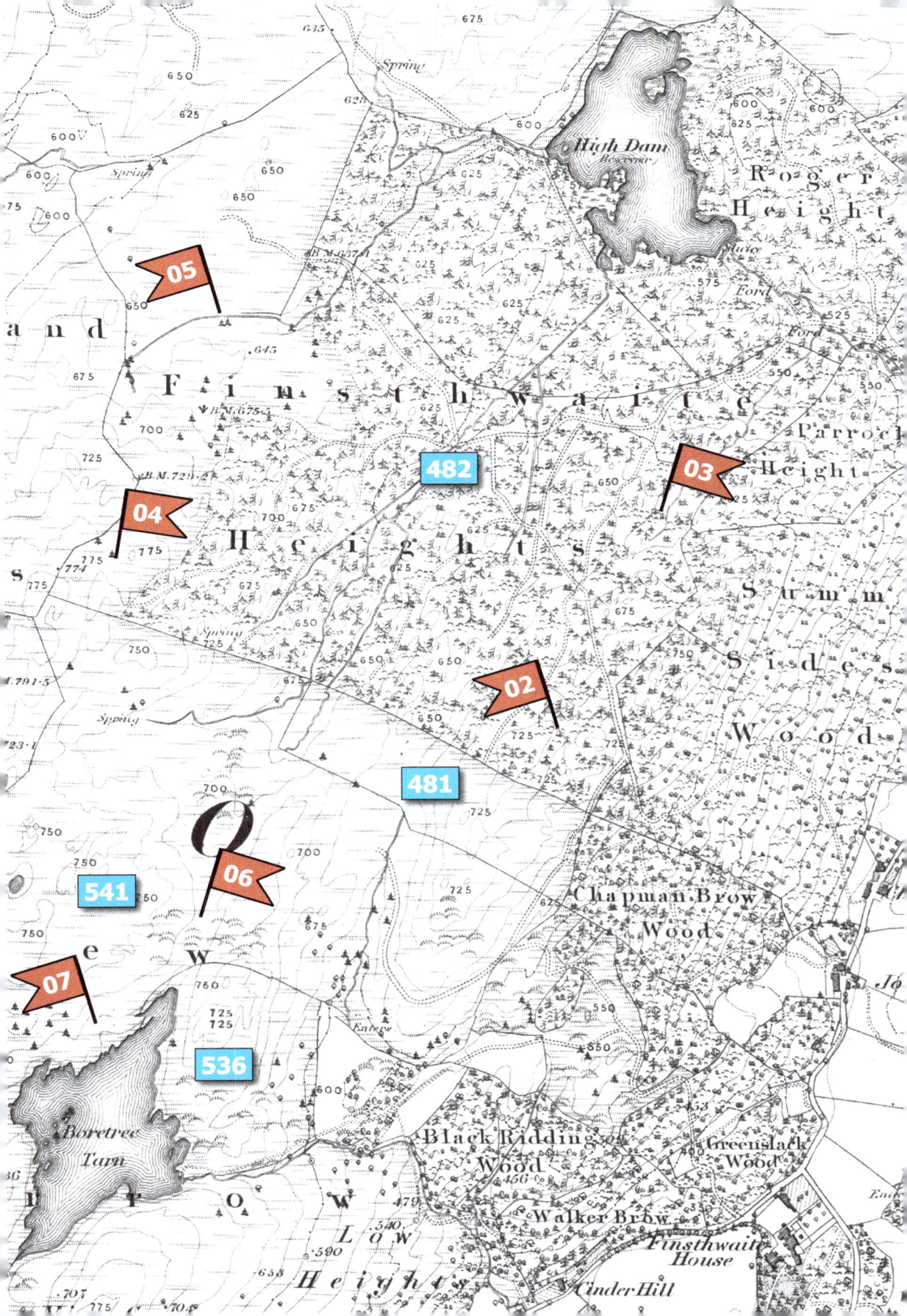

Boretree Tarn (542): a tarn (small upland lake) which may be the fresh-water fishery called **Dulas** in 1539, a name of Celtic or Gaelic origin meaning 'black lake'. It appears, as Boretree Tarn, in 1633 (DDPd 26/78) in connection with Tarn Haws, plot 536. In 1635 it is '**the Tarn of Borterie**' (LRO PR 2850/6/2 no 8c). The name on FHEP in 1851 is **Bawtry** but a pencil correction 'Bortree' is added underneath. Bortree is a dialect word for the elder tree. In 1843 (WDB/135/3/4) four detached plots of peat moss, claimed by the Landing estate under the name '**Burtree Tarn Moss**', lay within the area near Boretree, but they are not precisely located on that map.

Low Height (554): an area of fell to the south of Boretree tarn, named on FHEP in 1851, and also identified on OS 1890 as **Low Heights**. OS 1850 reserves the name Low Heights for the eastern end of the plot, which is lower down the fellside, and identifies the hill summit at the western end of 554 as **Sea View Crag**. The words '**Sea View Summit**' have been added, in pencil, to FHEP, but the name is not used by the Chaplin family. In 1684 the peak seems to be called **the High Crag** (DDPd 26/154). It is not included in the area of the enclosure award in 1771, and is marked on the map (DDPd 26/336) as High Crag, belonging to Mr Backhouse.

Hill Above Staff Gate (480): named in 1771 on the enclosure map (DDPd 26/336) this hill slopes down to Rusland, and is identified on OS 1850 and 1890 as part of **Rusland Heights**.

Little Ellerside (Flag 08): this plot is named Little Ellerside on the enclosure map (DDPd 26/336) a small plot where alder trees grow. (Great Ellerside is plot 767 nearby down the slope.) **Hurley Hall Tarn (Flag 09)** which we have named from a c1740 document (DDPd 26/332) which mentions the tarn in connection with Little Ellerside, one of the Jolliver Tree holdings. Wright's *Dialect Dictionary* gives the meaning of a 'hurley house' as an abandoned or derelict building, which we think may have been a hut near the little tarn to house someone working the woods on the fell or perhaps a shepherd. The tarn has no modern name.

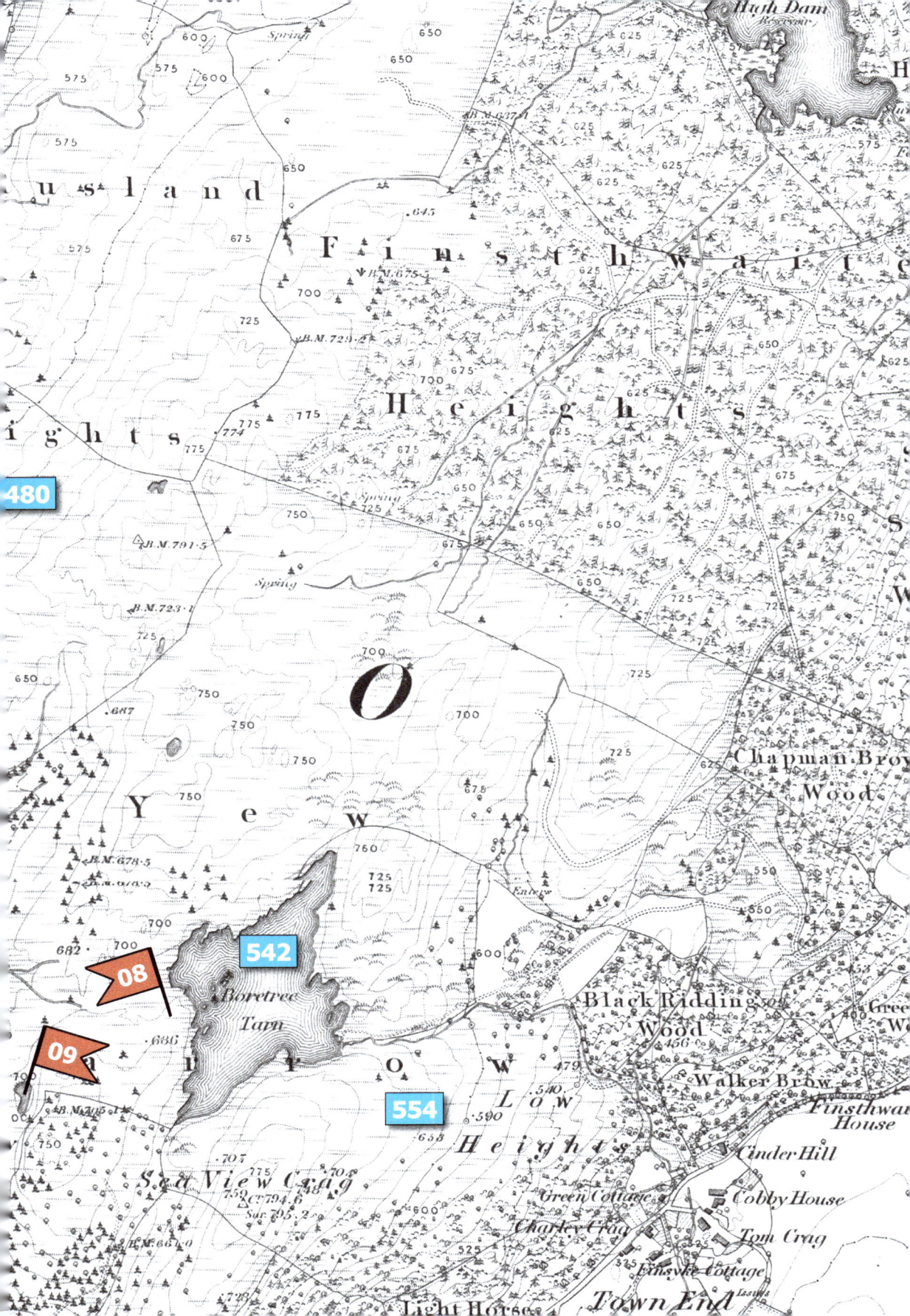

• Section 7 •

Newby Bridge and the Knott

Little Tarn Potts (797): a small corner field next to Tarn Potts 718, named in 1851 on the Finsthwaite House estate plan (FHEP), which shows how the railway line reduced it further in size. For an explanation of the name Tarn Potts see 718 and 728.

Tarn Field (728): a field which lies between Tarn Potts, 718 and Little Tarn Potts 797. It may have had a small pool in it (perhaps a post-glacial feature), although 'tarn' is usually a word reserved for a mountain pool. It is named on FHEP in 1851.

Wharf Field (727): a field by the waterside wharf near the Swan Hotel on the narrow lower reaches of Lake Windermere, named on FHEP in 1851.

Tarn Potts (718): pott is a dialect word for a hollow or a pool and has given this field (and by association also 797 and 728) its name. It is recorded in 1851 (FHEP). Tarn Potts is mentioned as early as 1582 (DDPd 26/15) and again in 1593 (DDPd 26/23) when it is the site of a dispute involving Peter Taylor of Waterside and two neighbours. In the agreed settlement Peter Taylor got the 'over end' or northern part, John Taylor the middle, and Richard Taylor the 'nether or south end'. Tarn Potts survives as the name of a modern house.

Tarn Potts Meadow (720 and 725): a meadow next to Tarn Potts 718, this field was one plot before the railway cut through. It is named in 1851 (FHEP). As it lies south of Tarn Potts 718, it may be the section allocated to Richard Taylor in 1593.

Tarn Potts Copy (part of **721**): a small wood within Tarn Potts field, part of the larger Newlands Head wood plot 721; named on FHEP, 1851.

Waterside Knott Pasture (717): an area of grazing at the southern edge of Waterside Knott (716) now completely wooded over, but named in 1851 (FHEP). OS 1850 shows an area of pasture with a few trees. It was wooded over by 1890, and remains so. The first archival reference to Waterside farm (by the river Leven) is in 1600 (DDPd 26/29) and this area of woodland pasture would have been part of that farm's holdings on the Knott hill.

Landing Knott Wood (459): a division of the wood on the Knott hill belonging to the Landing estate; it is named Landing Knott Wood on OS 1850 and 1890 but is called **Knot Breast Wood** in 1843 (WDB 135/3/4), denoting that it was in the Knott but on the breast or slope of the hill. The Knott, as the name for the whole of this hill, is a name which first appears in 1552 (DDPd 26/2).

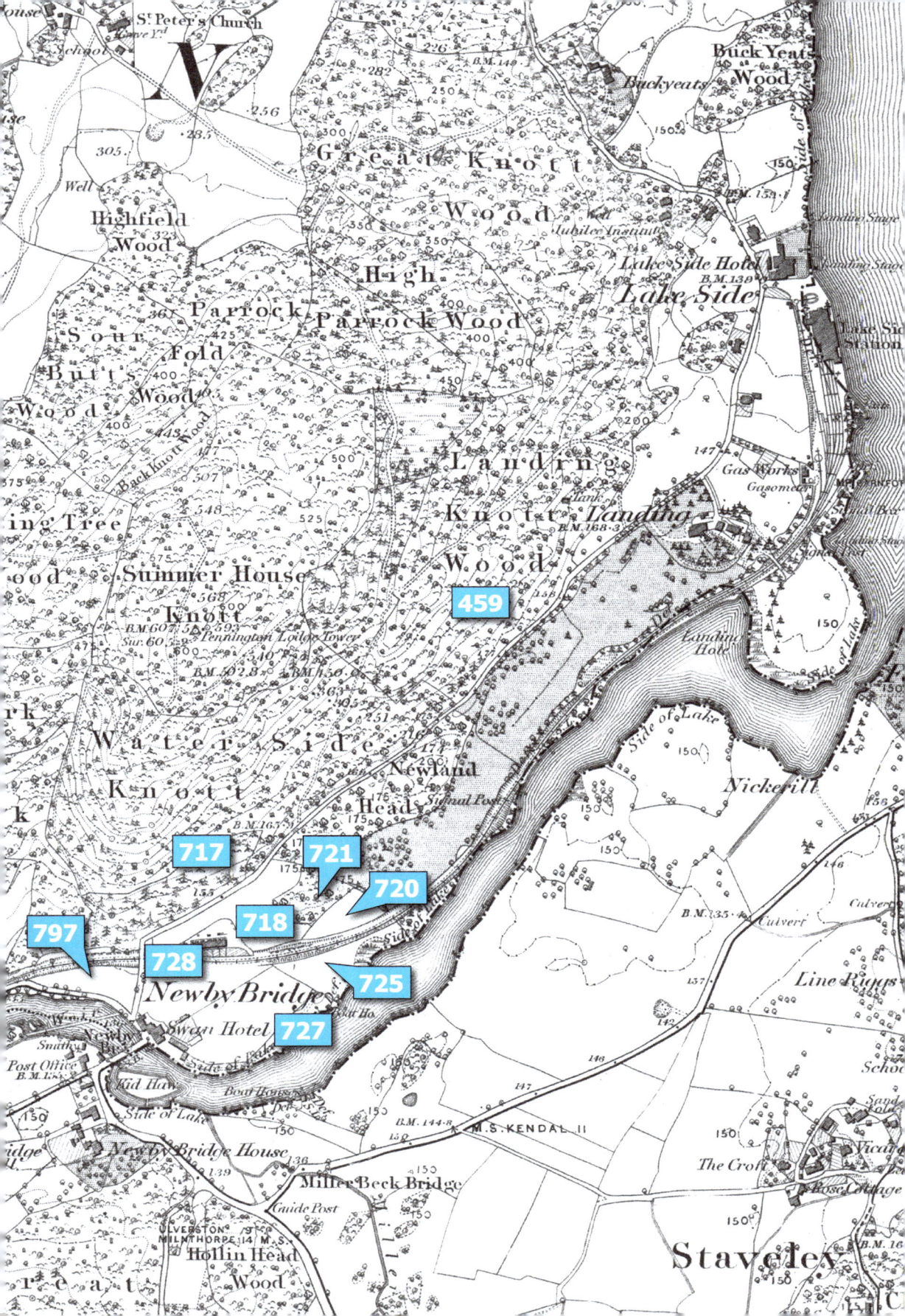

Knot Wood (715): a small enclosure of woodland in the Knott. This small wood is separately named on the 1843 map (WDB 135/3/4) but is a nameless plot on OS maps.

Knot Pasture (458): an area of grazing on the Knott hill near to Knot Wood 715. Although the plot has now been planted with trees, it is still possible to see one of the three small walled areas within it: a D-shaped enclosure plot **457** quite close to the modern footpath. The other two enclosures on the plot can be found, but are ruined. These three enclosures walled off trees from the pasture presumably to protect them from grazing livestock. The name Knot Pasture appears in 1843 (WDB 135/3/4) on a map which clearly shows the three walled features.

Summer House Knott (464): a wood which takes its name from Finsthwaite Tower, built by James King of Finsthwaite House in 1799 in commemoration of the 'matchless conduct and irresistible valour' of the Royal Navy. OS 1850 marks the tower 'Summer House or Tower' but FHEP in 1851 does not use the description Summer House (but just says 'Tower') and calls the plot on which it stands **Top 'oth Knott**. The wood is on the summit of the Knott and this is presumably the name of the wood before The tower was erected. The tower, although shorn of one storey, still stands and there are, in 2018, plans to create a viewing platform so that visitors can once again climb to the top. OS 1850 marks the tower 'Summer House or Tower'. The name Summer House Knott is given on OS 1890, but OS 1850 reserves the name for the southern end and used **Back Knott Wood** for the northern end of 464. FHEP also names the northern 17 acres of 464 Back Knott Wood but adds the name Summer House Knott in pencil suggesting the OS name was being used by the Pedders.

Back Knott Wood (547): a wood on the back or far side of the Knott, as viewed from Landing. OS 1890 only uses Back Knott Wood for this small plot, but OS 1850 includes the northern portion of plot 464. Roger Taylor's account book (DDPd 26/341) says that Back Knott Wood was coppiced in 1842. Roger Taylor lived at Finsthwaite House by 1842 and his continued use of the name 'Back Knott Wood', despite the wood lying on the Finsthwaite side of the Knott, is an interesting example of the persistence of woodland names. The name implies it was once owned and named by the Taylors of Landing.

High Parrock Wood (455 and 454): a wood near the summit of Great Knott, divided into two plots, or parrocks, which share a name. High Parrock wood is the name on both OS 1850 and 1890.

Great Knott Wood (459): the whole of this steep sided, craggy hill has been called the Knott since 1552 (DDPd 26/2) and this is the largest of the enclosures of woodland on the Knott. It is 66 acres, and spans the hill from Lakeside to the fields at Plum Green. The name has come to be attached to the whole hill, rather than this one big wood. Great Knott Wood is now in the care of the Woodland Trust.

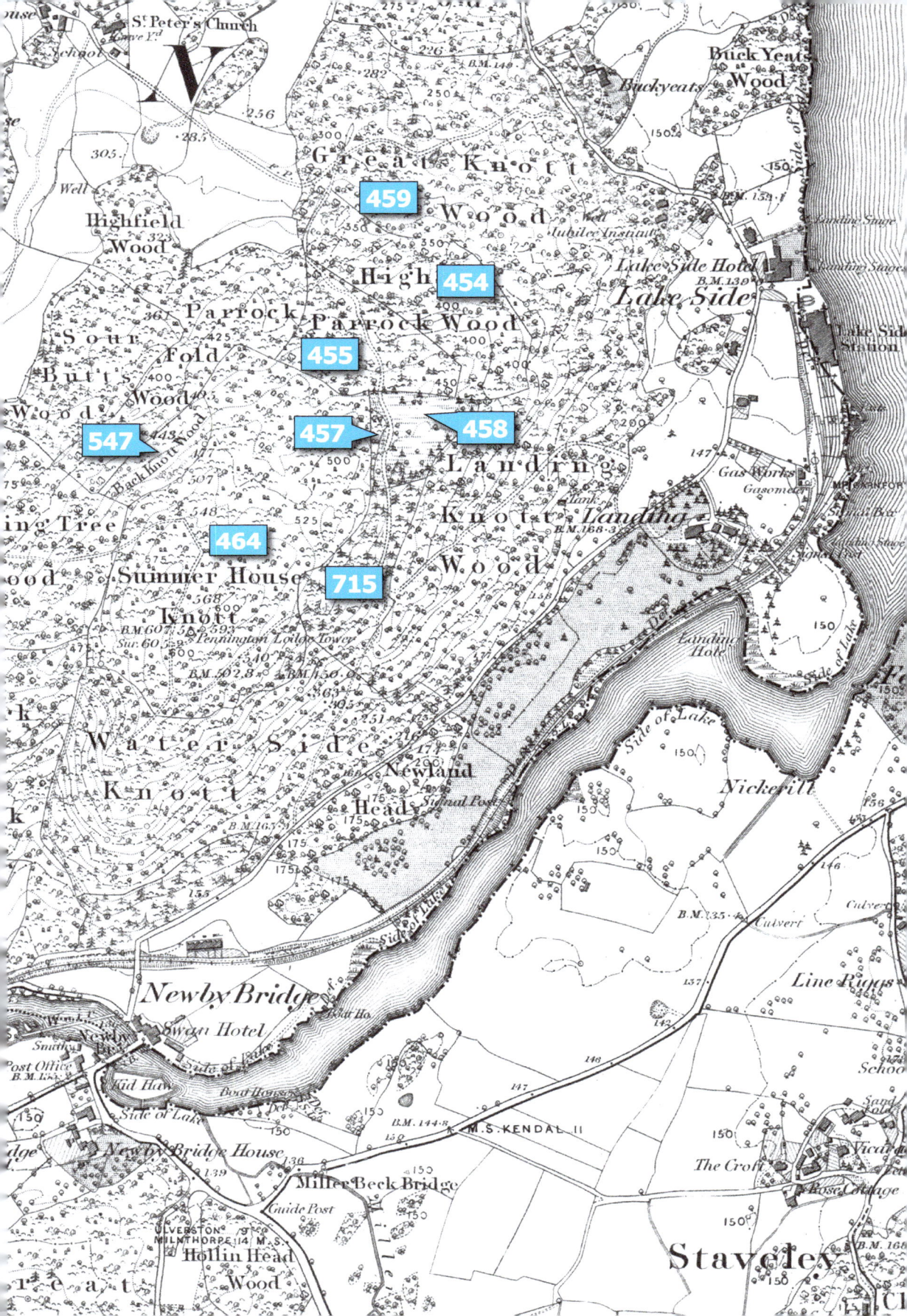

• Section 8 •

Landing and Lakeside

This section begins with land around the oldest settlement, the farm at Landing. Windermere is at its narrowest here, and as well as being a place where goods like charcoal could be landed and shipped on by road, there were also fords across the lake. Then we work north along the lane that runs up to Stott Park, naming fields and woods which partially still exist, but have also been built on during the late nineteenth century when Lakeside began to come into being. Names in this section have come from the estate papers of the Harrison family of Landing and from sales particulars for the house building plots.

Newland Head (721): a wooded crag next to the Lakeside road; 'head' or high place fits the hilly character of this plot. The name survives onto modern OS mapping and is on OS 1850 and 1890. We would expect the Newland element to refer to a piece of ground newly taken into cultivation, and although the adjacent field plot 722 is called Low Field in the 19th century, we think that the earlier, 1694, name for 722 is New Close (DDTy 2/2/1). Newland Head is mentioned in a list of holdings of Waterside farm in Clement Taylor's account book.

Low Field (722 and south-west half of 712): a field named on a map of 1843 (WDB 135/3/4) as extending over plot 722 and part of 712. It is 'low' in the sense that it is further from the house at Landing and the ground slopes towards the lake. Because Newland Head 721 is so called, we think that plot 722 is **New Close** in 1694 (DDTy 2/2/1).

Front Field (north-east half of **712**): a field at the front of the house and formal gardens at Landing. It is named Front Field in 1843 (WDB 135/3/4).

Park (712): the whole of plot 712 is named Park in 1920 (BDHJ/100/19) and is shown as parkland on OS 1850. It is now grazing land rented to Iain Kellett and known as **The Parks**. The plot includes a woodland strip, **711**, which was called **Park** in 1920 (BDHJ/100/19) and had ornamental planting.

Strip across the Line (724): a narrow strip of woodland cut off from the rest of the Landing estate by the railway, named 'Strip across the Line' in 1920 (BDHJ/100/19). Plot **713**, the strip of woodland next to the Park 712 and named **Park** in the same 1920 document, lies on the Park side of the railway line, but OS 1850 clearly shows 724 and 713 were once part of the same narrow wood running along the edge of the lake shore. **Park** is the name given to two strips of woodland bordering the edge of 712: one is 713 on the park side of the line, and the other is 711 at the side of the lane (see notes on 712).

Orchard (710): an area planted as orchard in 1843 (WDB 135/3/4). This plot does not have the symbol for orchard trees on OS 1850 when it shows as a clear plot, so it may have been grubbed up by the time of the OS survey in 1846. It was traditional to place an orchard by a farmhouse, and this one probably dates back to Landing's days as a farm. The plot is called **High Bank** on a sketch plan of 1881 (WD/AG Box 17/19), and is on a slope above the house. By 1881 the Webster mansion had no need of a traditional farm orchard on the plot.

Field behind House (463): a field behind the house at Landing named in 1843 (WDB 135/3/4). There is a 'Field beneath the house' in 1694 (DDTy 2/2/1), but much would depend on whether the site of the new house at Landing, built in 1830, was similar to the 17th century one. This field, or a one-acre portion of it, is known as **Pond Field** in 1920 (BDHJ/100/19) and the map shows a small pond by the lakeside. The same type of pond, possibly a left-over from glacial activity, gave Tarn Potts 718 its name. The name **Pond Meadow** is given in a sketch map of 1881 (WD/AG Box 17/19). The 1694 list of fields (DDTy 2/2/1) lists **Moss Closes** which may have been here, as this name implies that the closes were on marshy land.

Landing How (708): a small hill on a round promontory that sticks out into the lake by Landing. Called **Lendin How** in 1694 (DDTy 2/2/1), the usual older spelling of a name that means the hill at Landing. Landing How is the name on OS maps from 1850.

Gateside and Limekiln Close (460 and most of 453): named with this double name in 1843 (WDB 135/3/4). The 'gateside' element may refer to gates into the wooded area of the Knott, or may be derived from Old Norse *gata* for a track which ran through this field linking the woods and the old landing point on the lake. There are signs of a potash kiln, found by Vanessa Champion, in Great Knott wood near the south-west end of 460, which may have been misnamed as a lime kiln (potash kilns are used to burn bracken to make lye for cleaning wool, and 'lye' and 'lime' may have become muddled) . The field contains a small wood, plot 452, for which we found no separate name; the woods still exist, although houses have been built in part of the field.

Bull Copy (FLAG 01): a small field for keeping a bull in. In 1843 (WDB 135/3/4) this little triangle of ground is shown fenced off separately from the rest of 453 and called Bull Copy. **Bull Copy Wood (FLAG 02)** which is named on the map in 1843 (WDB 135/3/4) was a small 2 acre wood west of Bull Copy. This wood has now been built on, but stood on the site of the Jubilee Institute and houses to the south. The 1890 OS map also shows several quarries in the area which was Bull Copy Wood, a sign of the extensive house building that took place in Lakeside in the 19th century.

Great Field (461): a large field that would have once bordered the lake but was built over after the railway came. This is one of several examples in our survey area of a Great Field, and is a common name for a large field. It is named in 1843 (WDB 135/3/4) and is probably the same Great Field mentioned in 1694 (DDTy 2/2/1). In 1882 (BDHJ 310/354) it was referred to as **The Great Field** and had been divided into building plots for sale; it has now disappeared under housing.

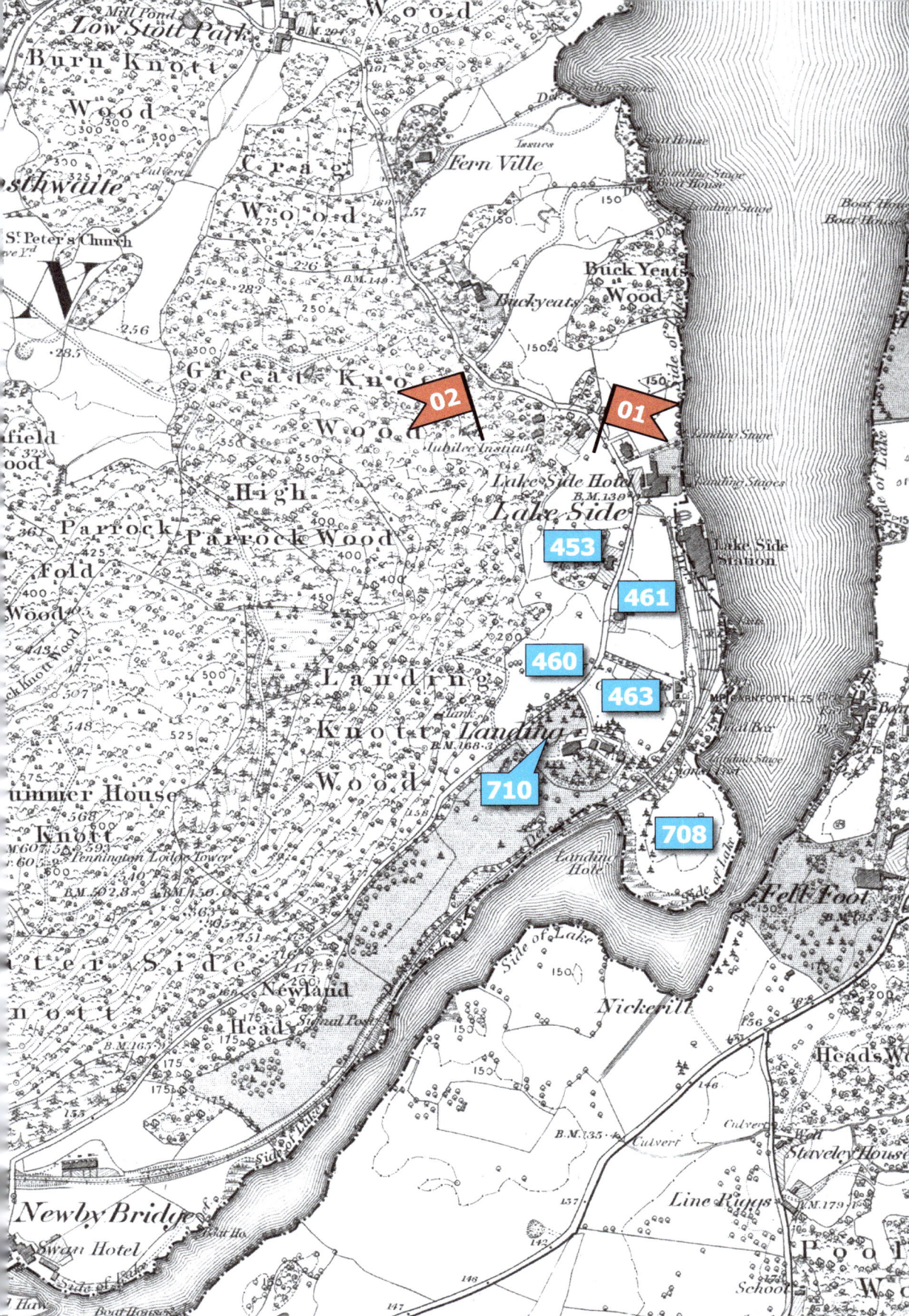

Buck Yeats (446 and 445): in 1843 (WDB 135/3/4) both these plots are called Buck Yeats. By 1882 (BDHJ 310/354) 446 is called **Buck Yeats Field** to differentiate it from Buck Yeats 445. Buck means either deer or goats, and in this area deer seems more likely. A yeat is a gate, used to control the movement of livestock into this area of grazing by the lake. The name Buck Yeats is associated with a large area of woods and grazing north of this point to nearly as far as Ridding Bay. Although our maps date to the 19th century it is a fair assumption that this name, and the management of livestock here, is much older. A **Buck Yeat Close** is mentioned in the will of Edward Taylor of Plum Green in 1626. In modern times it has become the name of a house set back from the lane in plot 441.

Buck Yeats Wood (444 and 443): two woods have the name Buck Yeats Wood, the main one being the four-acre 443. 444 is a small triangle of wood by a bend in the lane, and may be a remnant of the larger one. Plot 444 is named Buck Yeats Wood in 1843 (WDB 135/3/4). 443 is called Buck Yeats Wood on OS 1850 and 1890, but on a document offering building plots for sale in Lakeside in 1882 (BDHJ 310/354) it is called **Great Ridding Wood**.

Great Ridding (442): a large field or area of cleared land (*rydding* in Middle English) named in 1843 (WDB 135/3/4). The field shares a name in 1882 with Great Ridding Wood, plot 443 to the east.

Tarn Hole and **Sand Hole (420)**: the eastern half of plot 420 is Sand Hole and the map of 1843 (WDB 135/3/4) clearly shows a gravel or sand extraction hollow. The western half, nearer the lane, is **Tarn Hole**, named on the same map as Sand Hole. The Old Norse word *holr* means a hole or depression. This is a low lying field and may have had a permanent or seasonal pond or tarn in it. Although tarn usually means a mountain pool, this word is also used at Tarn Potts near Newby Bridge.

Magazine Wood (Flag 03): on the very eastern edge of field 420 on the lake shore is a narrow strip of wood called Magazine Wood in 1843 (WDB 135/3/4). On OS 1850 a powder magazine is marked, together with a pier jutting out into the water. This seems to have been a safe storage place for gunpowder that had been shipped here to help quarry stone for house building, or to blast holes for water tanks for the villas and new houses of Lakeside.

Tarn Hole Wood (441): a wood next to Tarn Hole field (western half of 420), named in 1843 (WDB 135/3/4). As we found so often at Finsthwaite, this is a pairing of wood and field names, although the two plots are now separated by Buck Yeats house. In 1882 a document listing building plots for sale (BDHJ 310/354) included this site.

Ridding Wood (440): an 1869 map (WDB 135/3/46) calls this Ridding Wood and shows it, together with field 421, as belonging to Chapman House. On the earlier 1843 map (WDB 135/3/4) it was not shown, as it was not part of the Landing estate. The wood takes its name from the field 421, Low Ridding, in another example of a paired wood and field.

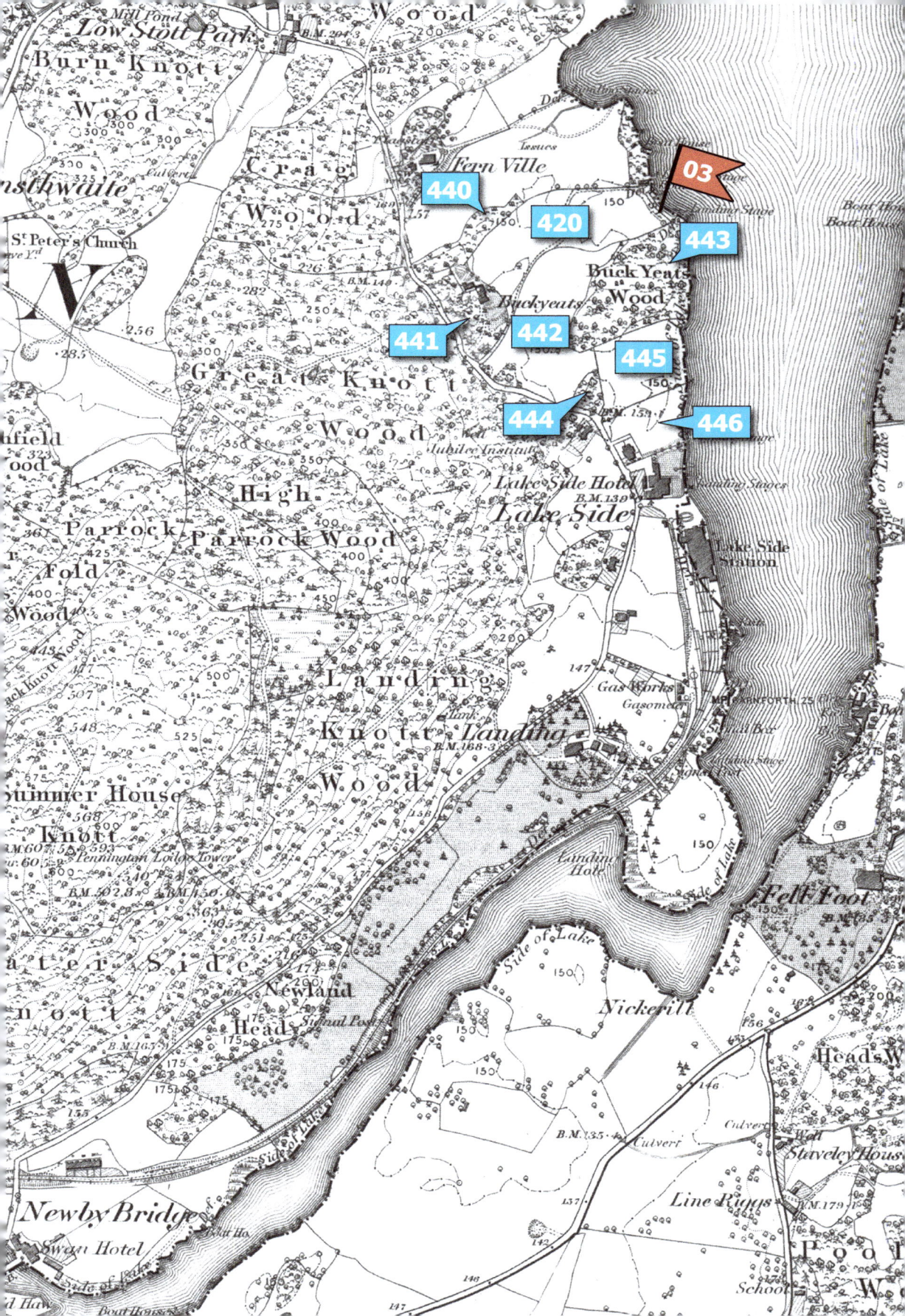

Low Ridding and **Far Low Ridding (421):** Low Ridding is the western half of the field, near the lane, and Far Low Ridding is further down the slope towards the lake (farthest from the lane), as named in 1869 (WDB 135/3/46). A ridding is a clearing, (from Middle English *rydding*) and this one is described as low because it is low lying. The two plots were farmed at one time by Chapman House, but were dropped from the estate in 1877 with a corresponding rent reduction (Janet Martin's notes of the Landing estate). The plots are now part of the gardens and lakeshore frontage of the villa Ridding Bay (built as Fern Ville, the first new development in Lakeside).

Far Low Ridding Wood (419): a wood name which is paired with the field 421, this strip of wood is on the lake shore at the eastern edge of Far Low Ridding, and named in 1869 (WDB 135/3/46).

Low Lands (428): a small field at the foot of the steeply rising ground of Crag Wood, named in 1843 (135/3/4). Angus Winchester suggests that 'lands' is an indication of strips of arable land in a common field, but a glance at this very small plot would confirm that it is not the case here. Its proximity to Low Ridding may be more likely to be a factor in naming it, or perhaps its position at the foot of Crag Wood. In the 1920 sale of the Harrison estate (BDHJ/100/19) it is called **The Croft**. It is now the site of a house and garden.

Knot Busk (425): a small wood or area of bushes (Old Norse *buskr*), named in 1843 (WDB 135/3/4). Rather than taking its name from the Great Knott this wood seems to be named in association with Twinmoss/Tweenmost Knott, plot 415. In 1937 (BDHJ/450/7), it is called **Wood in Turn Moss Field**, plot 426.

Twinmoss Field (426): named Twinmoss Field in 1843 (WDB 135/3/4). The name appears in the key although the number has been accidentally left off the map, although as the wood next to it, 415, is Twinmoss Knott there seems no mistaking which field is meant. In 1937 it is **Turn Moss Field** (BDHJ/450/7).

Twinmoss Knott (415): is the wooded hill, or knott, that shares a name with Twinmoss Field 426, in 1843 (WDB 135/3/4). It is a later version of a 17th century name **Tweenmost Knott** which is documented in 1692 (WD/AG Box 64/4) when it is described as 'two closes', and may therefore include plot 426. In 1616 (WD/AG Box 64/4) '**the Knott or Lamb Parrick**' seems to refer to the same closes of mixed 'arable, meadow and wood'. 'Tween' is a dialect word for between, and this hill runs from the farm at Low Stott Park to the lake shore, and perhaps is named to suggest that stretch between two points. Later the 't' at the end of 'most' has been dropped to become 'moss'. There are also mosses or marshy ground nearby. In 1843 (WDB 135/3/4) the eastern edge of Twinmoss Knott wood is named **Cowper Ridding Wood** where it wraps around Cowper Ridding field 418. OS 1850 and 1890 call the whole of plot 415 **Riddings Wood**.

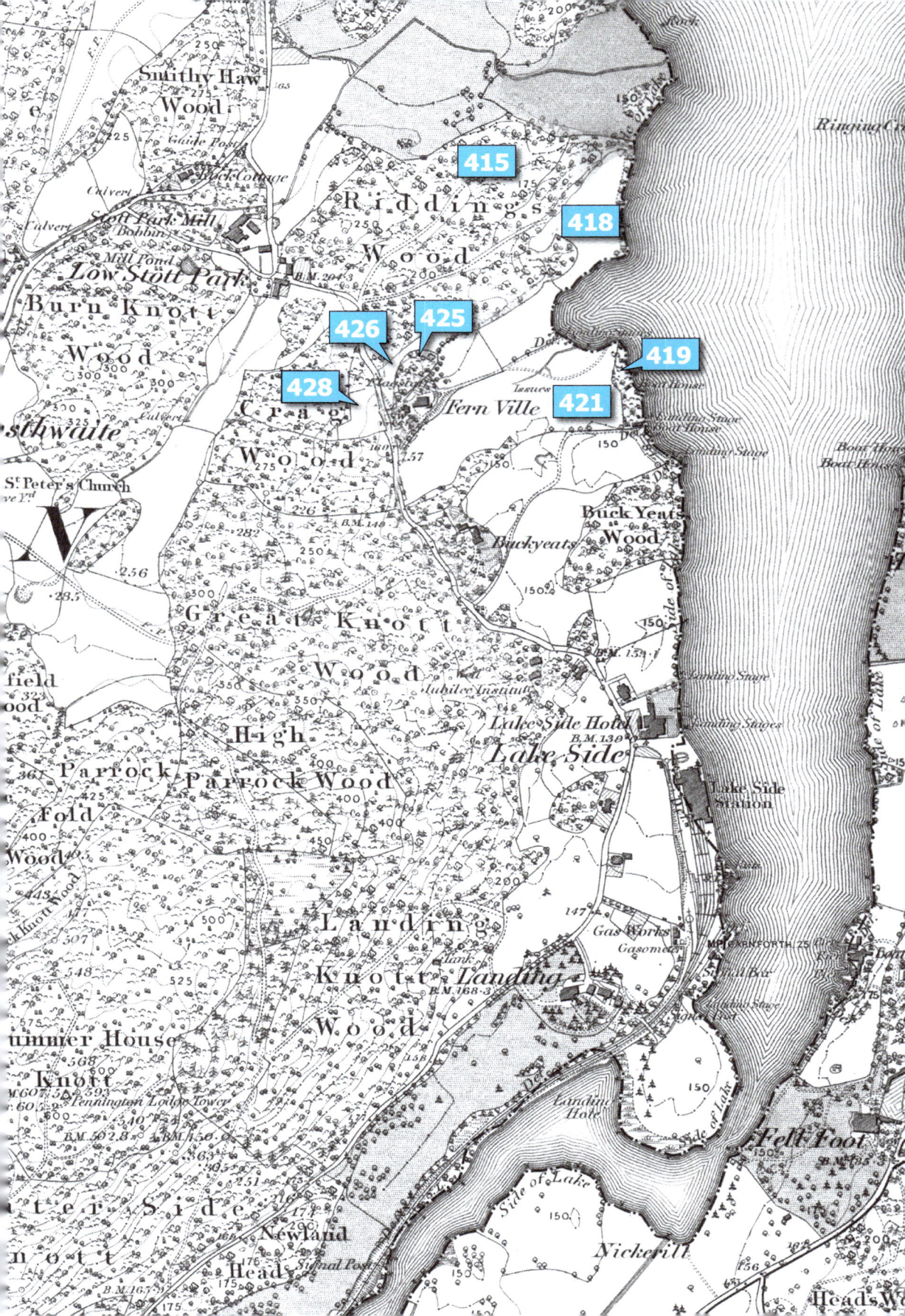

Cowper Ridding (418): the field next to Cowper Ridding Wood 415, in the now familiar concept of a pairing of wood and field. Named like Cowper Ridding Wood in 1843 (WDB 135/3/4) but the name goes back to 1692 (WD/AG 64/4). It makes an appearance in Clement Taylor's account book among a list of fields and woods 'sold at Plum Green' in 1734 when it is linked with the nearby Water Meadow 416 (see Stott Park map section). A ridding is a clearing (from Middle English *rydding*). The Cowper/Cooper element is an occupational name and men in both the Braithwaite and Harrison families, who farmed at Stott Park and held this land, were coopers.

Round Meadow (plots 422 and 423): named Round Meadow in 1843 (WDB 135/3/4). The two plots create a field that is far from round in shape (being a long oblong with a narrow point where it reaches the lane). It is possibly named in jest. Another possibility is that the name derives from the Old Norse *raun*, the rowan or mountain ash tree which may have grown here (it is prolific locally). 'Round' as a surname has not arisen in our researches. Again, this is a field with a longer history than the 19th century map. It is mentioned in 1692 (WD/AG Box 64/4) in two documents, both of which mention Round Meadow as providing an access route for hay carts bringing loads out of Cowper Ridding 418 'when Tweenmost Knott is ploughed'. At that time, Tweenmost Knott, a woodland name in the 19th century, then covered an area of arable as well as wood.

Crag Wood (429 and 430): a wood on a rocky hill at the northern end of the Great Knott. Both plots are named Crag Wood on OS 1850 and 1890. In 1843 only the northern plot, 430, was part of the Landing estate, and is named **Crag Head** (WDB 135/3/4). The name is now associated with a 19th century villa.

Cinder Nab (Flag 04): *Windermere Reflections* archaeology project has confirmed this as a bloomsmithy site.

• Section 9 •

Low Stott Park

At Low Stott Park we have identified names partly from a map drawn up for a proposed sale of the Landing estate in 1843, which named fields through Lakeside and also at the Harrisons' old farm at Low Stott Park. We have been able to work back from 1843 using other documents, for example the Braithwaite papers in the Hart Jackson collection, and earlier Harrison family papers, to get earlier dates for some plots.

Parrock (431): simply a small field adjacent to the farmhouse at Low Stott Park; it is named in 1843 (WDB 135/3/4). This is now the site of two houses. This plot may also be **Cowper Close**, in the list of Laurence Harrison's holdings in 1769 (WD/AG Box 64/4), listed as 'arable and coppice'. This second name is speculative, and based on the sequence of the fields named in the list.

Little Parrock and **Bobbin Mill (409)**: a small field, lying opposite the farm at Low Stott Park (in contrast with Parrock 431. Little Parrock is named in 1843 (WDB 135/3/4) and is now the bobbin mill's front car park. In a list of the holdings of Laurence Harrison in 1769 (WD/AG Box 64/4) there is reference to three orchards, one of which was next to Underside (plot 406) which makes it seem likely that the mill was built on what had previously been orchard sites.

Orchard (433): an orchard next to the farm at Low Stott Park. It is named Orchard in 1843 (WDB 135/3/4) and shows as orchard planting on OS 1850. Laurence Harrison had three orchards at the farm in 1769 (WD/AG Box 64/4) and the other two were, we think, opposite on the site later occupied by the bobbin mill.

Field above House (434): the field behind the Low Stott Park farmhouse, named in 1843 (WDB 135/3/4).

Barbary/Barbara Parrock (408): a small parrock or field named after a woman, probably Barbara, or Barbary Chapman who lived at Stott Park in the early 1700s. The field is Barbary Parrock in 1843 (WDB 135/3/4) and Barbara Parrock in 1868 (WD/AG Box 19).

Underside (406): the name Underside is the name of this plot in 1843 (WDB 135/3/4) but the name also appears much earlier in 1606, and again in 1769 (WD/AG 64/4). It would seem to refer to a wood on the lower slopes below Smithy Haw wood 403. The west corner of Underside is known to some locally (information from Denis Jenkinson) as **Gardeners' Corner (Flag 01)**, from its use as allotment plots.

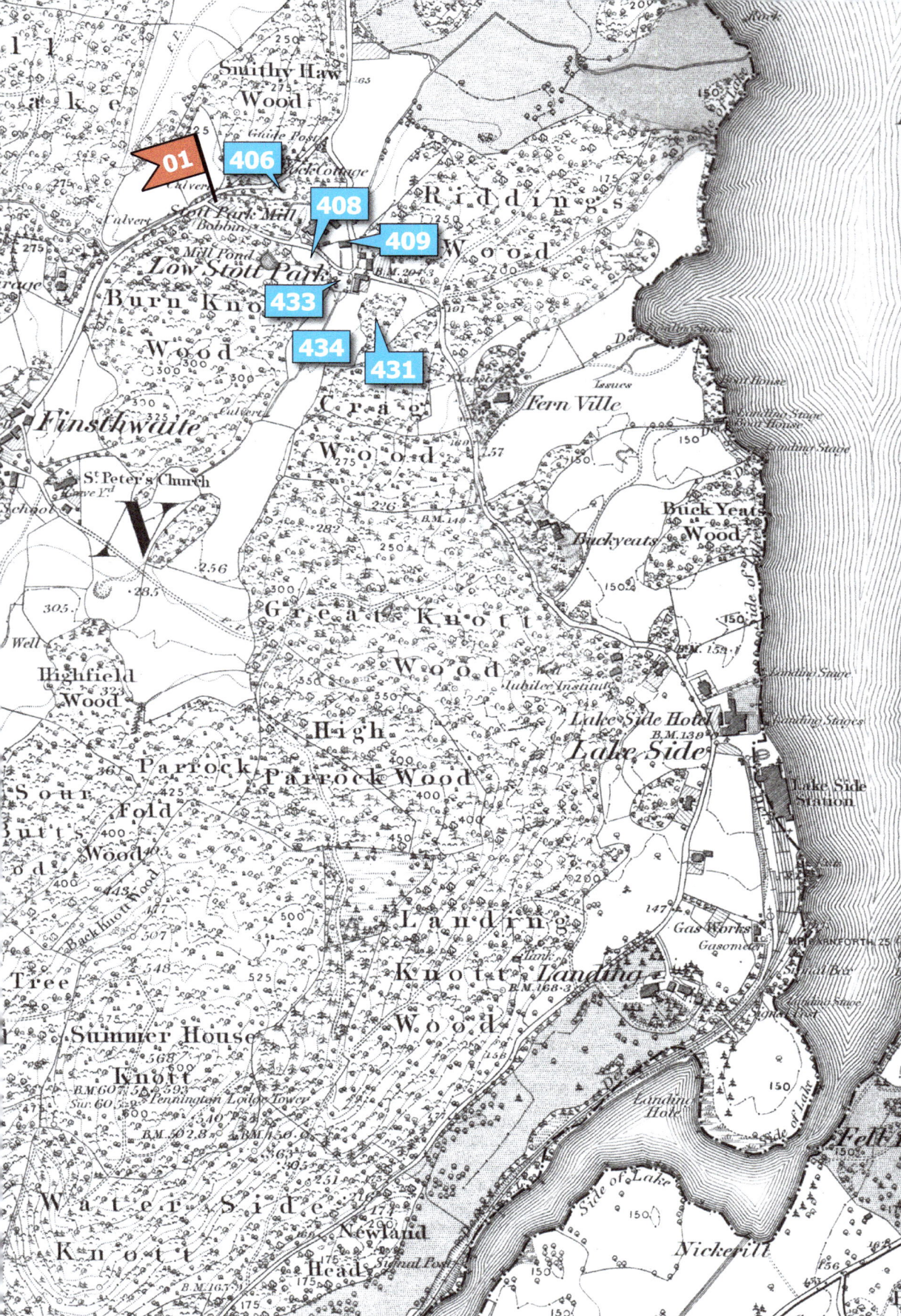

Smithy Haw Wood (403): a small hill (*haugr* in Old Norse) which may have been an iron-working site or which may have have belonged to a blacksmith. The 1643 will of William Taylor of Plum Green lists among his goods an anvil, bellows, tongs and hammers. At the lane side there is an odd indent in the wall, often used as a parking space by walkers, which Janet Martin suggested could be the site of the smithy – conveniently situated close to the beck for water and the road for passing trade. The name appears as Smithy Haw Wood on OS 1850 but as **Smithy Hall Brow Wood** in 1843 (WDB 135/3/4). The name first appears in 1686 as **Smiddy How** (WD/AG 64/4). **The Smithy How** is on the list of Laurence Harrison's holdings (WD/AG Box 64/4) when it is described as having 'oak timber of 2 years' growth'. The name Smithy Haw Wood appears on modern maps.

Smithy Hall Brow (404): a small area separated from the larger Smithy Hall Wood 403 and named on the 1843 map of the Landing estate (WDB 135/3/4), although the reason for the plot being separated is not clear. This is now the site of a house, built in 1882.

Beck Ridding (411): a field with a stream (Old Norse *beckr*) running through it, named in 1843 (WDB 135/3/4) and mentioned in 1769 in the list of the holdings of Laurence Harrison (WD/AG 64/4) when it is described as 'arable and meadow', but with 'two timber trees' standing in the meadow. The beck running through the field, and separating it from plot 410, is the same one which comes down from High Dam and through the bobbin mill site. In the 1769 list there is mention of a 'cottage, outhouse and garden adjoining Beckridding', all trace of which has disappeared.

Bonny Lands (410): a field which may in the past have been named 'bonny' (beautiful) because plentiful water from the beck may have made it a productive strip of ground. It is named in 1843 (WDB 135/3/4).

Holme Lands and **Holme Ridding** (southern half of **414**): these two plots are named in 1843, but even so, the names only cover the southern section of 414. The northern part was not owned by the Harrisons. Holme Lands (south-west portion of 414) and Holme Ridding (south-east portion) are named in 1843 (WDB 135/3/4). Holme derives from Old Norse *holmr* meaning land surrounded by water, which probably refers to the beck which circles the plot to the west and north. In the list of holdings of Laurence Harrison in 1769 (WD/AG Box 64/4) Holme Ridding is described as 'arable and woody' meaning that, as so often in local fields, there were trees in amongst the arable land, and 14 oak timber trees and 10 ash are singled out as being of value. In the Braithwaite papers in 1701 and 1636 (BDHJ/398/3/1/22 and 26) we have also found reference to **Longdale and Harrison Land**, a single close which lay to the south of Thomie Field. We identify the northern section of 414 as Thomie Field and Longdale and Harrison Land as earlier names for what later became Holme Ridding and Holme Lands.

The northern half of 414 is explained in Section 10.

• Section 10 •

High Stott Park

Names in this section come from archives of the Braithwaites, the Taylors and the Lewthwaites (who inherited land from Roger Taylor). Information from an 1890 map of the Lewthwaite estate has been included in its entirety to complete the picture of their holdings at High Stott Park, even though some fields and woods lay to the north of our OS sheet 11. In Roger Taylor's account book (DDPd 26/341), in use between 1794 and 1852, a map is sketched in the opening pages together with detailed notes of the Stott Park woodlands and their felling and coppicing dates. In 2019, just after our first edition was published, a map showing 'particulars of the Stock Park Estate in Finsthwaite', was released from a previously closed archive from Kendal Fisher solicitors. This plan (BDKF/plans/20) gave us 20 new names from the Braithwaite estate as it was in 1850.

Although we have named plots beginning on the west side of the lane, working north, and then turning back south through the plots east of the Hawkshead lane, this seemingly logical approach in fact moves in and out through lands which belonged variously to the Taylors, the Braithwaites and, in the seventeenth century, to Thomas Chapman (who gave his name to Chapman House farm in Finsthwaite). The two farms at High Stott Park had holdings that interlaced with their neighbours' lands. The resolution of the resulting disputes, in 1673 and again in 1751, generated archives which included field and woodland names.

Orchard (412): an orchard near High Stott Park House. This shows both in 1794 (DDPd 26/341) and 1890 (BDHJ/12/1/2). The earlier map also notes a 'Great Orchard' on a site north of the High Stott Park farm, but by 1890 this had disappeared, seemingly because of the building of a large new barn on the site.

Intack (398): a field enclosed or 'taken in' to cultivation from the waste or woodland surrounding it. Intack is named in 1794 (DDPd 26/341) and 1890 (BDHJ/12/1/2) but intakes were generally made in the 16th and 17th centuries, so this name may be much older.

Far Intack (399): a field enclosed or taken into cultivation, like its neighbour 398, but further away from the farm at Stott Park. The plot is named in both 1794 (DDPd 26/341) and 1890 (BDHJ/12/1/2).

Far Intack Wood (400): the wood in Far Intack field 399. It is named Far Intack Wood in 1890 (BDHJ 12/1/2) but is just 'wood' on the map in Roger Taylor's account book, although he includes a note that it was last cut in 1789 (DDPd 26/341). It is called **Fair Intake** in 1920 (BDHJ/12/1/17).

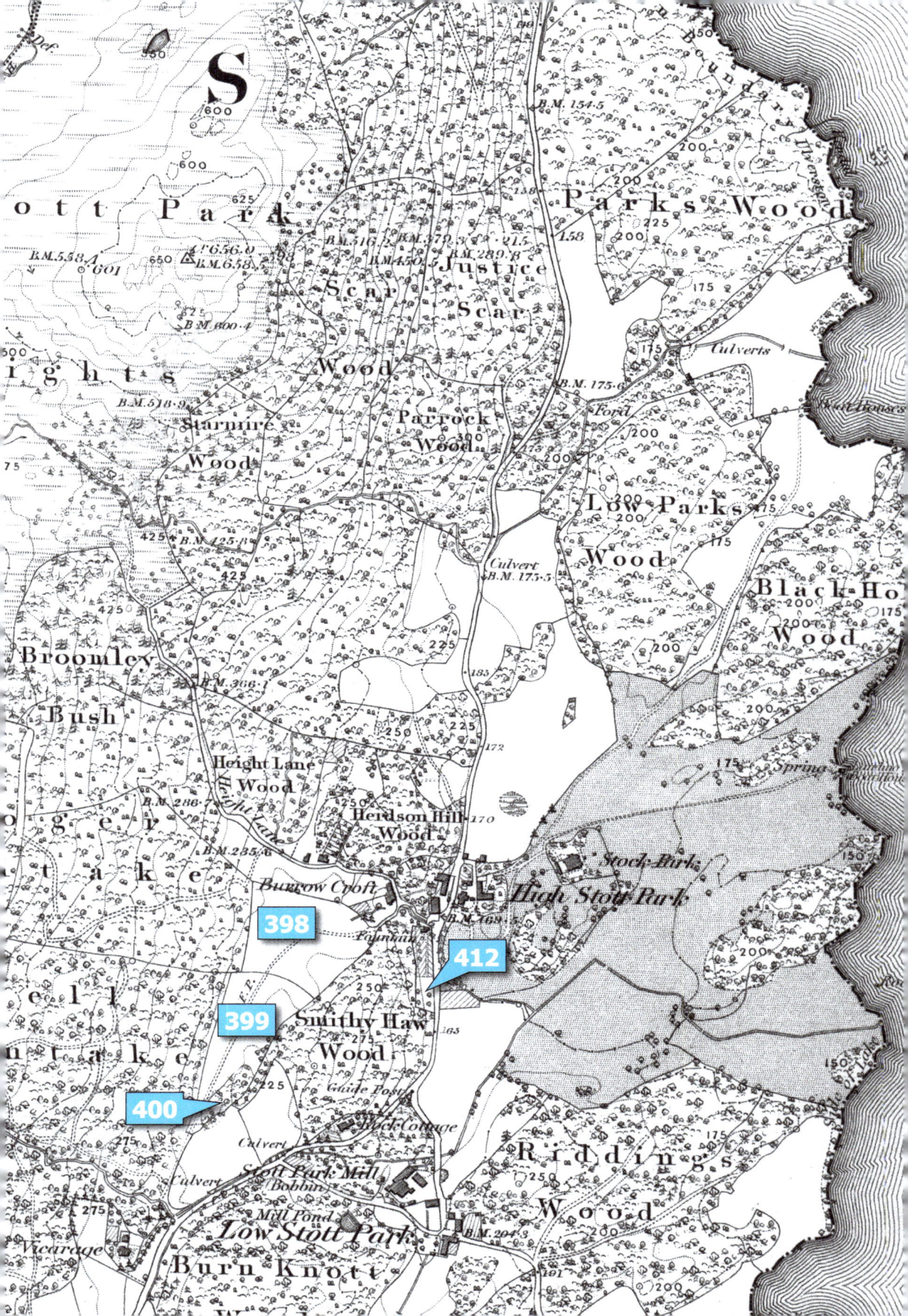

Burrow Orchard (393): this plot is called Burrow Orchard on the 1794 map (DDPd 26/341) but is now part of Burrow Croft house and garden. In 1890 (BDHJ 12/1/2) it is a plot marked as 'house, garden and orchard wood' so some memory of the old orchard survived. For notes on the name 'Burrow' see Burrow Newlands, plot 397.

Burrow Newlands (397): land newly taken into cultivation, although the date when this was done is uncertain; it is named in 1794 (DDPd 26/341) and 1890 (BDHJ 12/1/2). The 'Burrow' element in the name may refer to land purchased by Robert Taylor of High Stott Park farm, and mentioned in his will of 1670 when he identifies some land as 'lately bought of John Borrow'. We have other examples of the vendor's name being used in references to land. In 1769 the land was owned by the Harrisons of Low Stott Park and was mentioned then as being 'let to William Braithwaite, for 7 years beginning in February 1769, for £6 5s per year' (WD/AG Box 64/4). In 1850 (BDKF/plans/20) the plot is called Burrows Parrick on the Braithwaite's estate plan. By 1890 it was back in the ownership of the Taylors of High Stott Park.

Roger Intake (467 and 185): a wood called Roger Intake on 1850 and 1890 OS maps, named after one of the Roger Taylors who owned Stott Park farm in the late 18th and early 19th centuries. In 1794 (DDPd 26/341) the two plots are named separately, plot 467 being Intack Wood (last cut in 1781) and plot 185 being **Hog Parrick** (also last coppiced in 1781). In 1890 467 is Intack Wood and 185 is **Hogg Wood Parrick**. Hoggs are young sheep kept in a field or wood like this plot, away from the main flock until they are ready to bear lambs themselves.

Broomley Bush (174): a wood where broom bushes grow; they are still visible, although now less dense. The plot is named on OS 1850 and 1890. The 1794 map (DDPd 26/341) shows this as Braithwaite (Stock Park farm) land. The Braithwaite plan (BDKF/plans/20) in 1850 calls it Broomy Bush Coppice, and calls the northern end High Broomy Bush Coppice, 'high' in this instance seemingly referring to the more northerly location. (**Flag 01**)

Height Lane (396): a lane leading from High Stott Park House onto the fell grazing (the Height) and up to the mosses south of Star Mire Wood for peat cutting. The lane is named on OS maps in 1850 and 1890 but is likely to be an older, traditional route. The lane is lined by walls on each side and the upper part has been designated a public footpath. The ruins of a bark peeler's hut can be seen by the side of the lane near the top, bearing witness to a long history of both agriculture and industry in this area.

Height Lane Wood (104): a wood on the north edge of Height Lane, named on OS 1890 as Height Lane Wood but just as **Height Lane** on OS 1850. The Braithwaite plan (BDKF/plans/20) calls it **Miles Close Coppice** (in an interesting echo of the Taylor's use of the same name, Miles Close, for plots 94 and 103 nearby). For the Braithwaites there is a link with field plot 394, which they called Miles Close.

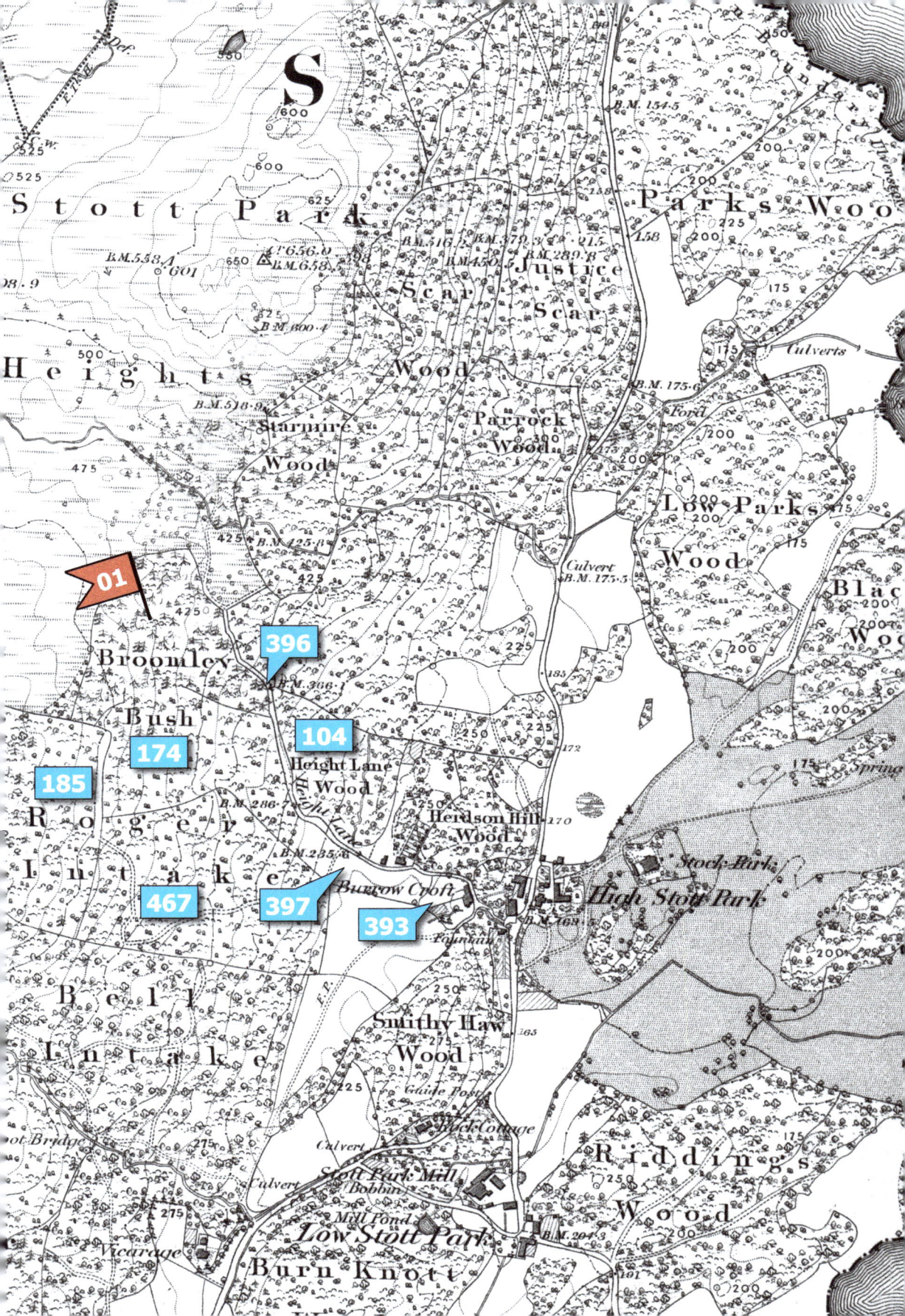

Miles Close (394 and 395): The Braithwaite plan (BDKF/plans/20) names plot 394 Miles Close and records it as arable land; the plan shows the wood in the field (plot 395) but does not name it separately. Although we are not certain of the Miles who is associated with these plots it is also a name used by the Taylors for another nearby field and wood pairing, 94 and 103. A line of pens marked on the OS 1890 we believe are pheasant rearing pens.. The mixed field and woodland would be ideal for the job according to Dave Wilson, the gamekeeper at Finsthwaite House. In the past, hens would be used to rear pheasant chicks. The hen would be tethered in an enclosure which allowed space for the young pheasants to roam and feed, and eventually to move out to the tree cover. The positioning of pens in 394 looking onto the wood in 395 follows this arrangement.

Herdson Hill Wood (392): named on OS 1850 and 1890, a wood on a hill probably named after a previous local owner called Herdson (the surname is common in the area). The wood is not part of the holdings of High Stott Park on either the Taylor or Lewthwaite family maps but is part of the Braithwaites' land. BDKF/plans/20 records the name as Herdson Hill Coppice, and says that it has 7 years' growth in 1850.

Spring Orchard (391): Spring is a name given to a wood that, having been coppiced or cut, has sprung back with new growth, but in this case seems to be a name for newly-planted orchard trees. In 1890 when this is called Spring Orchard (BDHJ 12/1/2) it may have been created to replace the 'Great Orchard' which shows on Roger Taylor's map. He had grubbed up the Great Orchard in order to build a very large new barn, also illustrated in his account book (DDPd 26/341). On the 1890 map **Spring Orchard Wood** is shown as a small wood, presumably with non-orchard trees, at the western edge of the plot 391. Both OS 1850 and 1890 show 391 as a field.

Myles Close Head Wood (103): a wood on a head (hill) next to Myles Close field plot 94. The name is given in 1794 (DDPd 26/341) although then spelt 'Miles', and noting that it was last cut (coppiced) in 1786/7. It is also named in 1890 (BDHJ 12/1/2). Wood in Myles Close is sold in 1713 (DDPd 26/191) by Clement Taylor for 'making charcoal and colliers' lodgings'. It is unclear whether plot 103 or 104 is indicated. The wood is not named on OS 1850.

Myles Close (94): a field named in 1890 (BDHJ 12/1/2), sharing a name with the wood further up the hill, plot 103. It is also mentioned in 1794 (DDPd 26/341) with a note that it was last cut in 1786-9 so it must have then been a wooded plot. Myles is a common Christian name in the Taylor and Harrison families and also with the Sandys family of Graythwaite, so it is not clear which Myles/Miles might be referred to. The Braithwaites used the name Miles Close for plot 394.

Close Lands (93): a field next to Myles Close 94, named in 1794 (DDPd 26/341) and 1890 (BDHJ 12/1/2). In 1890 (BDHJ 12/1/2) the field includes a wood, Close Lands Wood, on the border with Parrick Wood 92.

Parrock Wood (92): OS 1850 names this Parrock Wood using a standardised spelling of what in 1794 (DDPd 26/341) is **Parrick Wood**, and Roger Taylor notes that it was last cut in 1778. The 1890 map (BDHJ 12/1/2) also uses the name Parrick Wood.

Star Mire (107): Star Mire Wood is named in 1794 (DDPd 26/341), when Roger Taylor notes that it was last cut in 1782. The name appears in 1751 (BDHJ 398/3/2/9) in the arbitration of a dispute between two Stott Park landowners about access to the fell and its mosses. The wood is also named on both OS maps, and on the Lewthwaite map in 1890 (BDHJ 12/1/2). It is a wood at the edge of Stott Park Heights, plot 175. The origin of the name is uncertain; but likely refers to a plant, like the Starry Saxifrage which grows in profusion on upland mosses, or Star Moss.

Far Star Mire (91): Far Star Mire Wood lies adjacent to Star Mire 107, and is further away from High Stott Park farm. It is named Far Star Mire in 1890 (BDHJ 12/1/2) but is not separately identified by Roger Taylor. The wood is not named on OS maps.

Star Mire (FLAG 02 within plot 175): this may be the peat moss or mire called Star Mire, which gave its name to the wood plot 107. The 'mire' element in the name of the wood suggests it is associated with a peat moss, and flora like the Starry Saxifrage and Star Moss. The area at the head of Height Lane is suitably wet.

Scar Wood (90): a wood on a scar (very steeply sloping hillside) named on both OS 1850 and 1890. Roger Taylor's account book (DDPd 26/341) shows it as Braithwaite land. In 1850 the Braithwaite plan (BDKF/plans/20) records the name as **Scar Coppice**, and records 5 years' growth.

Justice Scar (89): a wood on a steeply sloping hillside, which in 1794 (DDPd 26/341), is identified as belonging to the Braithwaites. George Braithwaite, who died in 1814, has a marble memorial plaque in Finsthwaite church which records that he was 'a most intelligent magistrate', a biographical detail which may explain the 'justice' element in the name. Interestingly, the Braithwaites themselves record the name (BDKF/plans/20) simply as **Parrock Wood Coppice**. The name Justice Scar is used by OS in 1850 and 1890.

Stott Park Heights (175): the fell pasture and mosses on high ground above Stott Park which, like Finsthwaite Heights to the west, is 'common or waste' used by local farmers as summer grazing and for peat cutting. In 1673 (DDPd 26/133) Thomas Chapman of Plum Green asserted his rights to a share of the resources on the Heights, despite it having been 'lately enclosed' by the farmers of Stott Park. In 1751 Robert Taylor and William Braithwaite disputed about their shares of mosses and fell pasture and rights of way to them. The documented agreement which followed (BDHJ 398/3/2/9) outlined a lengthy process of marking out and valuing various parts of the Heights. Stott Park Heights is named on OS 1850 and 1890. The Braithwaite plan (BDKF/plans/20) calls the plot simply '**Intake**'. **Deer Lake Moss (FLAG 03)** is named in 1751 (BDHJ 398/3/2/9), on Stott Park Heights, and is presumably a pond where deer would drink.

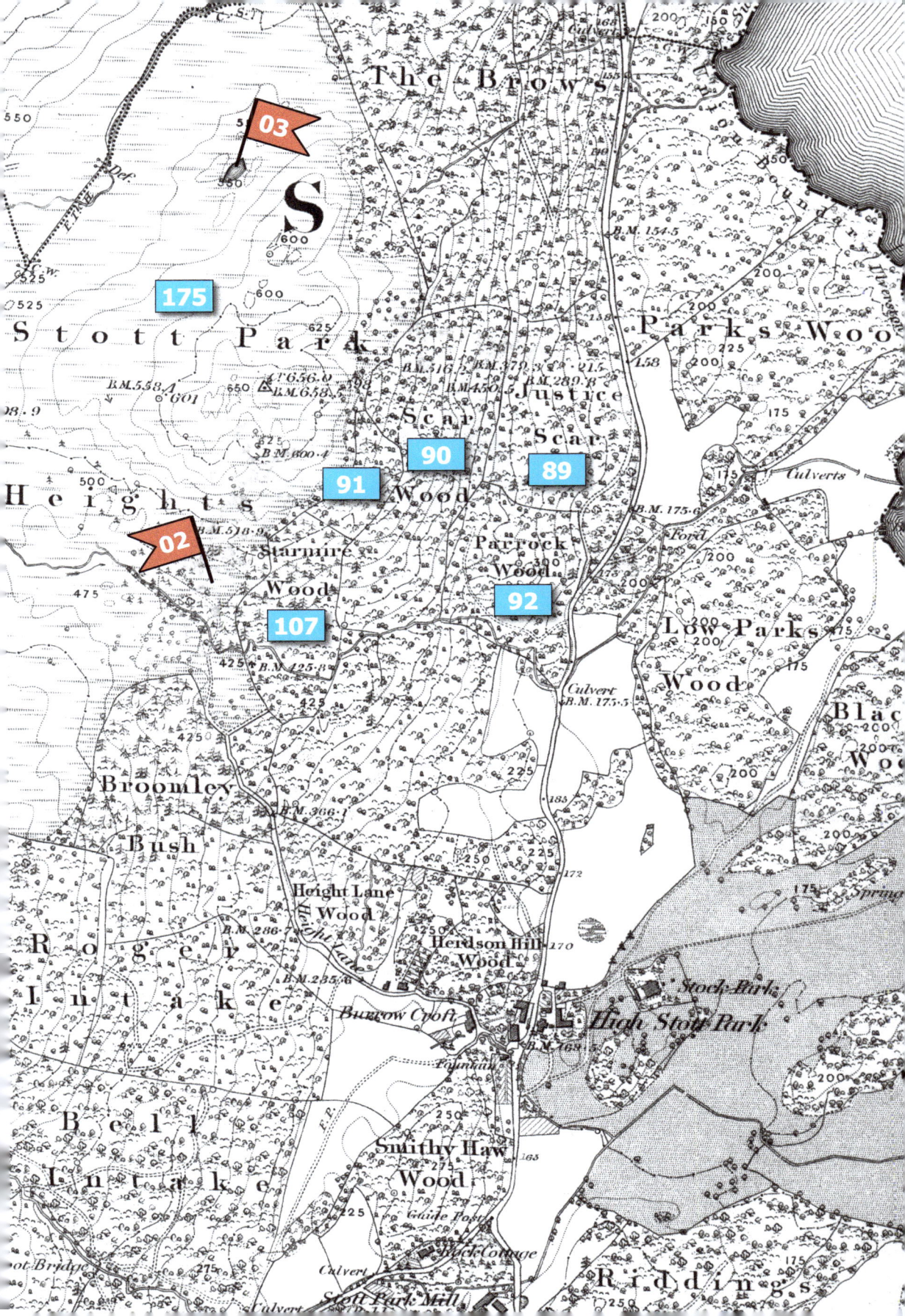

The Brows (77 and 79): a large wood on a brow (hill slope). It is named on OS 1850 and 1890, as well as in 1794 (DDPd 26/341) when it is just called **Brows**. In 1890 (BDHJ 12/1/2) **Brow Wood** matches the acreage of plot 79 and **Brow** that of plot 77. In 1751 the dispute resolution (BDHJ/398/3/2/9) included a requirement that Robert Taylor must allow a way for William Braithwaite to access Stott Park Heights at Brows Yeat (a track through The Brows, derived from Old Norse *gata*). On the Braithwaite plan in 1850 (BDKF/plans/20) it is marked 'wood and road', suggesting that 100 years later it was still the Braithwaites' route to the fell.

Parks Wood (80 and 81): a wood at the north end of the Low Parks 105. The name Parks Wood is used on OS 1850 and 1890. Roger Taylor's 1794 map (DDPd 26/341) calls the plot **Parks Head** and the entry in the account book that year says that **Park Head or High Wood** was last cut in 1792/3. 'Head' and 'High' indicate the wood is on a hill. In 1890 (BDHJ 12/1/2) the Lewthwaites owned a 19-acre wood, which we think is the southern plot 81. The acreages listed match plot 81 and an entry in Roger Taylor's account book in 1823 mentions that Parks Wood has been divided with Miss Braithwaite (of Stock Park) and that Roger Taylor 'retains the southern end'. On the Braithwaite plan in 1850 (BDKF/plans/20) there is water damage and the map is badly torn, but the key includes a 17 acre wood called **High Parks Coppice**, which if the division of Parks Wood follows the pattern we think, will be plot 80.

The Drain Field (87): OS 1850 shows the whole area of Parks Wood (80 and 81) as wooded; by OS 1890 there is a field plot, 87, carved out next to the lane. Roger Taylor's account book mentions '**New Close**' on the east side of the road, which may be this field. His 1794 map shows Parks Head as a single enclosure; the New Close was made in 1834. If it is plot 87 it cannot have looked distinctively enough like a field to the 1840s OS surveyors. On the Braithwaite plan in 1850 (BDKF/plans/20) plot 87 is called The Drain Field, which is explained by the culvert and ford at its southern edge on the OS 1890 map we have used, although when the field passed into Braithwaite hands is unclear.

Rudding (84 and 85): two field plots (rudding is a variation of ridding or reading, a cleared area). Rudding appears on the 1794 map in Roger Taylor's account book (DDPd 26/341) with a note that it was last coppiced in 1783, so it was then a wood. A plot called Rudding is mentioned in the 1721 marriage settlement of Henry Taylor of Plum Green (DDTy 2/2/2) and 'Redden' appears in 1694 (DDTy 2/2/1), again in a marriage settlement. If this is plots 84 and 85 then it is a distant holding for the Plum Green farm. In 1890 (BDHJ 12/1/2) Rudding shows as a field with woods on its north, east (lakeshore) and west sides. The woods surrounding these fields are all called **Rudding Wood**.

Low Parks Wood (98): Low Parks Wood is named on both OS 1850 and 1890. It appears on the Braithwaite plan (BDKF/plans/20) in 1850 as **Near Low Parks Coppice**. It is described as coppice of 15 years' full growth. It takes its name from its position south of Parks Wood/High Parks Coppice 80 and 81, as the Braithwaites in particular seem to use High and Low for north and south. The wood is also adjacent to plot 105, Low Parks.

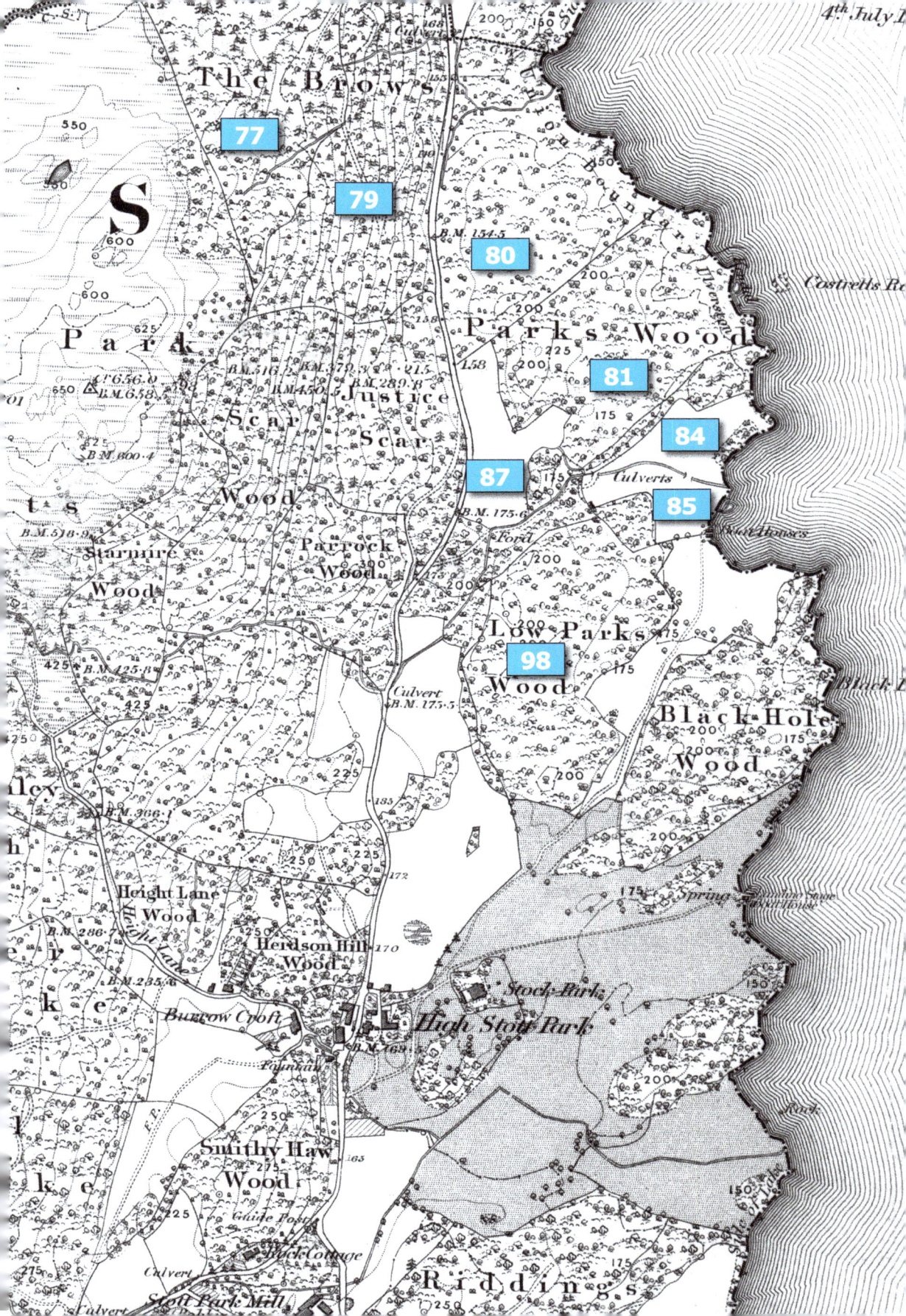

Black Hole Wood (100 and 101): a wood which is named Black Hole Wood on OS 1850 and 1890. The name may be derived from hol, Old Norse and Old English for a hollow or hole with deep water where a boat could moor. Black Hole is marked on the lake shore at the end of a track through the wood. The Braithwaite map of 1850 (BDKF/plans/20) calls this wood **Black Hole Coppice** and notes that it has 15 years' full growth.

Boat House Field (99): a field named on the Braithwaite map in 1850 (BDKF/plans/20). The field runs down to the lake shore where there is a boat house.

High Field (96): a field belonging to High Stott Park farm which is further north (higher) than Great Field 102, which lay opposite the farm. The field is named High Field on both Roger Taylor's 1794 map (DDPd 26/341) and the 1890 Lewthwaite map (BDHJ 12/1/2). **High Field Wood (95 and 97)**: two woodland plots surround High Field, 95 to south and 97 to north, and are both called High Field Wood in 1794 (DDPd 26/341) and 1890 (BDHJ 12/1/2). Roger Taylor's account book notes that High Field Wood was coppiced in 1784. OS 1890 uses the name High Field Wood; OS 1850 shows the woodland plots but does not name either.

Great Field (102): a large field. It is named in the 1794 map (DDPd 26/341) and again in 1890 (BDHJ 12/1/2).

Low Parks (105): the plot is shown as parkland on OS 1850, suggesting it was landscaped, but the name is considerably older. Descriptions of the positions of Tomie Field and Water Meadow (part of 414, and 416) in the late 16th and 17th centuries, refer to the Braithwaites' land of 'the Low Parks' (BDHJ 398/3/1). We concluded that the area could always have been extensive, ranch-style grazing and meadows, perhaps shared by the different farms at Stott Park (and by the Ashburners and Blumers before the Taylors and Braithwaites). The early Braithwaite papers refer often to the Low Parks, including land bought by the family in the mid-17th century (BDHJ 398/3/1), although the purchase may be an addition to their existing share of this large plot. In 1689 (BDHJ/398/3/1/14) 'Little Park and Low Park', both woodland plots, were also sold to George Braithwaite by Robert Taylor, but whether these correlate exactly to the wooded plots 106 and 386 is by no means clear. The Low Park plot may refer to Robert Taylor's traditional share of the larger Low Parks. On the 1850 Stock Park plan 105, largely cleared of trees, has been divided into two fields. **New Lands** is by the lake shore (**Flag 04**) and **Great Field** is nearer the lane (**Flag 05**). **Summer House Field (Flag 06)**: some 8 acres of pasture, is named on the Braithwaites' plan (BDKF/plans/20) in 1850. The site is now partially occupied by the Stock Park Mansion which was built circa 1865 and so does not feature on the 1850 plan. The summer house which gives the name to this field is marked on OS 1850 within the curve of the woodland plot 388.

Meadow Hill Wood (386): a wood named in 1733 (PR2850/6/2 no 9 at Lancashire Record Office) in the list of holdings of Henry Taylor who was declared bankrupt in this year. The documents list his land assets, and 23 creditors. Meadow Hill Wood is described as lying to the north of 'Water or Blomer Meadow' plot 416.

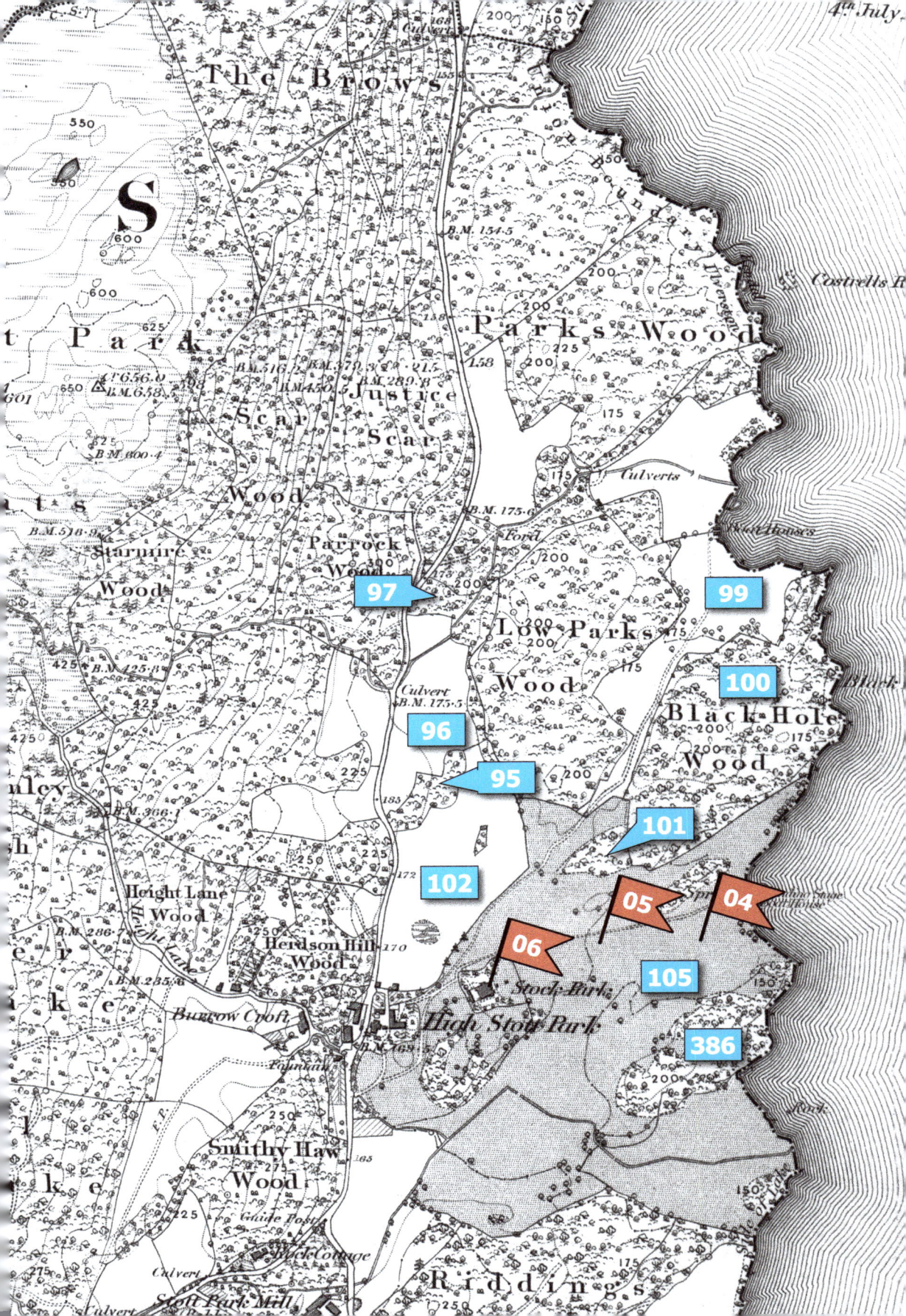

Water Meadow or Blumer Meadow (416 and 417): a meadow by the lake shore with a beck running through it. Either its position by the lake, or the beck, may explain the name Water Meadow. On the Braithwaite plan in 1850 (BDKF/plans/20) the field is called simply Water Meadow. The version Blumer Meadow has two explanations. Archaeology during the *Windermere Reflections* project has identified this as an iron-working (bloomsmithy) site but it seems possible that the name refers back to the Blumer/Bloomer family, who were living at Stott Park in the late 1530s and may well have sold the plot to the Braithwaites. Water Meadow appears in the Braithwaite archive in 1579 (BDHJ 398/3/1/12) and in 1604 (BDHJ 398/3/1/8). In 1701 (BDHJ/398/3/1/14) the plot is described as 'arable, woods and waste'. Plot 417 now shows as a small wood on the lake shore but as with the treed plots in 105 we cannot be sure that woods have survived in the same position. 417 may be a remnant of the 17th and 18th century woodland.

Pasture Meadow (northern part of 414): plot 414 is divided in two on a roughly east/west axis. The southern part of 414 is named in Section 9 (Low Stott Park). The northern part, which was bought by the Braithwaites, is called Pasture Meadow on the plan of 1850 (BDKF/plans/20). Not long after their purchase of the field in the mid-17th century, the Braithwaites called it **Thomie Field**, after the vendor Thomas Chapman. The earliest reference to Thomie Field is 1647 (BDHJ 398/3/1/24), but a detailed description of the position of Thomie field, meaning that we could know that it was this plot, occurs in 1682 (BDHJ 398/3/1/27).

Arboretum (388): an ornamental wood was commissioned by Col Dixon when he owned Stock Park, and planted by his brother. Bob Hull, who owns a flat in the Stock Park Mansion and has written its history, told us that planting included the first monkey puzzle trees, handkerchief trees and other exotics. A summer house and fountain are shown on the site on OS 1850, although these features have now disappeared. As the wood is always mapped in this horseshoe shape, including on the 1850 estate plan (BDKF/plans/20) which predates the mansion, it was presumably simply replanted for the Arboretum.

• Section 11 •

Linsty Green and Hill Top

Sources for this section include the Finsthwaite House estate plan of 1851 (FHEP), OS maps, and an early-nineteenth century map in the Hart Jackson collection which dates to sometime before 1821. It shows 'Mr King' as the owner of land on the borders of the map, and this is James King of Finsthwaite House who died in 1821. This map covers a large swathe of land outside our survey area (and so it was used by other Mapped Histories teams), but included the farm at Hill Top. Later archives from the Hart Jackson collection at Barrow Record Office confirm that the names of Hill Top fields were still the same in the early twentieth century.

Black Beck Mire (815): a wood through which Black Beck flows; this particular part of its route is low-lying and liable to flooding. Black Beck Mire is named in 1851 (FHEP) and gives its name to a pasture on the other side of the lane, plot 818. **Black Beck Myers** is first named in 1660 (DDPd 26/118).

Turner Wood (814): named on an early 19th century map (BDHJ/449/2/1/25) and on OS 1850 and 1890. FHEP has the name added to the plot in pencil and marks it as the property of G F Dickson Esq. Turner is presumably a local surname.

Fell Parrock (820): a small field on the side of Huddleston Hill. It is named in 1891 (BDHJ/398/4/31 and DDPd 26/426).

Top of Ealinghearth (822): a field at the top of Ealinghearth hill, named in 1851 (FHEP). In 1698 (DDPd 26/169) it is called the **New Parrock** (the site description matches this field). The 1698 document mentions the importance of the tenant maintaining ditches and drainage, and the west corner of this field is noticeably liable to flooding.

Huddleston Hill (821): a wood named on OS 1850 and 1890. The Huddlestons were a Millom family; Thomas Huddleston was a tenant of Town End farm in Finsthwaite until 1779. It is named in 1851 on FHEP. Roger Taylor's account book (DDPd 26/341) records that the wood was coppiced in 1834.

Back Lane (858): a lane which links Ealinghearth hill and the 'new', 1829, road to Backbarrow. Back Lane is the name on OS 1850 and 1890. Locals in Finsthwaite call it **Love Lane**. We have been too discreet to ask why.

Little Wood (859): a tiny wood set in a curve of Back Lane/Love Lane 858. The name is given on an early 19th century map (BDHJ/449/2/1/25).

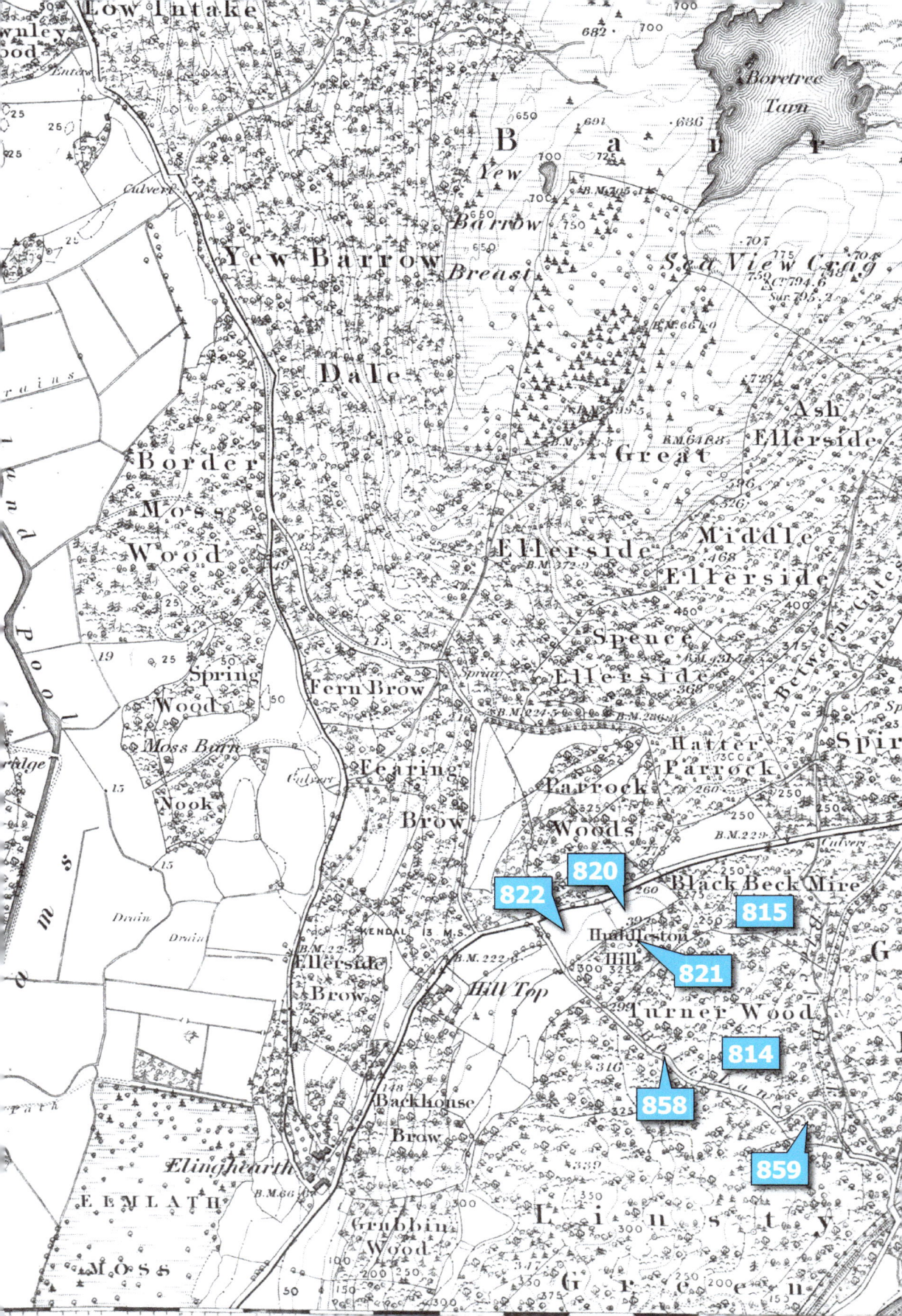

Cuckoo Bridge (Flag 01): this railway bridge is known to locals as Cuckoo Bridge, apparently because children used to stand under it and call 'cuckoo' to make an echo – something which the acoustics of railway bridges makes particularly satisfying. A report in the Ulverston Advertiser in November 1899 mentions a 'violent collision' on the Furness Railway line at **Finsthwaite Lane Bridge**, which gives us the official name.

Linsty Green (865): a large wood named on OS 1850 and 1890. It is also on FHEP in 1851 and earlier, as 'the Linstey Green' in the Pedder archive in 1683 (DDPd 26/149). Linstey, or Linstey-Wunsty, is a dialect version of Linsey-Woolsey, a kind of cloth made of a mix of linen and wool, or sometimes from wool gathered from scraps of fleece picked off up from the ground. This wood may be named in association with Linsty weavers living locally. The name survives for a row of cottages on the outskirts of Backbarrow. In 1683 (DDTy 1/3/12) the 'cropping of six holly trees on Linsty Green' is sold.

Higher Bloom Ridding (863): a field (ridding is a plot cleared of wood, from Middle English *rydding*) which was probably an iron working site, or bloomsmithy. Named in 1851 (FHEP) alongside its neighbour to the south, Lower Bloom Ridding, which lay just off the bottom edge of our map sheet 14. High and Low in this case refer to (roughly) north and south. Bloomer Ridding is mentioned in Clement Taylor's account book, as a charcoal burning site. The name appears in 1683, as **Bloomer Ridding** (in DDPd 26/149). The modern name for the field is **the Linsty Green Field** (Chaplin family) because it is opposite Linsty Green wood 865, and near the modern Linsty Green houses.

Far Acre (Flag 02): a small strip of field opposite the gate of Hill Top farmhouse, named on an early 19th century map (BDHJ 449/2/1/25). As this is a small plot, well short of an acre, and near to rather than far from the farm gate, the name is humorous.

Meadow above House (827): a field next to Hill Top farmhouse, named on an early 19th century map (BDJH 449/2/1/25).

Sunny Bank (828): a field on the slope above the house at Hill Top which presumably gets good sunlight. The field is named on an early 19th century map (BDHJ 449/2/1/25).

Hoggarth Field (856): a field for young sheep (hogg is a dialect word), named in the early 19th century (BDHJ 449/2/1/25). Hoggs or hoggets are kept separate from the main flock, until they are ready to bear lambs themselves.

Middle Field (854): it is not immediately obvious that this field is the middle one of a linked series, but 866 nearby is Far Field. The name appears on an early 19th century map (BDHJ 449/2/1/25).

Grubbing (855): a field which has been cleared of trees and their roots, and also of stones. The field is another entry on the early 19th century map (BDHJ 449/2/1/25).

Moss Field (853): a field in a dip or hollow which becomes marshy. Moss Field appears on the early 19th century map (BDHJ 449/2/1/25).

Far Field (866): the field furthest away from the farm at Hill Top (thereby also perhaps justifying the name of Middle Field, 854). It is named in the early nineteenth century (BDHJ 449/2/1/25).

Newlands (869): a field newly brought into cultivation or newly enclosed. This is named in 1928 (BDHJ/8/2/17), although when the field was made is not known.

Backhouse Brow (850): a wood on a hillside, probably named because of an association with the local Backhouse family. The name is on both OS 1850 and 1890.

Grubbin Wood (851 and 852): a wood with a name which implies that the plots have been grubbed up, and then replanted. The name appears on both OS 1850 and 1890.

Plot 847 – see **Great Ealinghearth** (846 and 847) in map section 14.

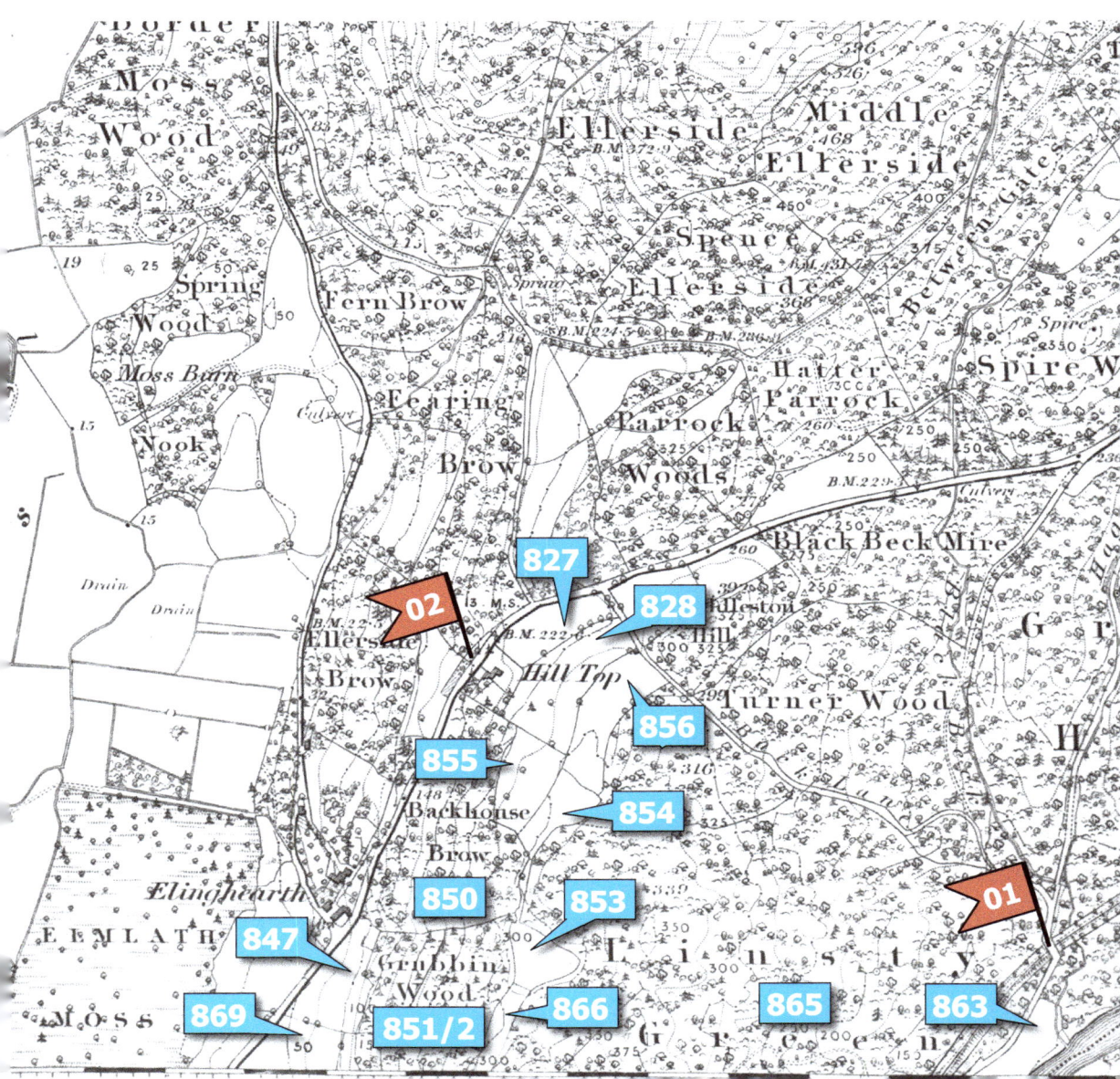

• Section 12 •

The Ellersides and Yewbarrow

The main sources for this map are OS 1850 and 1890, documents in the Pedder archive including the enclosure map of 1771, and the 1851 Finsthwaite House estate plan (FHEP).

Spence Ellerside (766): a hillside woodland where alder trees grow, sold in 1715 by Thomas Spence (DDPd 26/197). It appears as Spence Ellerside in 1851 (FHEP) and in the account book of Roger Taylor (DDPd 26/341) where he mentions the woods being worked in 1840. Roger Taylor had inherited the Finsthwaite House estate, in addition to his own land at High Stott Park, in 1821. He was the last of the Taylors to own the estate, and in turn left it to the Pedders in 1849.

Middle Ellerside and Ash Ellerside (768): the southern end of plot 768 is Middle Ellerside (it sits between Spence Ellerside and Ash Ellerside) and the northern end of 768 is Ash Ellerside. Ash Ellerside seems to mean a wood where alder trees and ash trees grow. The plots have their individual names in 1851 (FHEP) but are marked as not being then owned by the Pedders; a pencil note has been added to say they were purchased in 1936. Earlier references to this wood are simply as **Ellerside** and it appears in the Pedder archive in 1604 (DDPd 26/31).

Between Gates (769): a wood between tracks (Old Norse *gata*) which are to the north west and south east of this plot. One of these tracks is a public footpath through the wood. The plot is named in 1851 (FHEP), which also has a pencil note on the neighbouring plot 765 (Hatter Parrock) to say that this too is called Between Gates at that point. OS 1850 calls this wood **Lag Parrock**, and its shape is perhaps reminiscent of the stave of a barrel, for which 'lag' is a dialect term.

Great Ellerside (767): a large plot of woodland and fell ground, very steeply sloping, where alder trees grew. It is named on OS 1850 and 1890, and 'Great Ellerside' survives onto modern mapping. The name appears in 1604 in the Pedder archive (DDPd 26/31) as does Yewbarrow Scar which is the neighbouring plot 555.

Little Ellerside (Flag 01): at the north end of High Crag, 750, is a plot called Little Ellerside on the enclosure map of 1771 (DDPd 26/336).

High Crag (750): this upland plot, which lay outside the proposed enclosure wall in 1771 (DDPd 26/336) is called High Crag. In 1851 it is marked on FHEP as belonging to another landowner, but identified as a **Larch Plantation**. In 1895 (BDHJ 398/4/10) it is owned by Mr Backhouse.

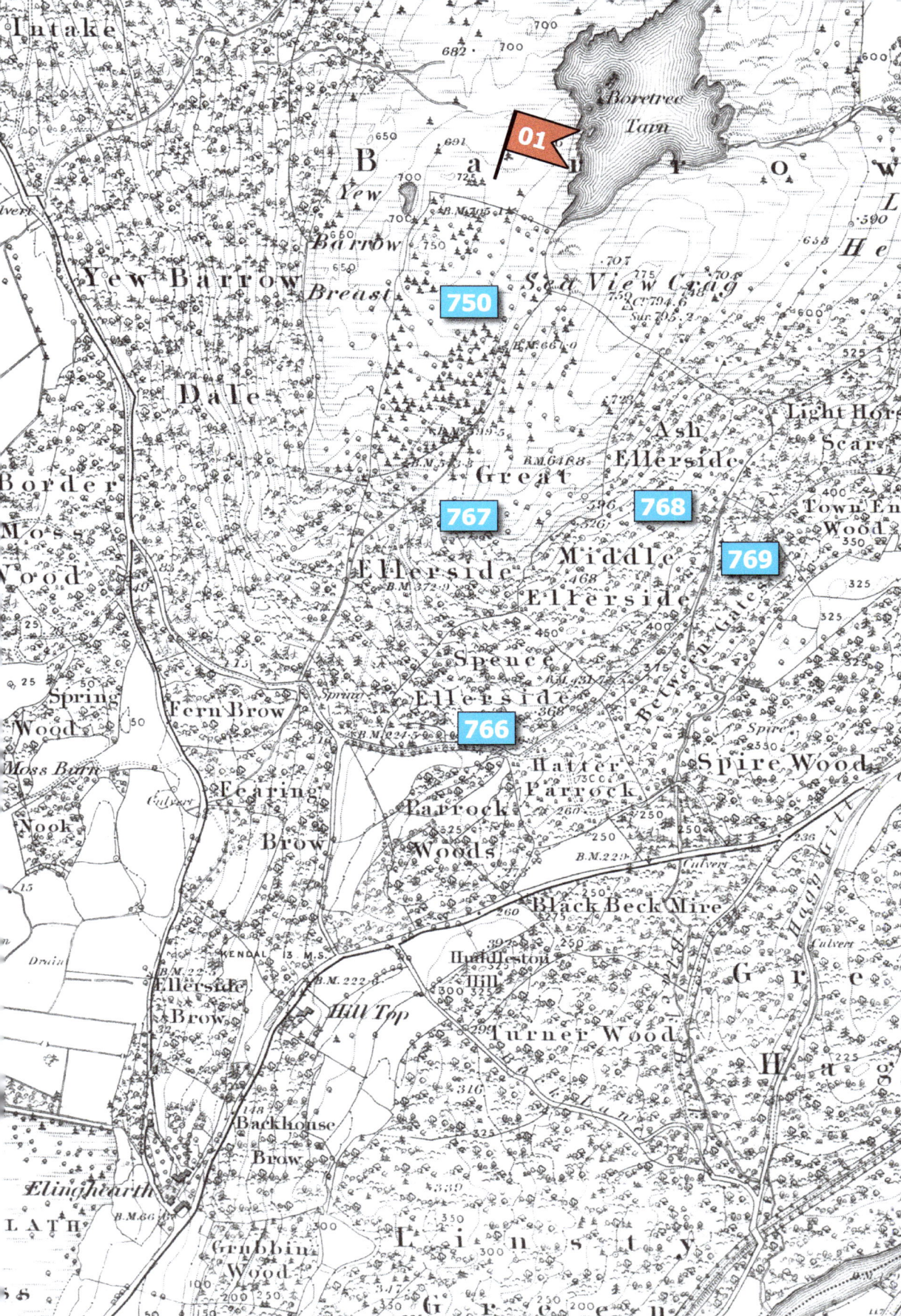

Yew Barrow Breast (Flag 02): in this narrow enclosure, made where the walls of the enclosure come together, is a plot identified on OS maps as Yew Barrow Breast and on the enclosure map in 1771 (DDPd 26/336) as **Top of Yewbarrow**. Yewbarrow might mean the hill where sheep (ewes) graze, but it may be named for the very prolific yew trees which grow all over the hill here. At the head of Yew Barrow Breast is a small tarn, which we have identified as being **Hurley Hall Tarn** in c1740 (DDPd 26/332) a name which suggests that a, then derelict, shepherd's hut stood nearby (a hurley house is a dialect term for an abandoned or ruined house). The tarn has no modern name **(Flag 03)**.

Yew Barrow Dale (555): OS 1850 and 1890 name this plot Yew Barrow Dale. Yewbarrow means either the hill where sheep (ewes) graze, or perhaps the hill where yew trees grow. It is heavily wooded, and on the enclosure map in 1771 (DDPd 26/336) was divided between the various signatories to the enclosure award to give each a plot of woodland as well as their shares of the fell grazing. The divisions between each plot were not marked with walls but with posts, and it is these multiple shares, or dales, which seems to give plot 555 the name, although the shares have become known by just 'dale' by the time of the OS maps. The name **Yewbarrow Scar**, meaning a steep slope or cliff on Yewbarrow (and it is very sharply sloping ground) appears in 1604 in the Pedder archive (DDPd 26/31), at a time well before the shares or dales were part of the 18th century enclosure agreement. In 1891 (BDHJ 398/4/31, and DDPd 26/426) a map which accompanied the notice of the auction of lands belonging to the Rev. Thomas Taylor, shows his 'Yewbarrow Dale' as a thin slice running up through 555, with an extension into plot 759 on the other side of the Fearing Brow lane. The enclosure map of 1771 (DDPd 26/336) also shows a parrock, which seems to have been unwooded and was called **Yewbarrow Parrick**. This may be a plot referred to in 1635 (LRO PR 2850/6/2 no 8c) as having been sold by John Walker of Sinderhill and in 1733 was called **Ewbarrow Pasture (Flag 04)** (BPR 17/M2/1-2).

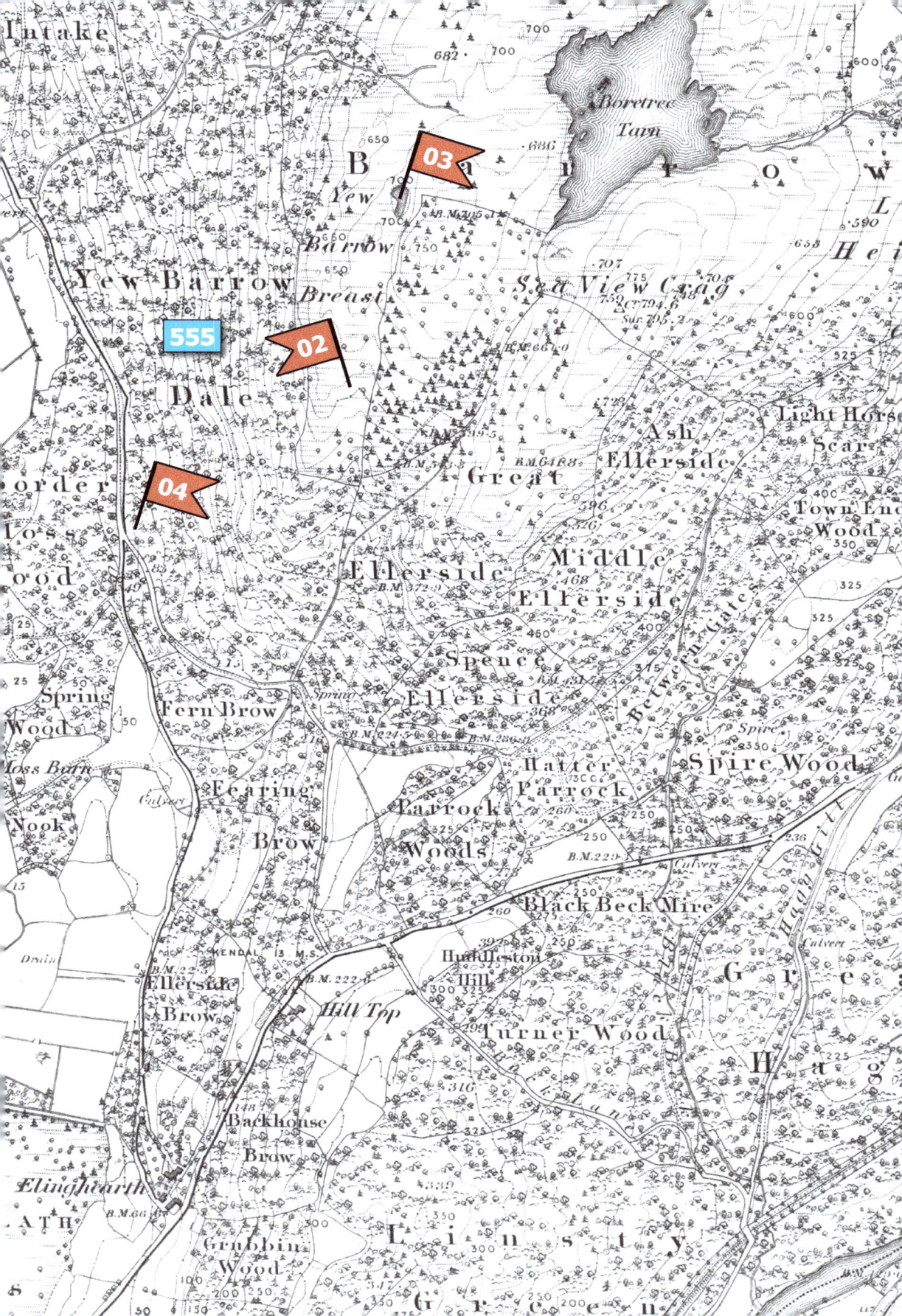

• Section 13 •

The Parrocks and Fearing Brow

An area of fields and woods at the top of the Fearing Brow lane, on the east side, is now known as The Parrocks. The area has been called Top of the Parrock or Parrock Head since the mid-seventeenth century (for instance, in DDPd 26/118 in 1660 and in the July Flower Tree estate book, DDTy 3/1, which dates to 1774-1790). The name Parrock Head is used as a woodland name on the Finsthwaite House estate plan of 1851 (FHEP), and The Parrocks is the Chaplins' modern name for the area. Other woodland names recorded here appear on OS maps.

Hatter Parrock (765): OS 1850 names this wood Hatter Parrock. The wood was sold in 1760 (DDPd 26/295) by William Braithwaite who was a hatter; he also gave his name to Hatter Hag near Waterside. FHEP, in 1851, marks this as belonging to another landowner, but adds in pencil the name **Between Gates** for this wood, also the name for the wood 769 to the north-east. When it was sold after the death of the Rev. Thomas Taylor in 1891 (DDPd 26/426 and BDHJ 398/4/31) it was divided in two by a footpath and the east portion is marked 'Hatter Parrock' and the west part 'Between Gates'.

Black Beck Mire (816): in 1851 (FHEP) this plot is marked **Pt** (part of) **Black Beck Mire**, in reference to the main woodland plot of Black Beck Mire on the other side of the road, 815. This small plot however has also been known as **Meare Parrock**, meaning that it marked a boundary (from Old English *meare*). It is named Meare Parrock in 1700 (DDPd 26/170) and the description of its position 'adjoining Little Close' (plot 771) is good enough to identify with this site. There is a very large stone in the plot, which might well have been a distinctive boundary marker.

Black Beck Mire (817 and **818):** two enclosures named in 1891 (BDHJ 398/4/31) as Black Beck Mire. OS 1850 shows this as a field, but in two sections and OS 1890 shows plot 817 as woodland and 818 as a field. OS names neither. The name comes because the plots are near (across the lane from) a wood called Black Beck Mire 815. The Black Beck runs down from Light Horse Scar 749, to the river Leven and the mire refers to the ease with which 815 floods. An 1802 archive (DDPd 26/346) mentions pasture shared between different owners and called Black Beck Mires, which pushes the name further into the past. In 1828, 817 and 818 (BDHJ 398/4/49) are called **Bracken Dales**, a field where different owners had the right to cut bracken (from *dael* an Old English word for a share). In modern times the field is known to locals as **the Pig Field** because it was once home to a very large number of pigs. The pigs have gone, but the name has stuck.

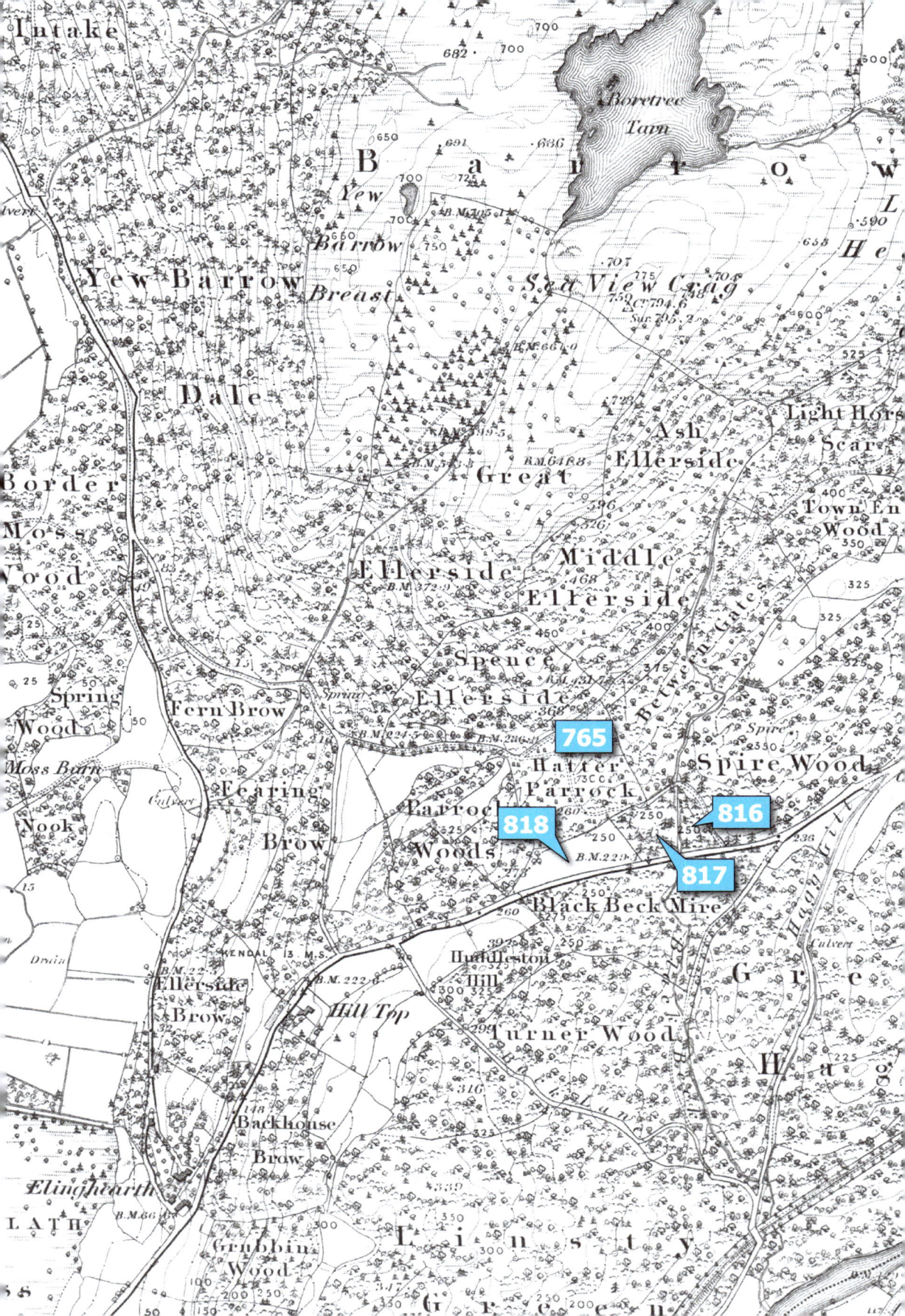

Hatter Paddock (764): a wood named in 1851 (FHEP) which may have had some association with land sold in the mid-18th century by William Braithwaite, a hatter. OS 1890 does not name this plot of woodland, but on OS 1850 the name **Parrock Woods** is extended to cover this plot and 823 and 819. The current name for this and all the neighbouring plots is **The Parrocks** (Chaplin family).

Paddock Head (763): a field named in 1851 (FHEP) as Paddock Head of a group of fields and woods on a small hill. Known now as **The Parrocks** (Chaplin family). In 1660 (DDPd 26/118) the name **Top of the Parrock** is given for this area, so the modern practice is to revert to seeing these as a group.

Paddock Head (824): this field is named in 1851 (FHEP) as part of Paddock Head, and shows as part of plot 763 (with the wood Hatter Paddock in the middle). The map shows a small enclosure at the west of this plot as separate, but also called Paddock Head. Now this is named, with its neighbours, **The Parrocks** (Chaplin family).

Paddock Head (823): a woodland plot at the southern end of Paddock Head field (763 and 824) and sharing a name with them in 1851 (FHEP). OS 1850 and 1890 uses the name **Parrock Woods** for 823 and its neighbour 819. OS 1850 also includes plot 764 under the name.

Paddock Bush (819): in 1851 (FHEP) this plot is named Paddock Bush. OS 1850 and 1890 sees it as part of **Parrock Woods.** These wood plots, like the fields, are known to the Chaplins by the group name, **The Parrocks.**

Sand Parrock (762): a field which may have had sand or gravel extracted from it. Two fields called Sand Hole are recorded at Plum Green and Lakeside and this may be named for the same reason. The name is used in 1851 (FHEP) and it appears earlier, in 1778 (DDPd 26/312). A late 18th century account book for July Flower Tree estate (DDTy 3/1) mentions a **Sands Parrock** alongside other fields and woods which they owned at Finsthwaite and at Top of the Parrock or Parrock Head. The Townley archive contains notes of land dealings in 1611 (DDTy 1/3/5) and 1704 (DDTy 1/3/13) with members of the Sands family from Bouth so it is possible that this was, before it came into the Finsthwaite House estate, a field named after an earlier vendor to the Taylors, and later the Townleys, of Jolliver. As the gravel extraction at the Plum Green and Lakeside fields is known to have taken place in the 19th century this Sand Parrock is perhaps more likely to have a much earlier vendor's name.

Lag Paddock (825): the *Dialect Dictionary* says the word 'lag' means the stave of a barrel, but unlike Lag Parrock wood (769 to the north east) it is not the right shape to have acquired the name for that reason. In Clement Taylor's account book there is an entry in 1726 recording the purchase of 1,000 sapps, some of which had been made at 'Top of the Parrock' (this area). Sapps are sapp-laths and are used in lath and plaster walls. In 1726 Clement Taylor was constructing his house, the present Finsthwaite House. The name Lag Paddock seems to memorialise this significant purchase.

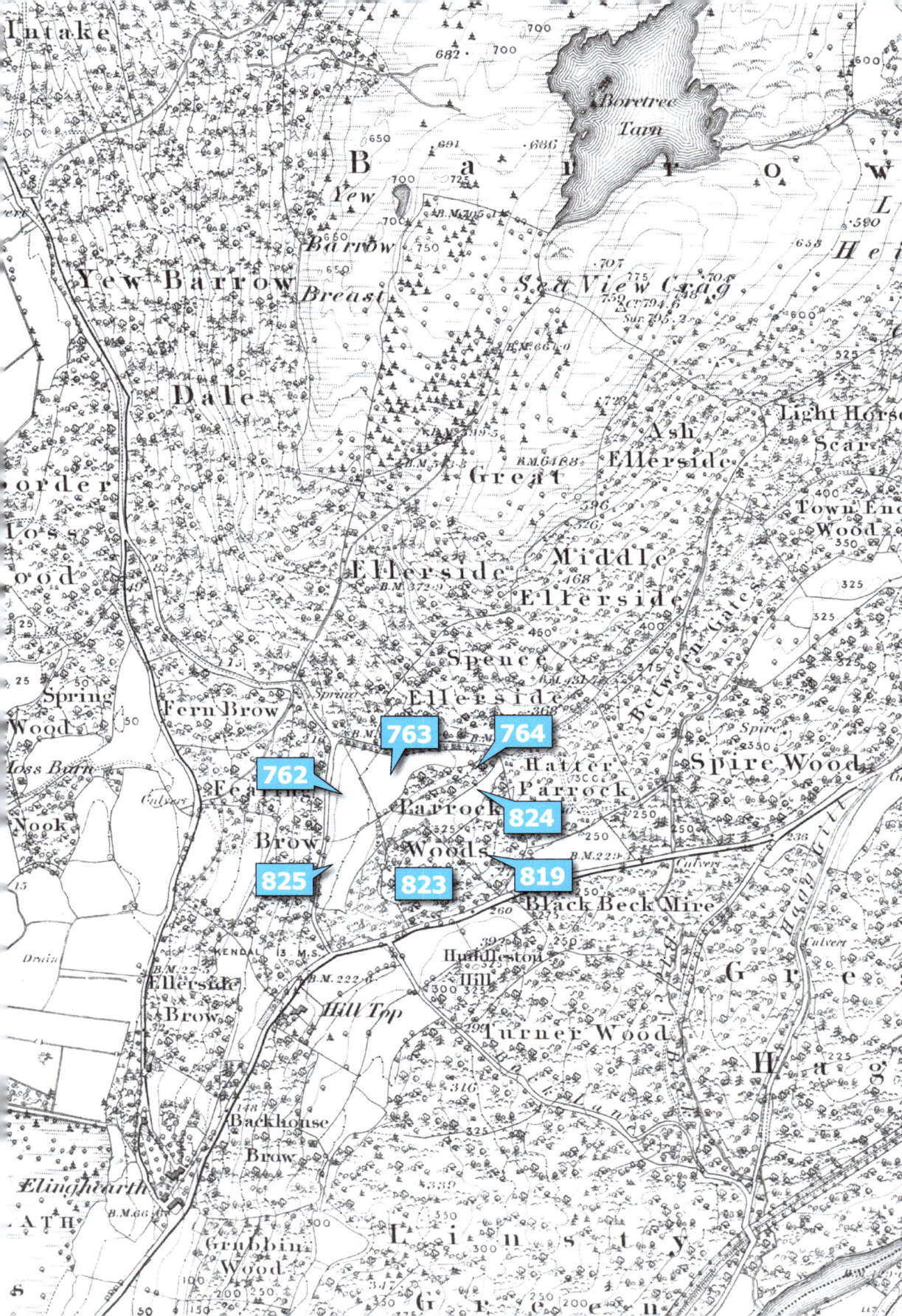

Lag Paddock Bush (826): an area of bushes or small wood next to the field Lag Paddock 825. OS 1850 and 1890 do not name it. Lag Paddock Bush, Lag Paddock and Sand Paddock are now included in the collective group **The Parrocks** by the Chaplin family.

Fearing Brow (761): the lane running down the brow (hill) at the back of Ealinghearth is called Fearing Brow, and takes its name from the wood 831. The dialect word 'fearing' means a ghost or evil spirit, and it seems that this lane has long been considered haunted. Stories about the 'Ealinghearth Dobby' connect her with this hill, and one of her chief characteristics is that she walks along with travellers, or hitches a ride on carts going up the hill. The modern name is Fearing Brow, or **Fairing Brow**. A well on the lane is known as **Peggy Taylor's Well (FLAG 01)**, after Margaret Lewthwaite (née Taylor) of High Stott Park (1771-1854) who used to stop when riding her horse on the lane and let it drink from the stream. The enclosure award and map of 1771 (DDPd 26/336) names the stream as **Yew Beck**. As does DDPd26/31 in 1604. Margaret's brother Roger Taylor owned Finsthwaite House estate, and the name of the well was remembered in the Chaplin family into the 20th century.

Fearing Brow (831): a wood on the brow (hillside) to the west of the lane which shares its name. A 'fearing' is a dialect word for a ghost, and the name appears as early as 1564 (DDPd 26/4) in reference to the wood, not the lane. It is later spelt **Fayre Aume** (DDPd 26/142), in 1676, and **Fairing Brow** in 1851 (FHEP). OS 1850 and 1890 settle on Fearing Brow. The Finsthwaite House estate map also calls the small wood plot 833 Fairing Brow.

High Newlands (832): an area of land recently taken into cultivation, or cleared of trees, higher up the slope than Low Newlands, 834. This field is named in 1851 on FHEP, but it is unclear when the land was cleared. **Low Newlands (834)**: an area of land recently taken into cultivation, or cleared of trees, lower down the slope than High Newlands, 832. This field is named in 1851 on FHEP, but it is unclear when the land was cleared.

Fern Brow (760): a hillside (brow) where ferns grow – and they still do, in profusion. The name is used on both OS 1850 and 1890. It is not named on FHEP because it belonged to another landowner. In 1895 (BDHJ/398/4/10) it is called **Rawlinson Parrock.**

Yewbarrow Dale (759): the end of a thin slice of woodland on Yewbarrow Dale, 555, was allocated to the Rev. Thomas Taylor's ancestors in the enclosure award of 1771. His share was sold after his death in 1891 (DDPd 26/426 and BDHJ 398/4/3). The map accompanying the sales particulars names this plot, along with the part on the other side of the lane, Yewbarrow Dale. 'Dale' means a share (and is derived from an Old English word *dael*). The strips of ground allocated to different people are shown on the enclosure map (DDPd 26/336). FHEP in 1851 shows the plot as belonging to the Rev. Thomas Taylor.

Low Yewbarrow (758): a small plot named in 1851 (FHEP) which may, like 759 next to it, be a remnant of a share of Yewbarrow Dale allocated to the Taylors as part of the enclosure award in 1771 (DDPd 26/336). It takes its name, like 759, from Yewbarrow Dale 555 across the lane.

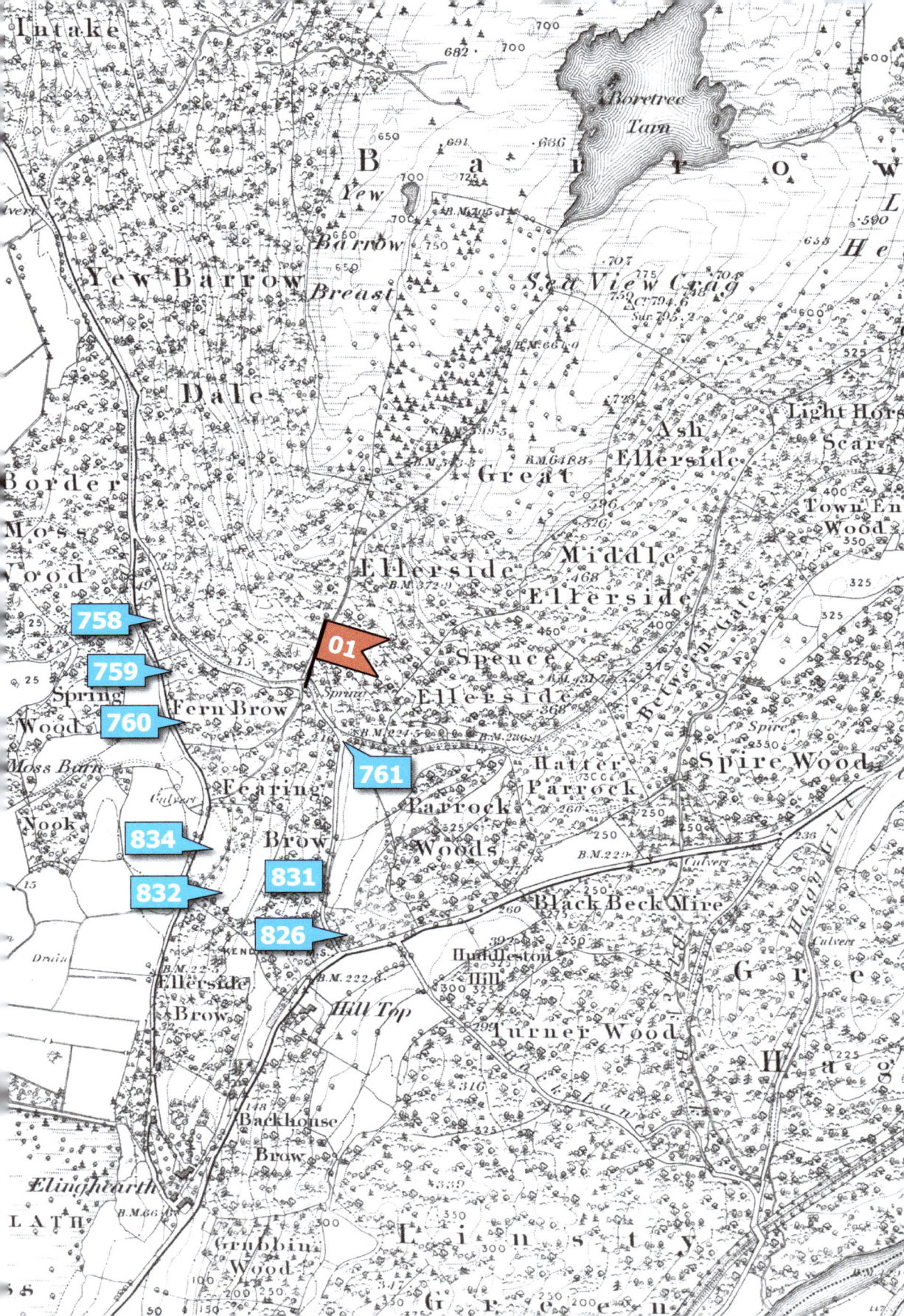

• Section 14 •

Ealinghearth and Border Moss

This map section begins on the west side of the lane, at the south of our map sheet 14, working up to Border Moss, and includes fields north of Border Moss Wood which lie west of our map boundary but appear on the Finsthwaite House estate plan, so these have been included for the sake of completion. Then we return to plots immediately by the Ealinghearth farms, at the foot of the hill.

Between Gates (868): a field between tracks (from Old Norse *gata*) into Ealinghearth Moss plot 867. The field is named in the early 19th century (BDHJ 449/2/1/25).

Great Ealinghearth (845, 846 and 847): we think that these three plots would once have been part of one large field, Great Ealinghearth. In his 1803 will, Thomas Taylor names the fields that he is leaving to his son beginning with Great Ealinghearth and Little Ealinghearth (844). Although both OS maps show two plots, 845 and 846, on the west side of the road these have now been put back into one field which is still known in modern times just as 'Ealinghearth' to Miles Saunders whose grandfather farmed it. The line of the road has changed too, and we think that it is this that severed the very steeply sloping part of the field, now plot 847, from the rest. After the turnpike road was re-routed there are complaints made in various documents relating to Ealinghearth farm about the destruction of **Ealinghearth Close** (DDHJ 8/13/1).

Moss Side or Low Paddock (844): this field stands next to Ealinghearth Moss, plot 867, and south of a wood called Moss Side Wood, 843, which explains the 'Moss Side' version of the name. 'Low Paddock' describes its low-lying character like the moss. It is named in this double way in 1891 (BDHJ 398/4/31 and DDPd 26/426) when it was to be sold after the death of the Rev. Thomas Taylor. In the list of fields in the will of Thomas Taylor in 1803, the Rev. Thomas's grandfather, this is probably **Little Ealinghearth**. In 1928 (BDHJ/8/2/17) the plot is simply called **Meadow**.

Ealinghearth Moss (867): a large peat moss at Ealinghearth, called Ealinghearth Moss in 1823 (BDHJ 398/4/47). On OS 1850 and 1890 it is given a truncated name, presumably based on pronunciation, **Elmlath Moss**. In 1741, it is called **Ealinghearth Moss or Low Moss** (DDPd 26/259) when divisions of the land are mapped and different local owners have a portion allocated to them. In 1851 FHEP shows some plots as belonging to named owners and marks others as **Common Moss**. The estate map also identifies the northern third as being **Big Hollin How Moss**. The name **Hollin Hall Moss** is mentioned in 1714 (DDPd 26/194), but this may relate to the wood plot, 842 which is adjacent. Hollins are holly trees, an important fodder crop. 'How' means a hill, and 'Hall' is used elsewhere in our survey as a version of 'how'.

Hollin How Moss (842): a hill where holly trees grow, next to the north end of Ealinghearth Moss 867. This wood is named in 1851 (FHEP) and elsewhere in the Pedder archive in the 18th and 19th centuries (eg DDPd 26/194 in 1714 and DDPd 26/352 in 1806). The name also appears in relation to a field, 841. Holly leaves were an important fodder crop (only the lower leaves tend to be prickly). Rights to cut holly were traded and sometimes holly trees are specifically excluded when a wood is otherwise being cut or coppiced (there are examples of this practice in Clement Taylor's account book).

Massick's Meadow (841): this large field plot has various names in 1851 (FHEP). At the north end is Massicks's Meadow, named after a member of the Massicks family who farmed at Town End, Finsthwaite, in the 18th century. Areas near to the wood plot 842, are known as **Hollin Howe** and **Higher Hollin Howe**, on the same 1851 estate map. John Chaplin identified these plots as part of the traditional holdings of Charley Crag Farm.

Moss Side Wood (843): a wood at the side of the peat moss called Ealinghearth Moss 867, or perhaps named because it is on the same side of the lane which runs north at this point. The plot is named in 1891 (BDHJ/ 398/4/31).

Moss Meadow (836): an area of meadow which takes its name from its association with Ealinghearth Moss, which lies to the south, and Border Moss Wood to the north. Two fields to the west and south of this plot are respectively **Ruff Moss (Flag 01)** and **Meadow (Flag 02)**, although their plot numbers are uncertain (they may be part of 841). All are named in 1891 (BDHJ 398/4/31 and DDPd 26/426) when they were lots for sale following the death of the Rev. Thomas Taylor. Moss Meadow is named in 1756 (DDPd 26/287). Ruff Moss was presumably a bit of rough ground in the mosses, perhaps in contrast to the grasses which grew in the section called Meadow.

Corn Moss (837): a field in the area between Ealinghearth and Border Moss used as an arable plot. Named in 1851 (FHEP) and as early as 1670 (DDPd 26/131) when it appears in the attempt to resolve a wide-ranging row between George and Richard Taylor. It is noted that Richard has the right to carry goods from William Bridge End (see 753) through George Taylor's 'close of Corne Moss, except when the corn is growing' when he must use a route further south, especially when he is driving cattle.

Round Close (838): a field that is not round in shape, so it may have reference to rowan trees (Old Norse *raun*). The field is named in 1851 (FHEP) and mentioned in 1662 (DDPd 26/126). Round Close and Moss Barn Field, 839 were identified by John Chaplin as part of the traditional holdings of Tom Crag farm.

Moss Barn Field (839): a field in the area between Ealinghearth Moss and Border Moss which is adjacent to a meadow called Moss Barn 756. It is named in 1891 (BDHJ/398/4/31 and DDPd 26/426) when it is to be sold following the death of the Rev. Thomas Taylor. This plot is identified as **Moss Barn Field No 2** in 1928 (BDHJ /8/2/17).

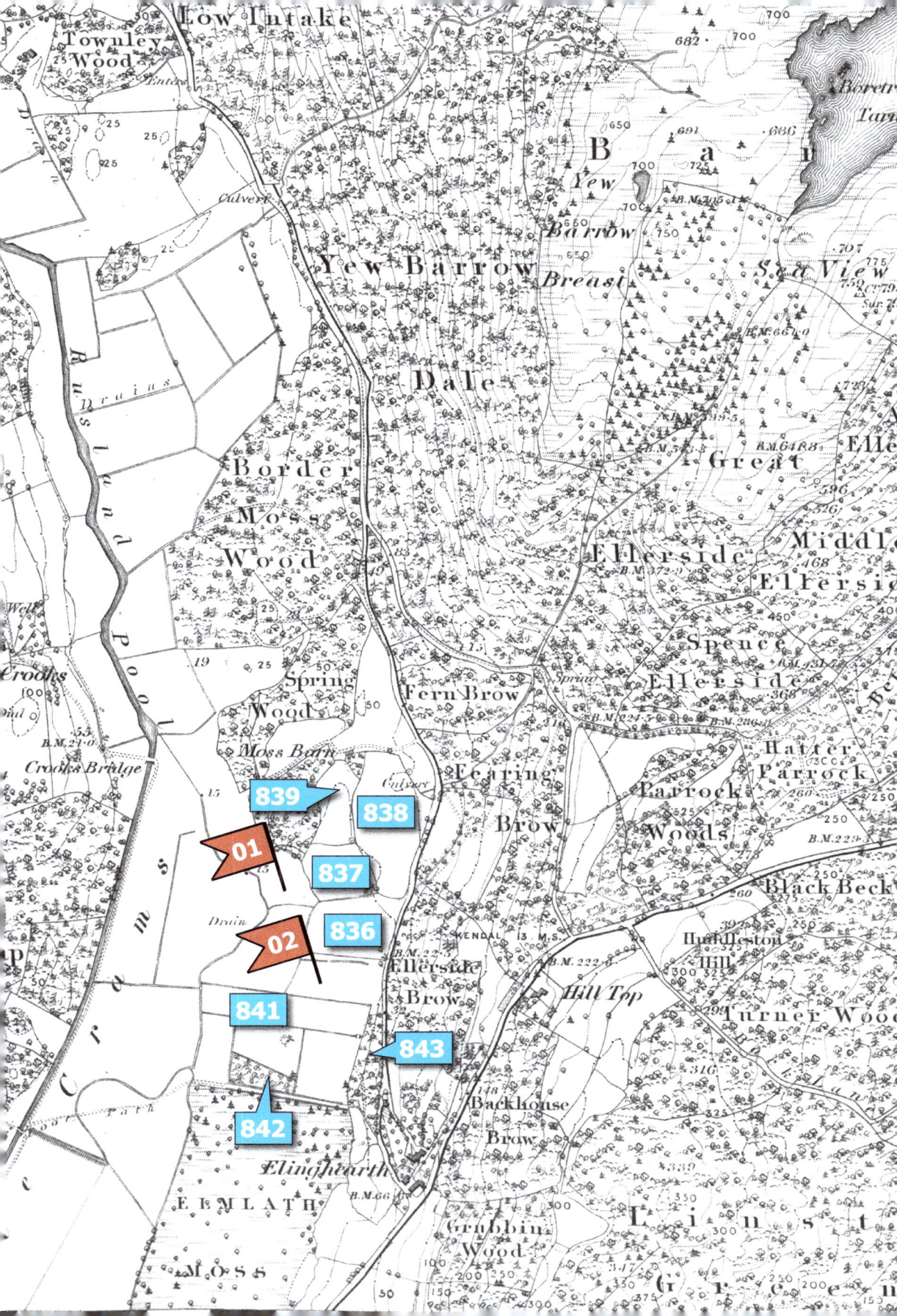

Nook (840): a wood in a secluded corner; the name Nook is used on OS 1850 and 1890. On FHEP in 1851 it is called **Moss Barn Wood**, a name which places it in the group with Moss Barn names. On the west edge of this wood plot FHEP also marks a wood called **Wild Brigg End**. The word 'Wild' has been crossed out and corrected, in ink, to 'Willy'. This plot is matched by another, 753, to the west of Spring Wood 755, and the name is interpreted under 753.

Moss Barn Meadow and Moss Barn Field (756): a field with a barn in it, next to Moss Barn Coppice. The meadow part, next to the lane side, is named in 1851 (FHEP) and the two sections, field and meadow, are named on the 1891 map selling the holdings of the Rev. Thomas Taylor (BDHJ/398/4/31 and DDPd 26/426). **Moss Barn** (as named on OS 1890) or **Moss Barn Coppice (Flag 03)** (BDHJ/398/4/31) is a tiny piece of wood, with a barn in it, at the southern end of this plot at the junction with 838 and 839.

Cram's Pasture (872): In 1891 (BDHJ/389/4/42) this plot (on the very edge of our map section) is named Cram's Pasture, a pasture within a larger section of fields called 'The Crams' by OS 1850. In 1928 plot 872 is given the name **Middle Crames** in reference to it being part of a larger group of fields (BDHJ/8/2/17). 'Cram' as a dialect word has the meaning of a food which is intended to be fattening, so this area was a place where sheep were probably brought for fattening and finishing after they had spent time grazing on the tougher lands of the fell. Another Cram's Pasture exists among the holdings of the Rev. Thomas Taylor (BDHJ/398/4/31) in 1891 **(Flag 04)**. A field called **New Pasture** is named in 1891 (BDHJ/398/4/3). **(Flag 05)**

Great Meadow (873): a large meadow (although as with 872 only a portion of it shows on our map sheet 14). It is named Great Meadow in 1851 (FHEP). As a Finsthwaite House holding, this may be 'Broad Meadow' or 'Meadow at Pul' which formed one of the traditional holdings of the Taylors of Lower Finsthwaite. Broadmeadow appears frequently in the Pedder archive from 1552 (DDPd 26/1), as well as in the 1570s (DDPd 26/10, 11 and 12). The broad character of plot 874 further north means that we prefer it as the site of Broad Meadow (see notes on Pool Meadow, 874).

Low Moss Barn (754): an arable plot near the Moss Barn group and nearly surrounded by woods 755 and 840. It is named in 1891 (BDHJ/398/4/31).

Spring Wood (755): a newly planted wood or a coppice wood that has been cut and the new shoots have sprung back. The wood is named Spring Wood on OS 1850 and 1890 and also in 1891 (BDHJ/398/4/31 and DDPd 26/426) when it was named as one of the Rev. Thomas Taylor's holdings.

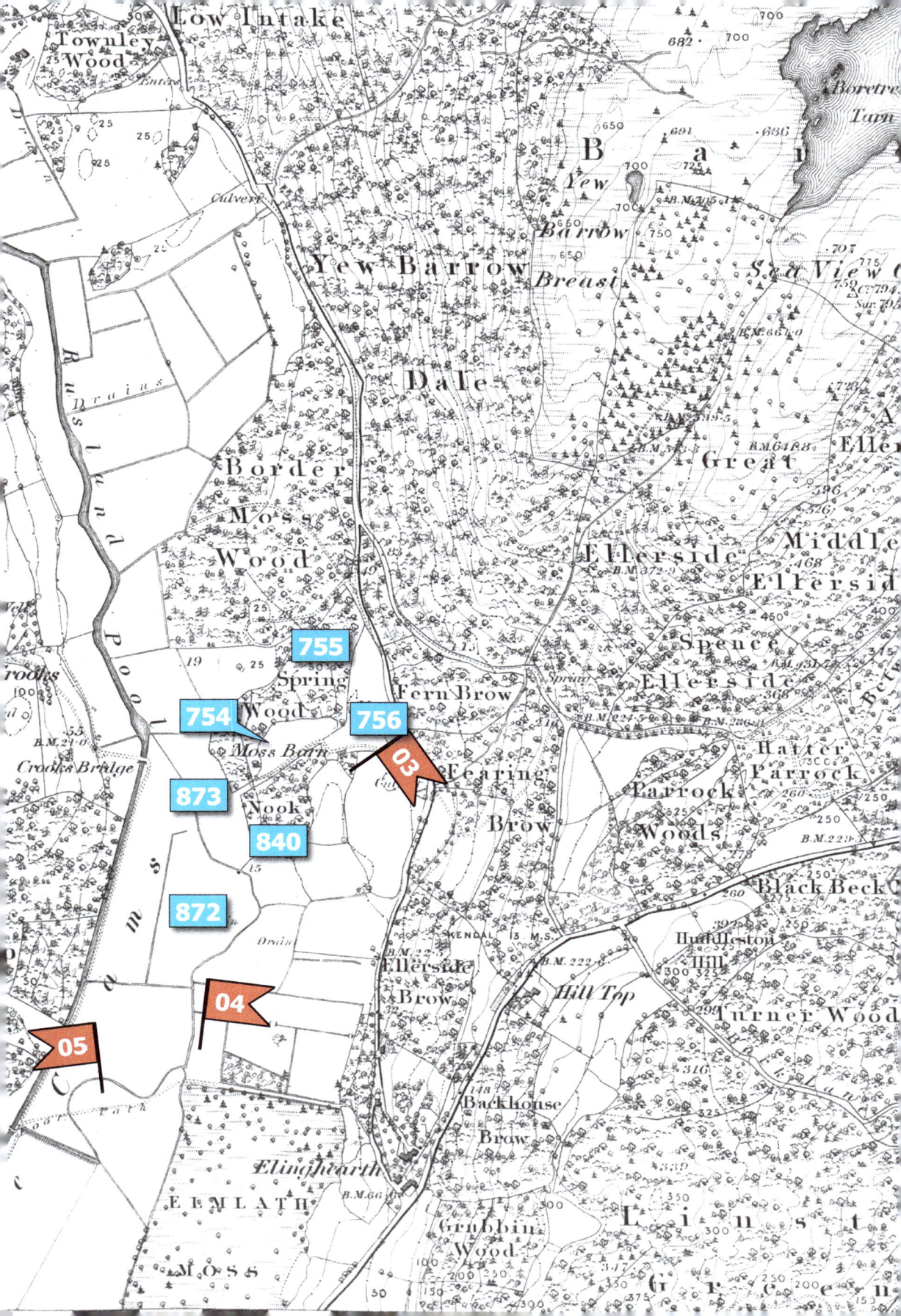

Willy Brigg End (753): this woodland plot is identified by the name **Wild Brigg End** in 1851 (FHEP), although it is corrected in ink to Willy Brigg End, like a similar shaped wood just to the south at the west end of 840, Nook. The two woods are separated by a track that runs between them, and leads to a bridge over Rusland Pool called Crooks Bridge on modern mapping, but simply identified as a foot bridge on OS 1850. In earlier documents of the Pedder archive this is identified as **Wright Bridge End** and the bridge may have had an association with a person called Wright (and maybe William, given the later name Willy). Diana Whaley notes that 'brigg' and 'bridge' are synonyms (derived from Old Norse *bryggja*). References to Wright Bridge End occur in 1662 (DDPd 26/126). By 1670 (DDPd 26/131) when it is **William Bridge End** when the plot is mentioned as a close of arable. Clement Taylor mentions Will Bridge End in his account book in the early 18th century.

Wool Moss (752): perhaps a field where common cotton grass grew (which has white fleece-like seeds). The possibility of it being a field where sheep were kept seems unlikely, given that so many fields would have had sheep on them. The plot is named Wool Moss in 1851 (FHEP), but a much earlier reference to Wool Moss occurs in 1608 (DDPd 26/36). Wool Moss was once one of the traditional holdings of Tom Crag Farm (John Chaplin), together with the northern end of plot 873 which lies just to the west, outside our map area.

High Meadow (873): FHEP names this High Meadow in 1851. The meaning of 'High' is unclear. John Chaplin identifies it as a traditional holding of Tom Crag farm.

Border Moss Wood (751): a wood by the Border Moss, which is named by OS in 1850 and 1890. The wood was not part of the holdings of Finsthwaite House when the estate map was drawn up but the name is mentioned earlier in the Pedder archive in 1658 when **Baldermoss Meadow** is recorded as being on the east side of Rusland Pool (DDPd 26/114).

Border Moss (in 874): areas of peat moss identified on OS 1850 (**Flag 06**). The border name implies a boundary feature, but 'bald' is a dialect word for tree-less and the moss may have been a place where trees struggled to grow.

Bailiff Meadow (southernmost plot of **874**): a meadow which probably belonged to an Abbey bailiff. Bailiff Meadow is referred to in 1741 (DDPd 26/259) and is on the map of the Rev. Thomas Taylor's holdings in 1891 (BDHJ/398/4/31). (**Flag 07**).

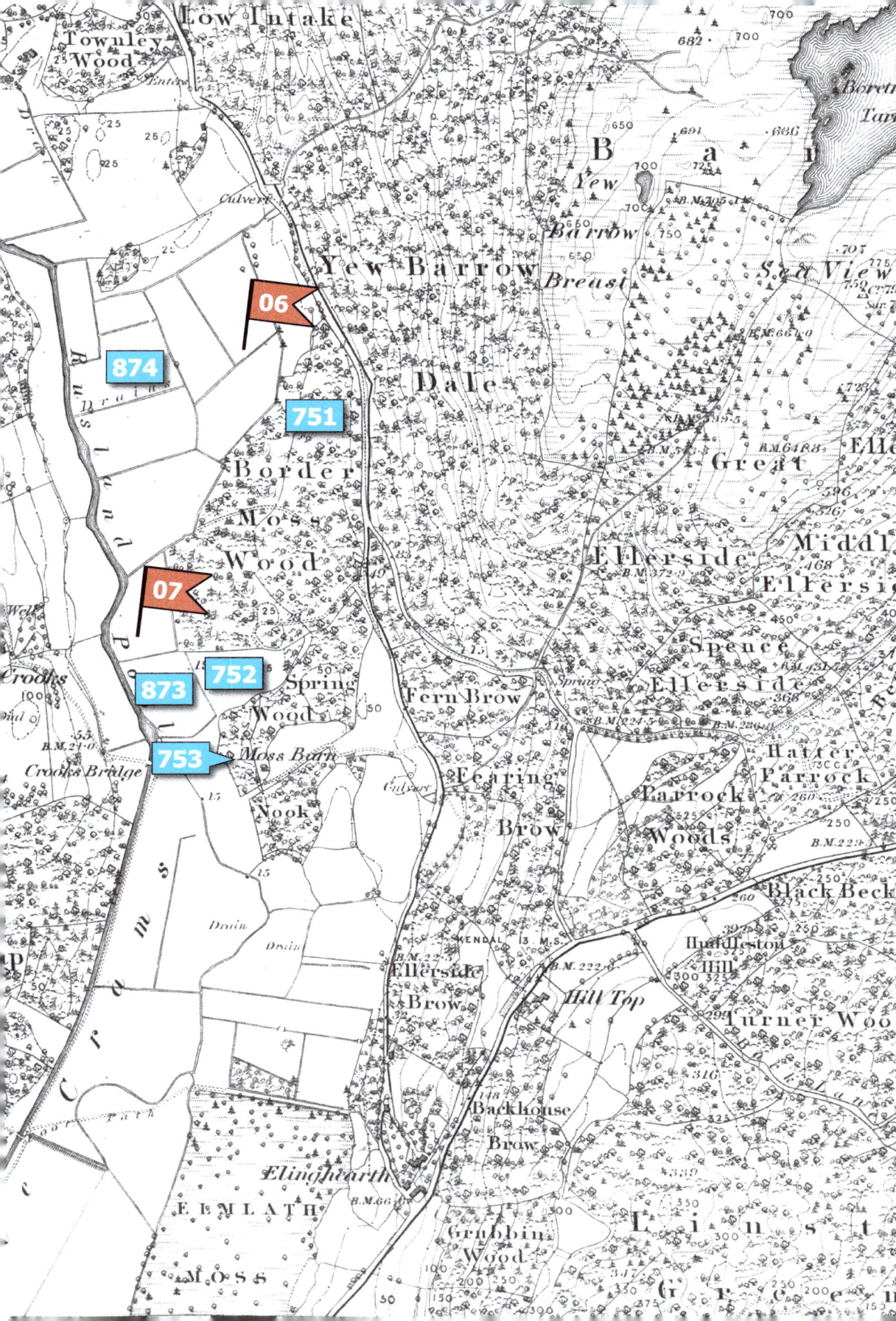

Pool Meadow (western part of **874**): meadow by the side of Rusland Pool (a 'pool' is a slow-moving stream). Although over the edge of our map sheet 14 we have included these Pool Meadows because they are illustrated on FHEP. The fields lie east of Rusland Pool and were traditionally owned by farmers from Lower Finsthwaite and would have been better arable and grazing land than the fields nearer their own farms. 'Meadows at Pul' are mentioned often in the Pedder archive from the 16th century. A **Broad Meadow** by Rusland Pool is mentioned, as '**Bradmeadow at Pulle**' in 1552 (DFDPd 26/1), and in the 1570s (DDPd 26/10, 11 and 12). Given the wide extent of plot 874, this may well be the site of this Broad Meadow. The large western plot is divided into smaller meadow sections on FHEP. Two plots are annotated as 'The Long One' and 'The Small One' and belonged traditionally to Charley Crag farm. One is marked as being purchased by the Pedders in 1876 from the estate of Philip Hartley. Another has 'John Fell Meadow' pencilled on it and belonged, with the meadows to the south, to Tom Crag farm.

Homestead Orchard (848): an orchard next to Ealinghearth farm (*stede* is a Middle English word for a place or the site of a house). The orchard is named in 1891 (BDHJ 398/4/31). OS 1850 shows extensive orchard planting.

Side Bank (849): a field on the side of the hill above Ealinghearth farm, named in 1928 (BDHJ/8/2/17).

Ellerside Brow (835): the hillside where alder trees grow. This wood is named on OS 1850 and 1890. In 1891 it is called **Ellerside Brow or New Barn Wood** and the 'new barn' is sited in Side Bank, plot 849 (BDHJ 398/4/31).

The Grubbing (830): a field which has been cleared of trees and stones, named in 1891 (BDHJ 398/34/31).

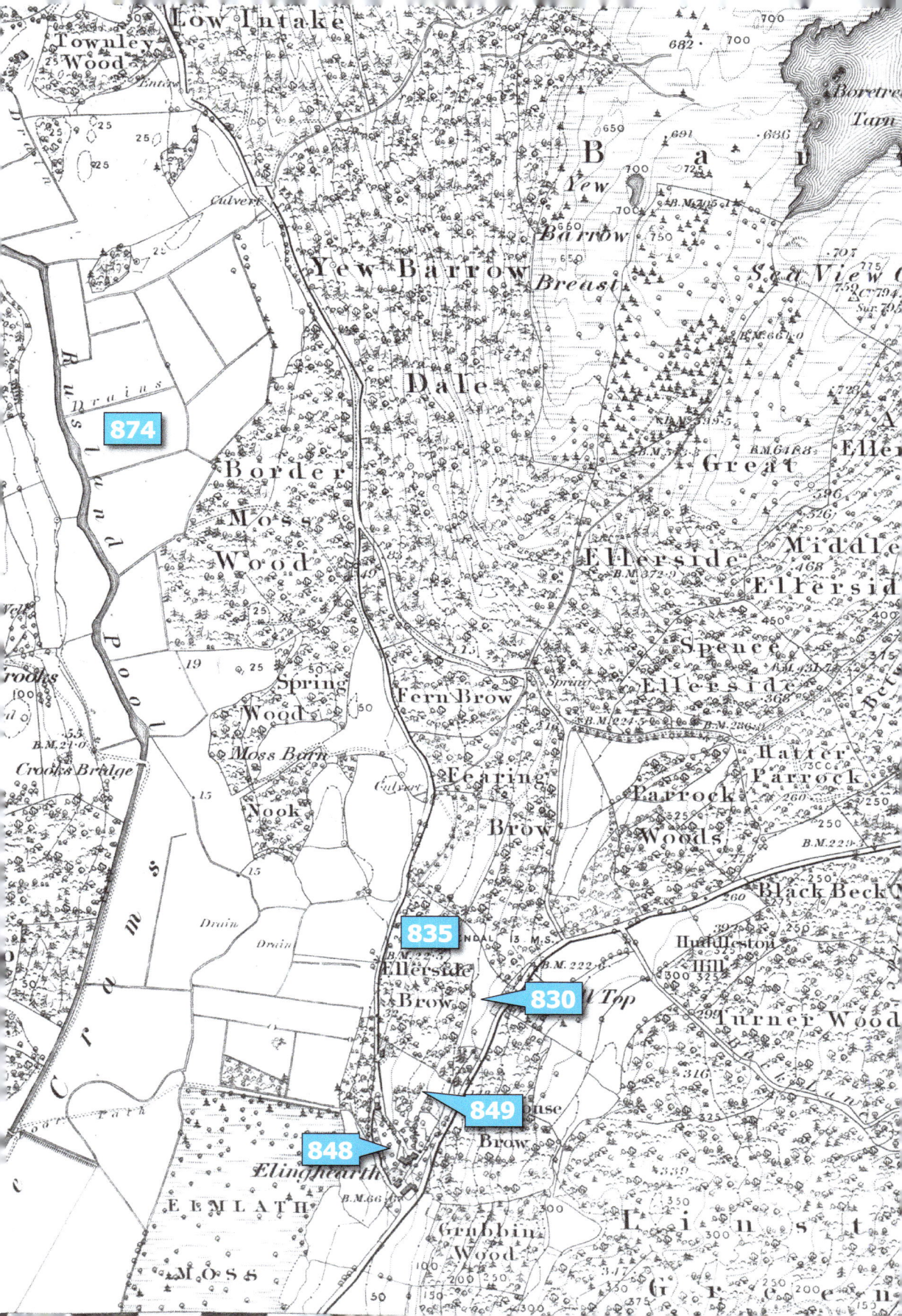

• Section 15 •

St Helens and Hall Brow Wood

Our final map section is mainly covered by woods, and we have largely taken their names simply from the OS maps. The survey for OS 1850 was carried out in the mid 1840s and for OS 1890 in the 1880s. We have named plots on our map sheet 14 but the illustration here shows plots to the west.

Machell Brow Wood (part of 181): a wood on a brow (hillside) associated with the local Machell family. It is named on OS 1850 and 1890, but has been dropped from the modern map.

Hall Brow Wood (181): the name Hall Brow is used on OS 1890 and seems to cover the whole of this wood, including the part which was Machell Brow Wood in the 19th century and the plots 473, 474 and 179 which lie east of Machell Brow Wood. Rusland Hall is nearby, and these woods may be theirs. Otherwise we have several examples in our survey of 'hall' replacing 'how' as a word for a hill. Plot 181 is on the steep slopes going up to Rusland Heights.

Birch Parrock (475): a small woodland plot or parrock where birch trees grow. The name is used on the modern map, as well as on OS 1850 and 1890.

Rusland Heights Moss (476, 477, 478 and 479): in 1726 DDPd 35/4 records the purchase of a 12-acre plot of turbury rights in Rusland Heights Moss from the owners of Rusland Hall. Plot 477 is just short of 12 acres. It is also named as belonging to Mr Strickland in 1895 (BDHJ/398/4/10). The rest of these plots are shown as mosses and so we assume that the Rawlinsons or other local landowners retained their rights on these. In 1895 478 and 479 are **Mr Drinkall's pasture** (BDHJ/398/4/10).

Resp Haw Wood (559): a wood named on OS 1850 and 1890, and also on the modern map. Resp is a disease of sheep and cattle, but also a dialect word used for plants that are fresh and full of moisture. The wood may be particularly verdant, or perhaps was the site of an outbreak of a livestock disease. Haw means a hill (*haugr* in Old Norse) and this is a hillside plot.

Walker Parrock (558): a wood associated with (probably sold by) someone called Walker, which is a common local name. John Walker of Sinderhill sold many plots of land in the 1630s, including one said to be near Border Moss, but this one would seem to be too far north to be one of his plots. It is named Walker Parrock on OS 1850 and 1890, but the name does not survive onto modern mapping.

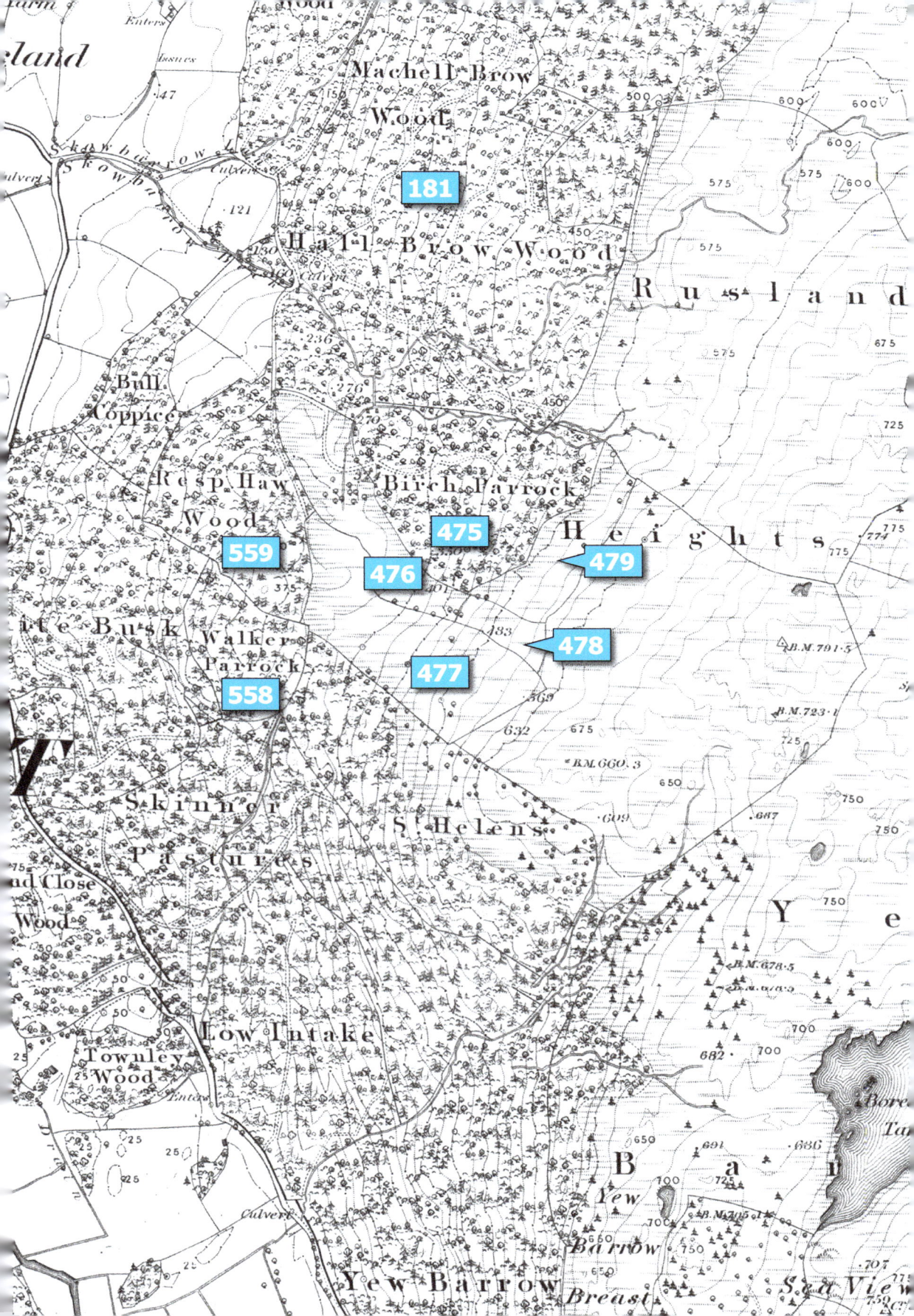

Rawlinson Intake (537): a wood named on OS 1850, which probably had an association with the Rawlinsons of Rusland Hall. On OS 1890 and modern maps it is called **St Helens**, for a reason which is uncertain.

Low Intake (539): a wooded intake or enclosure on the lower slopes of the hillside. It is named on OS 1850 and 1890 and survives onto modern mapping. It was one of various lots of fields and woods sold in 1868 (DDPd 26/427) and was then called **Intack Wood.**

Hill Above Staff Gate (480): named in 1771 on the enclosure map (DDPd 26/336). This plot slopes down to Rusland, and is identified on OS 1850 and 1890 as part of **Rusland Heights (472)**, a large area of fell grazing for Rusland farms.

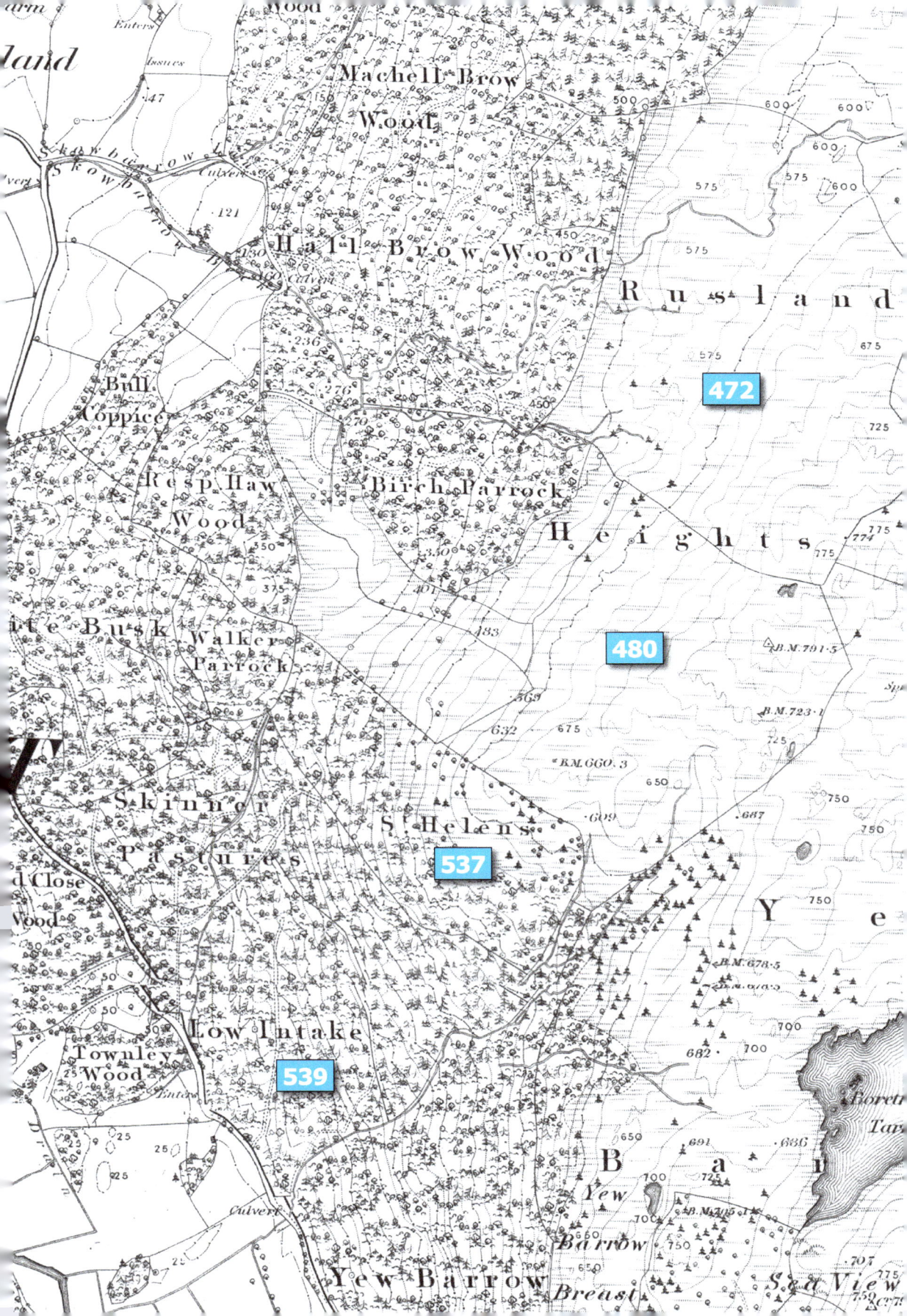

The journey continues....

We have had remarkable good luck in finding names for so many of the plots on our maps. This is due to the survival of so much archive material and to the work of Janet Martin, who pieced together information from many documents and let us rifle through her huge collection of card-indexed notes and copies of maps. We have also benefited from the interest (and patience) of the people who still farm the land in Finsthwaite. But we cannot have found everything, and it is highly likely that there are names known to people who live in the area, or have roots here, which we have not chanced upon.

The same is true of the areas of the Mapped Histories project which have been worked on by other volunteers. The work done so far is available on the Rusland Horizons website at www.ruslandhorizons.org which hosts a map with the names of as many plots as have been identified and interpreted. A group of volunteers are continuing the work, and would be delighted to hear from people who have information to share.

The archives also have secrets to yield up. Late seventeenth and early eighteenth century lists of the holdings of Plum Green farm include references to 'Ridding' or 'Rudding' which simply means a cleared field, and could be anywhere in our survey area – although we have tentatively associated it with land at High Stott Park where the Taylors farmed. The same lists also include Forest Parrock and Wilson Parrock, which would have been known to the writers of the lists, but, sadly, not to us as no descriptions of the position of these fields are given.

More intriguingly, a field named in the Pedder archive in 1571 as 'Sargalynhaw' has always puzzled us. Pat Jones has identified recently that a Scottish word, *sgalan*, exists which means a temporary shelter formed by roofing a shallow trench with branches. As 'haw' means a hill, we are now looking for the hillside site of a long-gone structure. We only know it to have been near Rusland Pool.

This book is dedicated to Janet Martin
an indefatigable, generous and inspiring archivist and historian.

Lightning Source UK Ltd.
Milton Keynes UK
UKHW050417170919
349882UK00003B/82/P